MW00640227

THE SHAAR PRESS

THE JUDAICA IMPRINT
FOR THOUGHTFUL PEOPLE

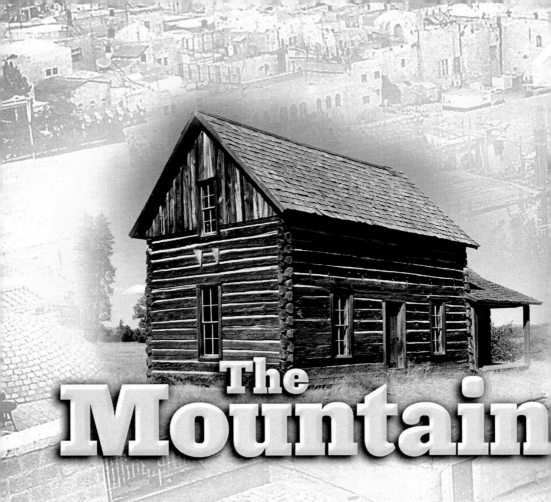

The Mountain

AN APPALACHIAN FAMILY OF 12 — AND THEIR FASCINATING JOURNEY TO JUDAISM

THE
SHAAR
PRESS

Family

Tzirel Rus Berger
with Penina Neiman

© Copyright 2013 by Shaar Press

First edition – First impression / November 2013
          Second impression / January 2014

ALL RIGHTS RESERVED
No part of this book may be reproduced in any form, photocopy, electronic media,
or otherwise without written permission from the copyright holder, except by a reviewer
who wishes to quote brief passages in connection with a review written for inclusion in
magazines or newspapers.
THE RIGHTS OF THE COPYRIGHT HOLDER WILL BE STRICTLY ENFORCED.

Published by **SHAAR PRESS**
Distributed by MESORAH PUBLICATIONS, LTD.
4401 Second Avenue / Brooklyn, N.Y 11232 / (718) 921-9000

Distributed in Israel by SIFRIATI / A. GITLER
6 Hayarkon Street / Bnei Brak 51127, Israel

Distributed in Europe by LEHMANNS
Unit E, Viking Business Park, Rolling Mill Road / Jarrow, Tyne and Wear, NE32 3DP/ England

Distributed in Australia and New Zealand by GOLDS WORLD OF JUDAICA
3-13 William Street / Balaclava, Melbourne 3183 / Victoria Australia

Distributed in South Africa by KOLLEL BOOKSHOP
Northfield Centre / 17 Northfield Avenue / Glenhazel 2192, Johannesburg, South Africa

ISBN 10: 1-4226-1455-7 / ISBN 13: 978-1-4226-1455-6

Printed in the United States of America.
Custom bound by Sefercraft, Inc. / 4401 Second Avenue / Brooklyn N.Y. 11232

PHOTO CREDITS:
Eric T Gunther: page 17

Table of Contents

Dedication

I would like to dedicate this book to my dear husband.

During his lifetime "Avrum" was the driving force behind many of my projects.

He was tremendously supportive of my writing, and it is likely due to his efforts that this book finally got written. About a year before his passing he sought the counsel of the Admor of Boyan *shlita* to clarify whether or not I should write a book about my life story. The Rebbe encouraged us in this endeavor as he felt that my experiences would serve as an inspiration for other Jews.

Yet he laid out two conditions: I must write the truth and I must do it anonymously. For this reason I have changed the first and last names of my children and family members.

It was just a few short weeks before my husband's passing that the two of us chose a writer, Penina Neiman, to undertake this project. In the wake of his sudden death, recounting my life story has given me some level of comfort and fulfillment. I am sure that Avrum's merit continues to impact upon my life and the lives of our children.

ת.נ.צ.ב.ה.

Acknowledgments

By Tzirel Rus Berger

Who lit the candles? The detective part of me has pondered many times the mystery of our family's journey. Was it the searching father, the children who raced ahead of us, the four pious grandparents? Or maybe it was a Bubby who long ago watched a child run from the path of the forefathers and streamed rivers of tears before her Shabbos candles? What part did I play?

Climbing to stand on a higher summit of this mountain range called life, I can look back with an increased clarity and see in greater ways the hand of G-d upon my life. I can see how every person, every day, every episode is part of a personalized life design: a gift of Hashem.

I thank You, My Creator, for giving me wholly and perfectly every person I needed for my life's journey —

The just-exactly-right:

parents I needed, my siblings, my aunts, uncles, nieces, nephews, cousins, friends, Lookout Mountain Family...

My beloved —

Children, grandchildren—my jewels, my *nachas*....

My soul mates, the Jewish people—

My friends, my guides, my late husband, our children, my father and mother-in-law, brothers-in-law, sisters-in-law, *mechutanim*, nieces and nephews...

My eloquent friend and co-writer of this book: Penina Neiman.

Those who helped me so much along the publishing trail:

Shmuel Blitz, Miriam Zakon, Avigail Sharer, Chaya Baila Gavant, and the entire ArtScroll family.

If I haven't achieved my potential, acomplished my mission or written in a way that uplifted others, the fault is only mine. I must also acknowledge that I am human, with human limitations. As we wrote the memories of my life sometimes I agonized, trying to remember exactly how it happened and who said what. I often felt like the policeman interviewing 15 people at the streetlight on the corner after the accident, with each eyewitness having different and even opposing views. My perspective is uniquely different from anyone else in my circle, and this book reflects that.

I am also very grateful as one who has benefited from thousands of authors and books in my lifetime, and longed to give back just one small book; this desire accomplished is sweet! I continue to long for the time when Hashem will let me sing my song for every unique gift with which He has favored me. May we continue to inspire one another in seeing how masterfully planned is our most beautiful, harmonious world, and join for all eternity in an expanding cresendo of praises to our Creator!

Tzirel Rus Berger

Preface and Thank-You's

By Penina Neiman

I t has been a tremendous privilege to have been honored with the writing of this very special book. Who would have thought that a Bais Yaakov graduate from the iconic-metropolitan city of Chicago would one day come to write the account of a family of converts from Appalachia?

At times I have been so deeply moved by the story, and its distillation from the ethereal world of memories and feelings into the more concrete realm of the written word, that the fine line between Tzirel Rus's thoughts and my words began to merge and blur. On some level I felt as though I myself was there right beside her, experiencing the extraordinary chain of events that make up the story of her life.

There is something here for everyone. The story of Tzirel Rus and her children touches upon the personal story of each and every one of us. This is a story of self-discovery, of devotion and deprivation and even desperation — yet never of despair. Through all her trials Tzirel Rus was able to maintain a clear sense of G-d's presence in her life, and I have been privileged to come along for the ride. She has brought me to places I never thought I would go, from the foot of snowpeaked Mount Baldy to the wilds of Appalachia and all the way to the Galilee. I have followed her to cities and towns in Oregon, Oklahoma, California, Washington, and Arizona.

We've traveled down to Mexico and then clear across to Georgia, Alabama, and Tennessee, with a stop along the way in Missouri and Idaho. Later still, we moved on to Maryland, which became the springboard for her journey across both the Atlantic and the Mediterranean on the way to the Holy Land of Israel.

It was there that our paths first crossed in 1997, when we lived on the same street. I was a young mother in my 20s, and she a seasoned grandmother spreading inspiration wherever she tread. As I struggled through sleepless nights of chicken pox and teething babies, juggling the needs of my growing family, I took much strength from her tales of raising her own brood on Lookout Mountain. What did I have to complain about when blessed with a wonderfully supportive community as well as disposable diapers, store-bought bread, and my own washer and dryer?

"You must write a book!" I enjoined her, and just as emphatically she insisted that eventually she would. Never in my wildest dreams did I entertain the thought that one day she'd choose me to craft her magnum opus.

Fast-forward nearly another 15 years. With the passage of time I gained even more common ground with my neighbor and heroine. Her book was still an elusive dream at best, and I had just been bitten by the writing bug. I became obsessed with the notion of writing up some of her stories, and she shrugged me off, insisting that she and her husband had decided that she wouldn't do any more interviews before writing The Book. But I couldn't take no for an answer. Her stories began to grow in my mind, pecking away at my brain until resignedly I was forced to put them down on paper, if only to quiet the nagging words that refused to be silenced. I wrote up some of her stories and shared them with her. She felt that I understood her, and was able to capture the essence of her experiences. In some strange twist of fate her thoughts and memories resonated with me. I felt as if I had been there with her and had actually experienced much of her life along with her.

When Tzirel Rus told me that she and her husband had decided to ask me to write her book, I didn't know if I could or even if I should. Not much more than a month later her husband suddenly passed away. At the *shivah* she said that the time had come for her to begin working on her book. Saying no has always been difficult for me, and how does one say no to a woman sitting *shivah* for her husband?

Two months later we began, and now a year and a half later the book is nearly done. By my estimate it has taken me over 1,200 hours, a massive undertaking that never would have happened without the support of my wonderful husband Eliyahu and my children. I would especially like to thank my daughters for all those times they pitched in and helped watch the little kids while I worked "overtime."

I would also like to thank my husband, for both helping me to interview Dovid Massey, and assisting me with "Project Galilee," which is the result of Dovid's interviews. My husband worked with me to make sure that all the halachic discussions in that chapter were written clearly and accurately, so even those who are not familiar with the Torah's laws would be able to understand the *mitzvos* under discussion. May Hashem grant us much *berachah* in our life together, as well as *nachas* from our children.

I would also like to thank all those who have helped me to develop my writing. First and foremost, my parents, Mr. and Mrs. Alan and Honey Aron, and my in-laws, Mr. and Mrs. Myron and Joan Neiman, who have been cheering me on from the sidelines. I'd like to thank the wonderful staff at *Binah Magazine*, and especially Sarah Rivka Kohn, for believing in me and granting me my first professional voice. The encouragement and practical guidance that I have received while on the job has taught me much both about writing as well as how to become a skilled interviewer.

It is clear to me that this book is the result of open Divine Providence. Just as the Master of the Universe crafted the fascinating twists and turns of Tzirel Rus's life, it is also He Who brought together a tremendous amount of talent to work on this book. Working with the staff of ArtScroll has been a pleasure. The professional guidance of Shmuel Blitz and the creative and insightful editing of Avigail Sharer have improved this manuscript incredibly. But I couldn't have done it without Miriam Zakon's invaluable guidance and input. While it was Tzirel Rus who was the inspiration behind this project, it was Miriam Zakon who provided the experience and expertise that made this book a reality. A special thank-you to Chaya Baila Gavant for her meticulous proofreading, I would like to thank all those who worked on the finishing touches in ArtScroll's New York office: including Eli Kroen for the magnificent cover design, Mrs. Tova Finkelman for the final editing of the manuscript, and Mrs. Estie Dicker for correcting and typesetting the book.

Last but certainly not least I must thank Tzirel Rus for entrusting me with her life story. Thank you for believing in me and for honoring me with this tremendous privilege. I shall always cherish the time we've spent together and the many life lessons you've taught me. And of course I'd like to thank your family for all that they have contributed to this project. My personal thanks to all the children of this very special family for their contributions. Special appreciation to Dovid and Estie for their insights and anecdotes, which added a special richness to this book, and Shoshana Bracha for her wisdom and advice.

And above all I would like to thank the Almighty for the privilege of establishing a home and raising a family in the Holy Land of Israel, as well as for the wonderful gift of writing.

May the words of the *pasuk* "… the earth will be filled with knowledge of Hashem as water covering the seabed" (*Isaiah* 11:9) be fulfilled speedily in our days.

Elul 5773/ August 2013

All translations of verses from the Torah appearing in this book are credited either to ArtScroll's *Stone Edition Chumash, Tanach,* or *The ArtScroll Tehillim.*

Prologue

I have traveled halfway across the world and now I have eyes only for a pair of brass candlesticks. Somewhere in the background, I hear my nephew wheel my suitcase into the house; my sister offers me a cup of coffee; children scatter. I take a step closer to the fireplace.

There they are. Tall, slender, dark brass. I pick one up; it's heavy. My sister crosses the room; she places her hand on my own and tilts the candlestick toward me. I see jagged indentations. "These marks show the old-time way that these candlesticks were carved," she tells me.

What kind of antique tool could have shaped the solid metal base? What other secrets are engraved within the marks? I cradle these family heirlooms in both hands. Why have I never seen them before?

"They really should be yours, Sheryl," my youngest sister Lesa says. "They've been passed down through the generations: Grandma Bowers gave them to

The candlesticks

her oldest daughter, Granma Grimm. She passed them on to Granma Carpenter, who passed them on to Aunt Hester, Granma Dugger's oldest sister. Mother got them next and she really should have given them to you."

I search my memory, but I can barely recall them. As a child, it had been my job to clean the living room in honor of the Sabbath. Though I always dusted the fireplace mantel, I never noticed the candlesticks, perhaps because Mother never used them.

You know, Mother and Daddy always said we were Jews from Spain. It was a casual comment made by my mother's sister, Aunt Mary, but when I heard it I was struck dumb.

I spent the first 40 years of my life investigating the religions of the world, in search of G-d's true people. Eventually, along with my 10 children, I converted to Judaism. After all I have been through, I wonder if it's really possible that my family had once been part of the Jewish nation. If so, how and why was this hidden from me for so long?

The mists of time have long since settled on any Jewish roots, obscuring them. Still, Lesa insists that although our family has been loyal to a small Christian sect for over a century, we in fact descend from Jews; hence our ironclad commitment to eating only "clean" animals and observing the Sabbath.

Did we descend from hidden Jews? Have I spent my life wandering and seeking—from California to the Appalachian Mountains, from Missouri to Atlanta, eventually arriving in the Holy Land—only to find the answers etched in a pair of brass candlesticks in my childhood home?

But then, throughout my long search, the brass candlesticks remained on the mantelpiece, unnoticed and unlit.

Mount Baldy

The highest point in
Los Angeles County, California
10,068 feet (3,069 meters)

As a child gazing at its awesome snowcapped peak,
I believed Mount Baldy was heavily forested and productive.
Until I hiked there in my teens and found it was barren at the summit.

CHAPTER 1

A Little Goat Girl Near Disneyland

I am 12 years old when my father brings home an expectant goat and appoints me caregiver. Along with the coarse-haired, lumbering mother-to-be, I am given a handbook written in the early 1900s. I pore over it, making a note to trim her hoofs every six months.

One goat soon becomes a flock. Each morning, my goaty friends gather around me in a semicircle, to welcome my morning arrival. As I descend down the ladder into the goat pen, they race forward, crowding around me. I pat a head or two and push through. They follow, dancing and nibbling at my clothes, shoving each other away as they vie for the privilege of strutting beside me.

At the barn they spring onto their small platforms. I fill their feed boxes: corn, oats, and molasses feed, two cups each. As they stick their heads through the two wooden slats to gobble, I lock each goat into place. Milking time.

Taking my pink bucket I sit beside a goat and milk. Swish, swish, swish, swish.

My goats and me

A neighborhood kitten comes to beg and I skillfully aim a stream toward its mouth. It laps hungrily. Swish, swish. I hold my left arm up at an angle to protect the steaming milk: in a split second, a swift kick can overturn the bucket or land a nasty foot inside—meaning I come home with no milk.

After milking I release the mothers and turn my attention to the small kids. I pour each a bottle full of milk, which they guzzle lustily. I throw a few flakes of alfalfa hay into the manger and as they eat I check the fence for weak spots. I open the kids' pen and they skip out to join the mothers. I open the main gate. Seconds later, the whole herd stampedes toward the gate, like schoolchildren running for freedom.

I let them play for a few moments and then, like some ancient herder, I grasp my stick in hand and stride toward our grazing land. My goats come running, walking beside me and falling into a line behind. The little kids skip and twist into the air, leaping from rock to rock.

In a few moments we reach our grazing acres, and I settle on a boulder to watch. The herd grazes contentedly nearby, biting and twisting off the dry desert bushes, crunching… Tilting my head upward, I gaze at the breathtaking beauty of Mount Baldy, one of the mighty Sierra Mountains. Rugged, snowcapped most of the year, it dominates the horizon.

Below us stand acres of massive lemon trees in green rows. I sit in my little self-made wilderness, an oasis where I can forget the four-lane boulevard of traffic that whizzes by our house, the mazes of highways, and the multitudes of cities that stretch out until the mighty Pacific Ocean. It is a shepherd's privilege to give herself up to her thoughts, and I grasp the opportunity.

Atheism and chaos surround me, thousands of voices, each screaming, "I'm right."

How can I know?

What do I know?

There is a Creator. His creations are gorgeous and majestic.

How awesome is Your world.

Sitting alone on the boulder, the sweetness of a Creator vibrates in my heart.

Soon, too soon, it's time to reenter the real world. "Let's go!" I call. Standing with my stick, my now-resting herd rises slowly, stretching, meandering about behind me, grabbing another mouthful or two as they slowly step by.

Mount Baldy rises above. Serene and rejuvenated, I walk up the foothill, coming home.

Coming home?

My father was a boy of 7 when a relative met him on his way home from choir practice and told him that his mother had died. Just two weeks before, she had given young Victor a baby brother. She had suffered a fatal reaction to an injection she received in her doctor's office. Little Victor and his baby brother, Ray, were sent to live with relatives until his father remarried.

The Great Depression and the devastating crop failures in Oklahoma due to the Dust Bowl took their toll on my grandfather's business. When he learned of job opportunities in the oil fields of Southern California, Grandfather and his new wife packed up their family and possessions and moved out to the West Coast. Against the backdrop of the breathtaking beauty of America's Pacific coast, the struggling family finally found some measure of success.

Yet even as my teenage father swam in the cobalt waters of California's beaches, tensions mounted. War erupted in Europe. Southern California was thousands of miles away from the fiery frontlines, but American anxiety was building. The debate raged: Should America enter the war or not? In 1941, my 17-year-old father enlisted in the Navy. If and when America would enter the war, he'd be ready.

Daddy was deployed to Pearl Harbor. The morning of December 7, 1941, found him on the *U.S.S. Hulbert*, eating his breakfast along with his crew members.

Sudden explosions thundered, and the smoky air was lit by huge tongues of flame. The Japanese had bombed the harbor. The sailors ran to arm themselves, but the huge guns had been in storage since World War I, and the sailors had to use army knives to cut away the canvas wrapping.

The *U.S.S. Hulbert* received the command to fire. The ship took aim and fired the first American shot of the war. The sea ran red with blood, and my teenage father witnessed a devastating loss of life.

The very next day, President Franklin D. Roosevelt declared war. My father prayed and pledged to G-d: "If You keep me through the war, I will serve You."

Daddy endured many harrowing experiences through the war. He fought more than 30 battles without being wounded, crediting his survival to the power of his vow.

My father lived through some of World War II's deadliest battles in the Pacific. At Iwo Jima, his ship "softened" the shore with its guns in preparation for the Marine landing. After the battle, he led a detachment ashore to collect dog tags off the American dead. The beach was so full of bodies that he couldn't see the sand, he told my Uncle Ray afterward. Later in the war he was in the ship's gunpowder magazine when a Japanese kamikaze dived onto the deck. Some of his men caught fire. They tried to flee into the powder magazine. Realizing that the

Daddy in uniform

men's smoldering clothes would cause a deadly explosion, Daddy blocked them from entering. His quick thinking saved both the ship and the lives of the other men on board. For this act of bravery, Daddy was awarded the Presidential Citation. It was too painful for him to think of a medal earned while listening to his own men burn, and he threw it away.

It wasn't just the Japanese that threatened America's Navy. The Pacific Ocean and her mighty storms were no less terrifying. Daddy often spoke to us about the typhoons he had survived. The terrifying waves "seemed a mile high, and all the men cried like babies and prayed to G-d."

Daddy's acts of bravery and leadership were acknowledged by the many medals he earned. These included 15 bronze stars, a presidential citation, a Philippine liberation medal, and a good conduct medal, as well as "stars" earned for participation in battle; more than 30 stars and medals altogether. He never discussed them with us, and we, his family, had no idea that Daddy had come home a highly decorated war hero, until a family member checked the records after his death, when he was given a military burial with an honor guard and a 21-gun salute.

The horrific scenes of war and the deaths of his comrades-in-arms left their impression on my father, convincing him that one has to be tough to make it through life.

At war's end he came home to his father and stepmother in California, devastated by the horrors of battle. His sister, after seeing he wasn't pulling himself together, invited him to visit her in Oregon, where he found a job hoeing corn. After each and every row he would look up to the heavens and beseech G-d to help him fulfill his vow. Daddy's parents had been Sabbath-observing Christians, but after his wife's untimely death, his father's devotion had waned. My father had to find his own way to serve G-d.

In Oregon, Dad made the acquaintance of my mother, Orabelle Dugger, a devout follower of the Church of God 7th Day and a daughter of one of the church leaders. When my father returned to California, they kept up a long-distance correspondence. After a three-year courtship, they married and settled in California. Ardent followers of their congregation, my parents observed the Sabbath on Saturday, avoided eating "unclean" meat, and were devoted to the study of the translations of the Jewish Bible. They were particularly inspired by the Bible's first commandment to mankind: "Be fruitful and multiply and populate the earth." I was the eldest of their 10 children.

One of my earliest memories is of being held in the thick arms of my 6-foot-tall father. I must have been about 2½ at the time. Normally I would have felt safe and secure in his arms, but on that particular day I was overcome by my father's intense emotions. He was attending the funeral of his mentor, Carl Stacy, a brilliant Bible scholar whom my father very much admired. He was killed in a car accident, leaving behind a wife and a small child. Daddy was devastated. I clearly remember how I was deeply affected by the sorrow around me and even began to cry. My father told everyone

My parents and me

I was tired, and I couldn't understand why he excused my tears.

Daddy searched all over Southern California, but he never seemed to find a new mentor. Instead of breaking him, this newest tragedy, after the early death of his mother and the loss of so many of his World War II buddies, only seemed to drive him on toward his search for G-d. He prayed and drove himself toward spirituality. He actually begged G-d to test him. Later, he was to say of that, "Don't ever pray that prayer — did I ever get trials and tribulations."

My parents were a very unusual couple. They were upright and moral people, and eventually Daddy became a pastor of his own parish. As expected, Daddy spent time visiting his congregants. Mother always accompanied Daddy on his visits, although this was not the norm. In retrospect, I realize that my parents wanted to ensure that Daddy never found himself in a position that would compromise his integrity. My parents lived their lives and raised their family in stark contrast to the prevalent values in Southern California of the 1960s and '70s. Deeply thinking and disciplined people, my parents stood behind their ideals and were not at all concerned about whether or not we fit in with others in our community.

My mother is a pious, organized, and hard-working woman. For as long as I have known her, she has risen in the silence of predawn to pray and study the Bible. While her family of 10 slumbered, my mother took time for herself and her spiritual and emotional needs. By the time she woke us, she had dressed and eaten breakfast and completed her daily letter-writing session. My mother was a devoted correspondent who kept up with a number of close friends and relatives.

Saturday was our official day of rest, and we diligently prepared for our Sabbath on Friday. I fondly recall how my mother enlisted the help of all her children in the task of cleaning our home in honor of the Sabbath. When we came home from school, she'd

The Youngs Family: Left to Right, back row: me, my mother and my father

say, "Here's your list. Take a snack and change your clothes." She handed each of us our individual list of tasks we had to complete before sundown.

As the sun began its descent, the youngest child was sent outside every few moments to observe the position of the sun and report back to us. He'd race back in the house hollering, "It's sundown, it's sundown!" Immediately, we would stop what we were doing and desist from working. We did not clean or shop on the Sabbath, but we did drive cars and use electrical appliances.

We ate dinner together as a family every day, yet Sabbath dinners were especially memorable. Mother served salmon soup every Friday night, and only on Sabbath did she serve dessert. After dinner all seven of us girls went to bed with our blond tresses wrapped tightly around little pink curlers, so that we would look our best at services the next day. Sabbath morning we would assemble to worship. The services were led by my father, Pastor Youngs.

My parents were very proud of their large family, even though it was seen as an oddity by the community at large. I remember hearing my father tell about church members who laughed at our family, saying, "Here comes Brother Youngs with his tribe, hah, hah!" Daddy wasn't bothered by the scorn of his congregants. He taught us to do what we felt was right and not pay attention to those who didn't understand our values.

Mother used to tell us about the shocked reactions of the women when they'd ask her how many children she had. When she told them she was the mother of 10, they'd put their hand on her arm and say, "Oh, you poor dear." She laughed and told us how she assured those startled women that she was truly blessed to have so many children. My mother was so passionately proud of our family that she submitted an article to our group's magazine lauding the benefits of having large families, concluding with the words, "Let the people of G-d increase and let the wicked decrease!"

My parents would often bring guests home after services, to partake of the sumptuous meals that Mother had prepared before the Sabbath. Mother always served homemade bread and salad with either roast or meatloaf. Dessert was always one of her three specialties: Jell-O with nuts and fruit cocktail topped with whipped cream, yellow cake with a crisp brown-sugar frosting, or date-nut bread. After lunch my parents would nap, and we were expected to either nap or play outside. Mother stressed that the Day of Rest should be spent studying the Bible, and absolutely forbade us from reading newspapers or novels on our holy day. Mother was careful not to wash the dishes on the Sabbath, a practice that left a huge pile of dirty dishes to be done on Sunday morning.

We were also scrupulous in our observance of the dietary laws. Pork and shellfish were completely off limits. I remember how we scrutinized the labels on all packaged goods in the grocery store. Only those products we were sure were free of the smallest trace of lard or its derivatives made their way into our home. To determine which animals to incorporate into our diets and which to avoid, we turned to the laws clearly spelled out in *Leviticus* 11. Cattle, sheep, goats, and deer were permitted. Only fish with fins and scales ever made their way into our home.

Birds and fowl were another story. While the Bible clearly states which birds are forbidden, we had a hard time determining which were permitted. We knew that chicken, turkey, and quail could be eaten, but Daddy wasn't quite sure about duck. After giving the matter much consideration, he finally determined that duck was fine. I remember the first time we were to sample this new delicacy. Daddy invested much effort in barbecuing his first duck. It was roasted to perfection. When he finally finished, he stepped inside for a moment to get a plate. When he returned, the duck was gone. Off in the distance, he saw a dog running off with our dinner. Daddy interpreted this incident as a sign from G-d that we weren't meant to eat duck after all.

Although Christians generally have no problem ingesting blood, Mother trained us never to eat blood. When we killed a chicken, we would slit its throat and hang it upside down to bleed.

After it was cut, the meat would be soaked to remove any blood that remained.

The two precepts, resting on the Sabbath and avoiding "unclean" meats, were shared by all the members of our community; however, my parents were exceptionally pious in their individual practice of our religion. We were raised and educated to maintain a higher standard of morality than anyone I knew. Additionally, Mother's exceptional organization skills and her large family made her a legend in our community. A visiting pastor often spoke in awe of how well run our home was. Everyone's chores were clearly listed; all 10 of us, from the eldest to the youngest, knew just what was expected of them.

When I was 7 years old, I was put in charge of the family's shoes. It was my job to collect everyone's shoes and bring them to the bathroom, where I set them out on some newspaper and carefully polished them in honor of the Sabbath. I worked hard to ensure that everyone's shoes were neat and clean, from Daddy's dressy blacks to the baby's little white ones. I lined up the freshly shined shoes and placed a clean pair of socks inside each set.

When I got older I was promoted and given the important task of cleaning the living room. This was considered a special privilege, which I had earned by being attentive to details. Armed with my little oily rag and bottle of Old English polish, I'd get to work polishing our antique coffee table and then reposition the stiff white lace doilies in the center of the table. The legs of our octagonal dark-wood table were adorned with intricate carvings, which I lovingly polished until they were clean of even a trace of dust. I well appreciated my mother's trust in my abilities, and I was happy to beautify our front room, which was only used on the Sabbath.

Mother was also a paradigm of modesty. She wore long dresses with long sleeves, thick stockings, and for a while covered her head while praying. As she aged, she began to cover her hair all the time, claiming that she felt cold and was more comfortable with her head covered. Modesty was very important to Mother, and

Mother with my oldest son

she insisted that my sisters and I adhere to her strict standards. Although we grew up near the beach, we were not permitted to go to the beach in swimsuits. Even at the beach we were, as always, different: covered up and separate.

Mother made sure that each of her sons was circumcised after birth, preferably on the eighth day. I had always assumed that this was another tenet of our religion. Only much later did I learn that our church did not endorse circumcision. For some unknown reason it was so important to her that she convinced Daddy to go along with this ancient Biblical practice.

My mother's example certainly left a deep imprint on me. One of the most compelling and impressive facets of her personality was her deep attachment to the Bible. My mother was the greatest scholar I knew. Never have I encountered another non-Jew who rivaled her erudition. After delving deeply into Scripture, Mother would come up with a number of questions that she would occasionally present to other learned preachers in the hope of finding an answer. Much of the time, these preachers didn't even understand her questions. During her pregnancies she would take 20-minute naps, and she would read the Bible until she dropped off to sleep. With very few exceptions, I cannot recall my mother reading anything else.

When Daddy prepared his weekly sermon, he would often call upon Mother's phenomenal memory to help him locate the verse he quoted. Her diligence was so inspiring and her perception so great that she often arrived at the true understanding of the text, even without the Oral Torah. For example, she taught me that the 400 years of Jewish enslavement in Egypt did not begin from the time that Jacob descended to Egypt with his family. She had done the math on her own, and she realized that the 400 years in fact began with the birth of Isaac.

I often wonder how my mother developed into such a serious scholar while simultaneously running her home in such an exemplary manner. I know that the answer lies in her deep love of the Bible and her single-minded devotion to living by G-d's word.

Mother was determined to imbue her children with her deep love of Scripture. Before school, she would wake us up early, and we'd all sit together before breakfast, singing Psalms. During our summer vacations she also taught us all about Joshua and the Judges, as well as the Books of *Samuel* and *Kings*.

Mother was a firm disciplinarian, and as a sometimes rebellious eldest child, I had firsthand experience of her disciplinary methods. Behind our home was a huge lemon grove, owned by a man we called Farmer Johnson. Realizing that the fragrant, sun-ripened lemons that littered the ground would go to waste, we asked him if we could collect them and bring them home. Mother would send us out to the lemon grove with empty baskets and boxes to collect the surprisingly sweet lemons she needed to prepare her refreshing lemonade and delicious pies.

One day, when I was about 6 years old, I had no patience to

comb the leaves for fallen lemons. Instead, I kicked the low-hanging, fruit-laden branches a couple of times. Lemons fell from the tree and I quickly filled my basket. If not for my sister's tattling I might have gotten away with my misdeed.

Once Mother heard of my misbehavior she insisted that I bring the stolen lemons back to Farmer Johnson and apologize. I refused. My mind conjured up all sorts of frightening images of an irate farmer getting even with a mischievous little girl, and I stuck to my guns. Mother didn't back down, and even threatened to spank me. With a heavy heart, I agreed to return the lemons. Mother drove me over in the station wagon and hid behind the bushes. I bravely made my way up to the front door.

With my heart pounding in fear, I knocked on the door. When it opened, I thrust the brown paper bag of lemons into Mrs. Johnson's hands, gabbled off a promise never to steal again, and scampered back to the car. Meanwhile, Mother apologized to Mrs. Johnson. As I waited for her, I firmly decided never again to take what didn't belong to me!

Daddy also left a deep impression on me. As Mother often told me, Daddy was "a deep thinker." He certainly invested a lot of thought in searching for the correct path in life. As his eldest child, I held a special place in his heart, and he'd often motion to me and call out, "Come on, let's go!" I'd run out to his pickup truck and we would go for a drive. While we drove, he'd chew his nails and stare off into space. I didn't know what he was thinking and certainly never thought to ask, but it was clear that he was trying to make sense of life.

Daddy loved history and would often be found reading one of his favorite books, Myers' *Ancient History*. I remember sitting at the kitchen table and listening in utter fascination as he told Mother the tragic story of Chanah and her seven sons. At that time, I had no idea that the heroine of the story was Jewish, but I was certainly impressed by the tenacity with which this ancient family held onto their convictions, even at the cost of their lives.

Daddy enjoyed fixing things around the house, and occasionally he would make repairs or home improvements on our property. I loved helping him, and made sure to be around to hand him whatever he needed. My father was a huge man with the thickest hands I had ever seen. He would call out gruffly, "Bring me those boards from over there. Now get me some nails!" and I would go running. After working for a while, the command came: "Now go tell Mother that I am hungry." I'd be off again. Mother had a stash of frozen hamburgers in her freezer for just these occasions. In no time she'd send me back outside with a mouthwatering hamburger sandwich. I'd hand Daddy his sandwich. He'd grasp it in one hand, look up to the heavens, and exclaim, "Thank G-d!" With just one bite, half the sandwich would be gone. The irony of my intimidating and taciturn father stopping to thank his Creator before devouring his sandwich made an incredible impression on me.

We weren't allowed to watch TV, and we certainly didn't attend movies. We did own books, toys, and games, but I have little recollection of my parents playing with us. In every way we were very different from our peers. We were Christian, but we did not celebrate any of the seasonal holidays, as our community realized they were of pagan origin. My parents even forbade us from participating in any preholiday activities that centered on these taboo festivals. This fastidiousness isolated us. Surprisingly, instead of feeling embarrassed or resentful, we absorbed a deep-seated pride in our way of life.

Since we didn't observe Halloween, my parents had to figure out how to respond when the neighborhood children knocked on our door and asked for the proverbial "trick or treat." One year, in addition to our standard apology of "I'm sorry, I cannot give you any candy," we handed out little pamphlets containing an illustration of Daniel's vision from the Old Testament. The following morning I wasn't surprised to see our front lawn littered with dozens of pamphlets.

Although my parents raised us to stand apart from most of

our peers, they were by no means antisocial. I well remember my parents' joy when friends and relatives would drop by unexpectedly. Daddy would happily run out to the grocery store and return home loaded down with paper bags bulging with everything Mother needed to serve her guests. I excitedly watched as packages of hamburgers and potato chips, loaves of bread, and cartons of ice cream emerged from those large brown paper bags.

Not only did my parents like to host their friends and family, they also reached out to strangers in distress. It seldom rained in Southern California, and so the day my father brought Bill and Margaret home is clear in my mind. Driving home from work in a heavy downpour, Daddy came upon a transient couple hitchhiking along the Los Angeles freeway. Without hesitating, he pulled over for the drenched couple and brought them home with him. Mother was completely unfazed by her soggy guests. She dug up dry clothing and prepared a warm meal for them. For his part, Daddy put them up in a nearby cabin and even found Bill a job. Our new neighbors stayed for a number of months under the watchful eye of my parents, until they were once again struck with wanderlust.

My father was bothered by the sight of the down-and-out drunkards living in Los Angeles, and so he joined a group whose aim it was to rehabilitate them. As a young girl I occasionally accompanied him on his trips down to skid row to preach to the drunks. Those able to participate were rewarded with a meal, and after a time, Daddy was able to weed out a few men he felt were the most likely candidates for rehabilitation. Finally he chose two men to bring home with him. As they did for Bill and Margaret, my parents rented a cabin and provided new clothing, jobs, and even haircuts. That first day, everyone was so excited to see the men's transformation. Unfortunately, my father's hopes for these two men weren't fulfilled. After a few weeks they were once again hopelessly drunk and back on the streets of Los Angeles.

Life with my parents was anything but typical. They were serious, hardworking, and driven; recreation was not an important part of their lives. Despite growing up in Southern California in the '60s, I was no all-American girl. At one point we lived a mere six miles away from Disneyland. As we drove by, my nose would be pressed to the window, staring wistfully at the Matterhorn. My parents stared straight ahead, as if Disneyland didn't even exist. Not once did we ever enter those magical gates. What's more, none of us ever dreamed of asking our parents to take us there!

Although we never did visit Disneyland, we did have family trips. Southern California has no shortage of sights, but my parents chose to take us on a yearly trip to the San Diego Zoo.

The night before our trip, my siblings and I were put to bed in the family camper. At 4 a.m. my parents would set off for San Diego. We drove for two or three hours, arriving at our destination at daybreak. We ate breakfast in the camper, and then we headed off for the enormous zoo. There we rode on giant, 100-year-old tortoises and bought cones filled with carrots and celery to feed the baby goats and sheep. There was even a lady holding a baby tiger or lion that we could pet. How I remember buying candy, either Red Hots or candy corn, and peanuts to feed the monkeys. In the afternoon we would get back into the camper and cross the border into Tijuana, Mexico.

Until we crossed that border, I never realized how rich we were. The contrast between affluent America and the third-world country just over the border shocked me. I took in the sights: a destitute little girl dressed in rags, a man with empty eye sockets staring sightlessly into space, an amputee with both legs missing hoisting himself up over the curb onto a wheelchair consisting of a piece of plywood nailed to a skateboard.

Why was no one else shocked? No one paid these people any attention, as if the raw pain and deprivation that I was witnessing was in fact a normal part of life in Mexico.

In Tijuana, my parents would give each of us kids 50 cents and let us explore. Although I could have bought myself a treat, the sight of the beggars, sitting with hands outstretched and pleading eyes, convinced me to break my quarters into pennies to alleviate some of their suffering. I would make my way along the row of beggars, trying to decide how to distribute my money. Inevitably, my money would run out and I would feel very bad that I had nothing left to give. This was my first experience with charity, and it made a tremendous impression.

When I was a little girl of about 5, we went on a weeklong camping trip to California's Yosemite State Park. I can still see the majestic trees and rugged mountains. Beautiful hiking trails and refreshing rivers crisscrossed the park, providing the perfect opportunity to fish, swim, and hike. We camped out in tents, enjoying the pure mountain air. To deter the small black bears that roamed the camp, we made sure to keep our trashcans closed and our food put away.

One day, my father stopped at a lodge to buy us all ice-cream cones. I excitedly made my way down the steps of the lodge, eagerly licking my ice-cream cone. Noticing a group of people surrounding a black bear, I went over to investigate. As soon as I approached, the bear raised its paw and tried to swipe my cone! I pulled it away. In an instant my father came bounding down the stairs of the lodge, grabbed my ice cream, and handed it to the bear. My quick-thinking father surely saved my life, but I lost my long-awaited treat. He didn't buy me a replacement cone. My father's motto seemed to be, "Life is rough so I'm gonna raise you to be tough!"

For all of my parents' heroic efforts in their parenting and role modeling, the years of tough disciplinary measures, including corporal punishment, resulted in my becoming a sullen and angry teenager. They pulled me through those awful years by having a lot of patience. My mother came to me once privately to tell me how much I was hurting my father, and my father came to me one day and said, "Your mother stays up every night, crying and praying for you."

My parents were deeply religious individuals. They lived to serve G-d and bring others close to the Creator. They worked hard to provide us with a solid upbringing, and instilled in us strong moral values that buffered us from the world's depravity. Still, I did not find lasting fulfillment in the religion I was offered. As I grew into adolescence, I became aware of a nagging emptiness inside. And the skills my parents nurtured were vital in my search for my soul's true path.

I was not privileged to be born a Jew, but I feel fortunate to have been born to such discerning parents. Although I am saddened at the thought of all that I have missed out on in my lonely years of searching for the truth, what I regret the most is not being given a Bais Yaakov education. How I wish that I was fluent in our Holy Tongue and could quote verses in their original Hebrew. Yet, for all my lack, I know that my parents managed to instill in me a deep appreciation of and knowledge of *Tanach*. Due to Mother's efforts, I was spared the fate of growing up an ignoramus.

CHAPTER 2

Beginnings of a Search

Public school, California, the '60s. Not the most conducive time, place, or setting for instilling moral values. And yet, despite the prevailing lack of principle, my parents succeeded in maintaining their standards. I couldn't have been older than 8 or 9 when my mother sat me down and said, "You won't be allowed to date until the age of 18, and then you'll only be allowed to date and marry members of our church. Better not to accept even an ice-cream cone from someone you wouldn't date and marry." With my parents providing such an example, I had no problem accepting their way of life. At my own initiative, when I was 13 I vowed to be moral, and not to marry outside of our religious group.

Among Mother's considerable talents was an affinity for music. Before her marriage she had been a piano teacher, and when I was 5 I became her pupil. I was not an eager student; in fact, I was so stubborn and disagreeable that our lessons became almost unbearable. When I was 6 years old, I refused to continue learning the piano, insisting that I wanted to play the violin instead.

A few days later, Daddy appeared with something hidden

behind his back. With a flourish, he held up a violin. My heart dropped. I would have to thank my parents, and worse still, learn to play the thing! I wished I had never claimed to want violin lessons! Despite my reluctance, I learned to love playing the violin.

Years later, a violin led to my first encounter with a Jew. Growing up in an anti-Semitic culture, I had absorbed a mistrust of Jews. Where I came from, Jews were considered stingy cheats, and we were wary of doing business with them. The pawnshop where Mother and I searched for a new violin, though, was definitely owned by a Jew. We had made the rounds of a number of pawnshops in Los Angeles, searching for a dream violin to replace the instrument I'd played for the past eight years. The violin we found had a beautifully mellow tone. This was the instrument we had sought.

We approached the Jewish proprietor. "How much?" Mother asked. On the counter beside her, I stroked the warm wood and ran my fingers up and down the strings.

A cigar clenched between his teeth, the owner said, "Sixty dollars." His voice was gravelly.

Mother firmly responded, "That's too much, I don't have it."

"So how much do you have, lady?"

Mother emptied her change purse and counted out her bills and coins. Forty. Fifty. Fifty-five dollars and every last cent she had was piled up on the counter. She looked up.

"That'll do," said the old man. The coveted violin was mine. Was I ever surprised. It was the first time I had ever done business with a Jew — and he had shattered the "stingy Jew" stereotype. Decades later, I was still able to detect a faint scent of the man's cigar smoke on my prized instrument.

I grew up at the foot of Mount Baldy, a snowcapped mountain that was the tallest of California's San Gabriel Mountain Range. Our home was on a piece of land owned by our "adopted" relatives, Uncle Russell Norton and his Sicilian wife, Aunt Eva. They owned two and a half acres of land on which sat two homes and eight cabins. We lived in one home; Uncle Russell, Aunt Eva, and their six children lived in the other. The one-room cabins were usually rented by the Mexicans who worked in the lemon groves nearby for $10 a week. In the center of all this was a large patio with a basketball hoop, round patio tables, and garden plots.

Aunt Eva, Uncle Russell, and their family were central figures in my childhood. They also belonged to our religious group, and since we didn't live anywhere near our extended family, they became our family. True to her Italian roots, Aunt Eva made the most wonderful spaghetti, lasagnas, and ravioli for Sabbath dinners. She was a nurse and an incredibly warm woman. She taught me to pray "with all your heart and tears, until G-d hears your prayers."

On the outskirts of our land, my father built a pen for our family's goats. My little brother was only able to tolerate goat milk. The high cost of commercially prepared goat milk prompted my father to acquire a small flock of our own. From the age of 12, I

That's me in the black dress, front row, third from left, standing next to my cousin Sharon Norton, fourth from left.

was placed in charge of our flock. This turned out to be one of the greatest gifts of my childhood.

We started out with just one goat, but in time the numbers increased until we had 10 goats to care for. Morning and evening I milked the goats, fed and watered the animals, and bottle-fed the babies. In time I became very devoted to the wily little creatures. Caring for them helped to develop my capacity for love and gave me the opportunity to meditate. I enjoyed taking my goats out to graze upon the craggy brush between our home and the lemon groves. Being alone with my flock, gazing at the beautiful mountains of Southern California, gave me time to think. Before long my thoughts turned to G-d and spirituality.

Spending time alone in nature, communing with myself and G-d, became a favorite experience of my adolescent years. Whenever my family went camping, I would wander off on my own in search of a little gurgling brook. There, I would sit and reflect and pray. These were precious and enduring moments, and I felt close to my Creator.

When I was 14, I attended a youth camp with a group from our assembly. One night, everyone sat around a campfire, singing and praying. Somehow, the very beauty of the service did not satisfy me; if anything, it only intensified the relentless yearning within me. I wanted something more.

I walked up a wooded hill and peered up at the heavens spread out above the towering pine trees. The flickering stars felt so close; I felt deeply connected to G-d. Deep within, a new thought welled up. G-d, Creator of the magnificent heavens above me, was surely great enough to hear my prayers. I said to myself, *If the G-d of the universe is so powerful as to make these heavens, then I know that He can listen to my prayer. I need no mediator! From now on, I am only going to pray to G-d Himself!*

Despite moments of deep inspiration, my teenage years were intensely lonely. I felt deeply disconnected from both of my parents, and I had no one with whom I could share my intimate thoughts. At high school, I felt alien from my fellow students. Knowing how I loved nature, my parents would send me up to Yakima Valley, Washington, to spend the summers with my mother's sisters. I relished every day spent in the company of Aunt Naomi and Aunt Mary. They were warm and uncritical, and they even fought over who would get to host me. Most of my time spent up in Washington I stayed with Aunt Naomi and Uncle Gordon on a ranch out in White Swan.

Aunt Naomi and Uncle Gordon had 10 children, and their eldest son Gordon was something of a prodigy. He dropped out of high school to continue his education at his own pace. At first, the truant officers tried to force him to return to high school. Gordon's principal intervened, explaining that he was incapable of providing the level of education Gordon needed. Already in his teens Gordon took college correspondence courses, eventually attending law school at Harvard — while working for NASA! This was the first time I heard of homeschooling.

The summer I was 16, Uncle Gordon gave me two wild horses to break in. Those horses were so untamed they were even afraid of a rope, and so my first task was to get them used to being led. I would feed them grain, and while they ate I slipped the rope on them. Once they were used to the rope, I wrapped it around them. At first, they trembled in fear. When they became accustomed to the rope, I introduced the bridle, and then the saddle.

My next task was to mount the horses. They would often rear up unexpectedly, which frightened me. When the time finally came to ride one of my horses, it took off at a gallop. I held on for dear life and prayed that it would soon calm down and slow to a trot. I knew that I had better gain control over those horses, and so I spent another few days getting the horses to walk in a square under my firm hand. It took weeks of training, but I was finally able to ride both horses without them getting out of control. My weeks with the horses taught me not to let a situation get out of control, and instead to invest whatever time and effort was necessary to address issues before they became harder to handle.

I was deeply touched by the beauty of the countryside. Miles away from the smog and neon lights of the city, the brilliance of the stars filled me with awe. I remember riding horseback with my cousin, the scent of freshly cut hay perfuming the nighttime air. Above my head, the Milky Way was suspended in all its glory. I felt so closely connected to G-d, spellbound by the awesome vastness of His world!

I was not charmed by all of G-d's creations, however. In fact, there were a few I would have rather not encountered. Uncle Gordon had warned me to watch out for rattlesnakes, which were often found in the fields where we worked. One year, my 9-year-old sister joined me up in Washington. She accompanied me to the alfalfa fields where I was moving irrigation lines. One day, a snake slithered unnoticed through the greenery and made its way up her leg. She let out a chilling scream and I ran to her. Grabbing a wooden slat, I beat that snake to death. Just a few moments later we stumbled upon the snake's mate. Once again I raised my make-shift weapon above my head and slammed it down. I had been entrusted with my little sister's safety and was relieved to bring her back home safe and sound.

Although I would have been happy never to have made the acquaintance of a venomous snake, our terrifying encounter did teach me something. A breach had been made in my youthful feeling of invincibility. For the first time I became aware of my human vulnerability. I was simultaneously aware that in that huge field, it was the Hand of the Divine that placed those two snakes just where we would encounter them.

Back in California my peers also enjoyed spending time out in nature, but it wasn't quite the allure of meditation that attracted them. They were passionate about watching the surfers at the beach. I also found it fascinating to watch the surfers wait for a good wave, hop aboard their surfboards, and ride the wave out till the end. Many years later, when going through a particularly rough time, I'd recall the Pacific Ocean and its powerful breakers, feeling that G-d was calling upon me to ride the waves.

A few times I joined my cousin Sharon and her brothers as they trained for long-distance running. While speed is the main goal in short-distance running, I learned that endurance is the key word when it comes to long distance. My cousins taught me how to pace myself so that I could maintain my stamina over time. I also learned that when you're breathless and feel that you just can't go on, if you can just manage to push yourself the adrenaline will kick in and you'll get a second wind. Years later, when my children were small, I found this technique invaluable.

Although I truly loved nature, reading was my first love. My passion for books stemmed from the restless brooding that filled my soul. I felt empty inside, and I was uncomfortable with the knowledge I had been given both at home and in school. Something inside told me that there existed a greater body of truth out there, and I was determined to find it.

I never had my fill of books. I read in class and during recess, and in every spare moment at home. My high school boasted two large libraries, one specializing in fiction and the other in nonfiction. Fiction did not interest me at all; I frequented the second library daily.

I was in ninth grade when I discovered Tolstoy. The following thought-provoking questions contained in his books set me on a path of contemplation. "These are the great questions of life that everyone has to answer: Is there a G-d? Is there life after death? Is there reward and punishment? What's the purpose of life?" These questions fueled my desire for more knowledge. The more I read, the more I realized that there was much more to know. I began to keep a list of books that I was determined to track down and read. My father once joked that I reminded him of an alcoholic pining for a drink, and there was truth to his words. I read like one possessed, devouring book after book in my search for answers.

I have always considered my thirst for knowledge as the single most important factor in my lifelong quest for truth. Yet perhaps it was the other way around. Perhaps it was the restlessness of my sensitive soul that inspired my thirst for knowledge. Either way, it was the voice of my intuition that held me back from fully committing myself to the religion of my parents.

My father, Pastor Youngs, was a very inspiring and successful member of the cloth. Tall and broad, he cut an imposing image. Daddy was a natural leader and had conducted many baptismal ceremonies. I, his eldest child, was a thorn in his side, testimony of his failure to "save the soul" of his own child. The vast majority of our community's children had been baptized; some even at the age of 9. I, however, was the exception. From a very young age I stubbornly refused to be baptized. Since baptism was intended to be a voluntary expression of religious commitment, Daddy could not coerce me to comply.

When I was 16, my Uncle Gordon took me aside and gently told me that the time had come for me to be baptized. My parents were thrilled that I had finally come around, yet when my father asked me to add my signature to the lifelong commitment detailed on the baptismal certificate, I blanched. There was no way that I would sign. Somewhere deep within my being, the pure voice of truth urged me not to make a vow that I might not be able to uphold. Something told me that there might be more to serving G-d than what I knew. I refused to sell myself out to a religion that I couldn't be 100 percent sure was true.

Like many teenagers, I was consumed with a strong need to find myself and my own unique place in society. My search led me to explore a number of different churches, but I grew disenchanted. I searched further afield. When I entered college I decided to study all the religions of the world. I began with Islam, but I could not get through the Koran. Two weeks into my college career, my sociology professor made the following pronouncement: "First of all, you must face the fact that you belong to the animal kingdom." That was my last day in college.

I went to work in a nursing home. That year, I learned more

about life than I ever could have learned in college. It wasn't easy spending my days with the elderly residents. Many of them were depressed and lonely, and it hurt me to see them live out their last days in sadness. They shared with me their pain and disillusionment, and I cried with them.

There was one old woman whose face was a mass of wrinkles. "I used to be beautiful," she told me. I believed her; there were still faint traces of beauty in her features. Still, I clearly saw that beauty is fleeting and has no long-lasting value.

One of the residents was a retired naval officer. He loved to brag about the good old days, when he was an honored admiral in the Pacific. Though he had once been awarded much honor, he was no happier in his old age than the lonely man sitting next to him.

My most poignant memory was of the old man who had yet to fulfill his dreams. "When I get out of here," he would tell me, "I'm going to sail down the Mississippi on a flatboat." There was no chance of his dream coming true.

Each day I encountered living testimony to the futility of beauty, honor, and even one's goals and dreams. If none of these accomplishments brought lasting benefit or comfort, what would bring man contentment and happiness in his old age?

There was one woman in the nursing home who bubbled with life. The wife of a poor coal miner and the mother of 14 children, she certainly hadn't lived a charmed life. And yet, she was so much more pleasant to be around than many of the other residents. She never complained, and she had the most upbeat attitude I encountered. I began to think that maybe a large family was the key to happiness.

What I saw most clearly in that nursing home was that just wanting to live a good life was insufficient. Up until that point I had thought that since I wanted to live a righteous life, things would turn out well for me. Now I realized that I needed a plan to set my dreams in motion.

I began to drive out to beautiful, secluded places, where I would meditate for longer periods. "G-d, help me in this journey of life. Help me to serve You. Help me not to make mistakes," I prayed. But I had absolutely no idea how to pursue my dreams.

CHAPTER 3

Coming to My Doorstep

A

At the end of my stint working in the nursing home, my family attended a summer conference of the Church of God 7th Day in South Dakota. There my father introduced me to his cousin, a member of the board of the Midwest Bible College in Stanberry, Missouri. "Maybe you should think about going there to study," my father urged. At the time, I was at an impasse, unclear as to what I should be doing with my life. The thought of continuing my education appealed to me. After all, I loved to learn; I just refused to compromise my religious values.

A few weeks later, my parents bought me an airline ticket and sent me off to the college in Missouri. It was up to me, however, to find a job in order to finance my schooling. Not long after my arrival, I got an afternoon job on a chicken farm, collecting eggs and transporting them to town.

As a teenager, I had struggled with doubts and fears about religion, but Christianity's overblown reaction to questioners who thought out of the box kept me from ever verbalizing my troubling thoughts. For years I turned them over and over in my mind as I continued my lonely search for answers. Ironically, it was at missionary college that I came upon the first few holes in my belief system. There, I learned that the Christian Bible had evolved out of a collection of letters that mere men decided to write: men who, with only one exception, had not even claimed to have received prophecy!

And it was in missionary college, at the age of 19, that I finally found someone I could talk to. It was difficult for me to adjust to being away from home, and I was extremely homesick. But I had a wonderful creative-writing teacher named Jewell who took me under her wing. She was the first teacher I ever encountered who saw teaching as more than just imparting information. She actually took a warm interest in her students' welfare. Jewell reached out to me and took me into her home and heart.

One summer night, Jewell and I stood together under the oak trees in front of her home. We were talking about the Bible, and Jewell told me that she was troubled by our religion's practice of extracting just a few commandments from the Jewish Bible while ignoring all the rest. Her words struck a chord. I had grappled with this question for years. This was the first time I had ever heard anyone verbalize it.

It was Jewell who first suggested that I date John Massey. Limited as I was by the vow I had taken at the age of 13, I knew that my future husband would have to be a member of our religious group. Still, I felt lost. How could I, with no one to guide me, figure out who would be a suitable mate? I had no choice but to put my trust in the A-mighty. I turned to G-d and begged Him to help me find my intended. I specifically asked G-d to bring my future husband right up to my doorstep.

Of all the men studying at our small missionary college, John Massey was by far the most learned. He was very serious about religion, and his Bible was worn out from heavy usage. During my second year, Jewell mentioned that she and some others thought we would make a good match. One evening, John offered to drive a few of us students to a social gathering. I needed to pick up something from my apartment first, and John accompanied me to my front door — right to my doorstep! There, he asked me out.

On our very first date, John asked me to marry him. I readily agreed; I knew he was for me, and the fact that he actually came up to my doorstep seemed to be a G-d-given answer to my prayers.

John took me down to Georgia to meet his parents. Although I realized that his family lived a simpler life than I was used to back in California, my first impression of his family was quite positive. It was only after our wedding that I became aware of the differences in our families' lifestyles.

Before our marriage, I held an imaginary picture of the home we would build. It would have a white picket fence out front, and would be neat and clean. No luxuries, nothing fancy, just a safe little nest to raise our family. While I planned our wedding and prepared myself for marriage, I left our future living accommodations to John down south in Georgia.

By this time my folks had moved from California to Idaho, since, as Daddy had concluded, "Southern California is no place to raise children!" Knowing that I would soon be moving away to build a life of my own, I flew home to spend some time with them. I must have sensed that my future would not be a painless voyage out into the sunset, for I felt a need to fortify myself before I sailed into uncharted waters.

I made the most of this time with my parents; it was a closure of sorts. My identity of Sheryl Youngs, daughter of Pastor Youngs and his faithful wife Orabelle, was about to morph into that of someone more mature and sophisticated, for soon I was to become Sheryl Massey, wife of an exceptional minister.

I approached my upcoming marriage with the same deliberate concern that had characterized my life until then. I was standing upon the threshold of an important future, and to prepare for it, I felt that I had to do more than just shop. I looked for some sort of guidebook to prepare me for marriage, but there was very little written material published by members of our assembly. The lack of literature led me to seek the counsel of three women I most admired.

I approached my youth leader and asked her to share some words of wisdom. She told me: "When you dress your child, don't just put his pants on; make the most of this daily opportunity to teach him the difference between right and left." Her simple words were far off the mark in terms of the marital guidance I sought. I crossed her off my list and went on to wise woman number two, my aunt. She, too, came up lacking. Finally, feeling I needed to be more specific in my quest, I consulted a preacher's wife. I asked her to explain some of the Biblical verses that refer to a woman's relationship with her husband. The meaning of the text had been lost on me. Sadly, she, too, was unable to answer my question.

As had been the case up until then, I was on my own when it came to developing my outlook on life. There was nowhere to turn, no one to guide me on how to successfully live my married life according to G-d's Will. And so I looked for answers in the Bible itself. The most potent recipe for a successful marriage I found was in *Proverbs* 31. I read King Solomon's "Ode to the Virtuous Woman," meditating on these verses each night. That way, I hoped, I would cull the answers I so desperately sought. But alas, I had no commentaries. Somehow, I sensed that there must be more, that there was a greater body of religious thought alluded to in the words of the Jewish Bible. But until Judaism provided the key — the Oral Torah — G-d's wisdom was hidden from me.

There was one particular line of *Eishes Chayil* that held great meaning for me: "Her husband was known at the gates, where he sat with the elders of the land." Within those words, I felt, I could find my answer. This verse became the goal of my marriage; I was going to help my husband grow into an influential scholar and leader. With his erudition and intelligence, coupled with the passion of my single-minded vision, I knew that this goal was well within my grasp.

I looked forward to a bright future together with my husband. No longer would I be alone, and left to fend for myself. Soon John and I would be married, and together we would study the Bible and grow together.

All of my and John's immediate family gathered in California for our wedding. It just so happened that our religious group had their national meeting for the first time in Southern California, so it was convenient for those who wanted to attend. My parents, with seven daughters, had always told us that it would be up to us to pay for our own weddings. My main expense was a new pair of shoes; I borrowed a dress. Usually, brides and grooms in our community asked their best friends to stand up by them as they were married. I didn't see the point in this, as I was closer to my family. So the day of the wedding John's family and mine stood up by us as we were married. The preacher preached a sermon and my father pronounced us man and wife. "No flowers for this bride"; I carried instead a brand-new Bible with an inscription of appreciation. After the short ceremony, in which everyone came through a line to shake our hands, I presented this beautiful leather Bible to the one who had encouraged our match, Jewell.

Even though I was 21, I had only been to about two other weddings. In our circles these were quite dry affairs. After the ceremony they would have a reception where the bride and groom would cut and serve the traditional white wedding cake, which I never liked. Then for an hour or so they would stand in front of everyone and open their gifts, thanking the giver and trying to make witty remarks. I always found this rather boring.

I didn't have money for such a fancy cake anyway, so I skipped this part. We had our quick ceremony, shook hands with the small crowd of guests, and made a quick exit, traveling back with John's family to our cousins' place, where his family and mine had stayed for this week.

Sheryl Massey was about to begin her new life.

Lookout Mountain

Appalachian Mountains of Georgia

It is said that seven states can be seen from this vantage point. During the Civil War, soldiers clambered up to scan the area below.

Now my days crawled by as the Southerners rocked on their porches and drawled, "How y'all doin'?" Even the dog lying on its dusty spot of the road lazily arose, stretched, and found no reason to hurry as the car sped toward it.

As difficult as the adjustment was, this experience was a gift from Above, slowing me down to look into the valley of life and search for another trail to take.

CHAPTER 4

No White Picket Fence

The next morning, the Massey clan loaded all our still-packed wedding gifts into their camper, and we set off for the 2,000-mile drive back to Georgia. I was a bit disappointed with our traveling arrangements. We had been married for a matter of hours, and I was uncomfortable having all these people around. Having grown up in an oppressive environment, though, I didn't even think of complaining. I consoled myself by thinking of the privacy awaiting us in Georgia. My little fantasy home still shimmered before me, in all of its inviting warmth.

Sometime during that three-day drive in the Massey camper, I found out where we would be living: in a small bedroom at the back of my in-laws' bustling household in the Appalachian Mountains that had been set aside for us newlyweds.

My dream of a home of my own was fading fast.

After days of traveling, I emerged from the claustrophobic camper tired, yearning to freshen up, and longing for some quiet space of my own. But upon entering the Masseys' house, I was surprised to see that things looked very different from the way they'd appeared to me back in December, when John had brought me to meet his parents.

The house was far simpler than I remembered. It was not as tidy or organized as my mother's well-run home. Worst of all, there was no bathroom, just an outhouse. I had known that the Masseys lived a simple and non-materialistic life, but I hadn't realized just what that meant. I had grown up in a nice, middle-class home. This was light-years away from what I was used to.

After all the time spent on the road, I had been looking forward to a good hot shower. When we finally arrived at the Massey home, I asked where I could wash up. I was handed a little pan of water. I looked down at it and wondered: Just how was I supposed to go about washing with it? Was I supposed to dump its contents over my head or somehow stand inside it? Somehow I got through that, but soon another surprise awaited me.

As a Westerner, from clear across the other side of the United States, I had always been taught in school that the Civil War was over. Well, maybe there was a copy of a surrender somewhere, but it hadn't reached this part of the Deep South. The resentment over the way the Northerners had treated the Southerners in the war and the way of life they had forced on them had seethed beneath the surface for over a hundred years. Now that they had an outsider in their midst — that is, me — they vented their rage. At first I feebly tried to defend what I had always considered the right side, the North. But in the days to come there was a part of me that felt so attacked, especially on this issue, that I, the real me, went underground. I was careful to never again put myself into such a position of vulnerability as to tell what I really thought. I kept my true feelings inside, all locked up.

In the weeks that followed a thousand questions formed in my mind. *How on earth had I ended up here? Why had G-d led me to this far-flung place, deep in the Southern wilderness?* Looking back, I understand that I was completely disoriented by my shocking new way of life. To top it all off, I had very little time alone to think.

With so many people living under one roof, I had no personal space. Located in an isolated part of the Appalachian Mountains, we were surrounded by nature, and I longed to retreat to a private place in the woods outside. Unfortunately, the menfolk told me that the woods were infested with venomous snakes, and I shouldn't enter them alone.

My life had turned out to be a far cry from anything I had ever envisioned, and yet the thought of leaving my husband never entered my mind. It was clear to me that this was the man G-d had intended me to marry. My only question was: What did G-d want me to learn from my new circumstances?

I had no choice but to overcome my culture shock and adjust to my new reality. Determined to make the most of my challenging situation, I soon became familiar with the Massey way of life. As I did, I realized that although I could cultivate some common ground, in many ways we would always remain worlds apart. In the years to come, as my children were born, I comforted myself by resolving that if I couldn't change the things I really disagreed with, at least I could teach my children differently — and I did.

To be fair, the Masseys were moral people, and like my own parents they were more righteous than the people in their community. Though further away there were good, simple people to be found, the mountainfolk in our area were mostly a bunch of crooks, and I soon learned that anything left outside was sure to be stolen. Granddad — as we called my father-in-law — would never take anything that didn't belong to him, and he prayed frequently that his children grow up to be G-d-fearing individuals.

At first I held my mother-in-law personally responsible for the family's rigid mentalities. She seemed totally locked into her mindsets and had absolutely no interest in change. We developed a typically negative relationship. I thought that if only she had better homemaking skills, would read a book now and then, or have at least one close relationship outside of her family, it would have made my life easier. Yet I recognized that it was G-d Himself Who placed me where I was, and so I decided to learn what I could from the situation. Not wanting to remain locked in negativity, I decided to improve our relationship. I figured that there must be something about Granny that was worthy of my admiration, and I was determined to find out what it was.

It wasn't really all that hard to appreciate the considerable time and effort my mother-in-law invested in cooking for her family. This was who she was and how she showed her love. On the first morning in my in-laws' home, I woke up to the delicious smell of Granny's wonderful biscuits. Every morning, the Masseys sat down to an elaborate breakfast, consisting of the lightest biscuits imaginable, homemade sausages and gravy, fried sweet potatoes, potatoes, and Granny's homemade jam.

After breakfast, Granny would rest up in her chair while Granddad went out to the garden. That first summer the garden was in full bloom, with cornstalks nearly eight to ten feet high. Every day Granddad would bring in fresh, homegrown produce: armfuls of green beans, huge luscious tomatoes, okra, potatoes, or sweet potatoes. As soon as Granny finished her rest she'd begin preparing lunch. She'd snap the beans, mix them with oil and salt, and cook 'em down, chop up the okra and roll it in cornmeal before frying it up. Peel the tomatoes, slice the corn from the cobs and cream it with milk, and prepare a perfectly browned pone of buttermilk cornbread fried in her skillet. Everything was scrumptious and cooked to perfection.

On particularly hot summer days, after a satisfying meal, the entire family would often nod off in the comfy chairs and couch in the living room. I was surprised at how well they slept, oblivious even to the odd fly lazily buzzing about. Life in the mountains was relaxed. No one was in a hurry; there was nowhere to run. It was nothing like my childhood back in Southern California, where life was all about accomplishment. My parents were incredibly driven workaholics, and my ever-efficient mother was always trying to cram more and more into her already busy days. I remember how they'd race past the living room and, seeing one of us sitting on the couch, they'd say, "Get up — there's work to be done!" At one point, as my mother worked nights, she ate raw Quaker Oats right out of the canister for breakfast as she drove home.

It wasn't just what we ate that was so different; the whole atmosphere was new to me. In the evenings, the entire Massey family would sit around and talk. Back in California, I had never seen anything like that. Where I came from, life was serious business. Children were to listen to their parents and not talk back. If the toddler did cute things, we were told, "Don't laugh or look at him, he just wants to get attention."

Our family dinners were quite formal, and they were more of an opportunity for my parents to train us in proper etiquette than to create family togetherness and connection. We were taught how to take a bit of butter from the butter plate and put it on our own plates before spreading it on our bread. Of course we were to say please and thank you, and never, ever chew with our mouths open. For spilling or chomping on our food, we were liable to be banished to our rooms without finishing our dinner.

At the Masseys' home, everyone joined in the dinner conversation, and they often continued to converse even afterward as they wandered slowly back into the living room. If someone felt particularly passionate about something, he'd claim the floor by getting up and standing in front of the wood stove. I wasn't accustomed to families spending time together talking.

I watched this relaxed atmosphere of my new family, and particularly appreciated how my in-laws took the time to converse with their children on a daily basis. I suppose that is one of the key reasons why there wasn't much of a generation gap on the mountain as compared to the faster-paced culture of the big cities.

Occasionally, there would be a heated discussion about some passage or another from the Bible. I enjoyed listening to my husband, father-in-law, and brother-in-law passionately debating the

Bible. Later, as my sons were born, I couldn't wait for the day when they'd join in the family's Bible Battles.

Even the humor on the mountain was different. Back in California, people often enjoyed a well-placed barb at someone else's expense or a joke of intellectual wit. On the mountain, amusement consisted of telling over comical antics of someone they knew.

At first, as they told a story and erupted into hysterical laughter, I would sit stony-faced, wondering, *What on earth is so funny?* As different family members continued to repeat and embellish the story in different ways and the belly laughter subsided into chuckles, there would be a few quiet moments of, it seemed to me, pure pleasure. And sooner, or maybe later, someone would remember yet another story…

Later, as I came to know these mountain personalities, I understood the humor a bit more. Granddad loved to tell one such story about a fellow who'd climb up a tall tree from time to time and threaten to jump. All the womenfolk, including the fellow's mother, aunts, and sisters, would run out, waving their aprons, surrounding the tree, and cry, "Don't jump, don't jump!"

"Yeah, I'm gonna jump," he'd go on threatening. After a while he'd have enough and come down, only to continue his theatrics on a later occasion.

One day, one of Granddad's brothers joined the crowd, and as the fellow threatened to jump, he called out, "Jump! I said, *jump!*" It was the last time the man ever tried that stunt! Even though they'd heard the story hundreds of times, the family laughed again and again.

Occasionally, Granddad's great-aunts would invite their friends and family to a "musical." The table would be laid out with roast turkey and dressing, coconut cake, German chocolate cake, and all sorts of goodies. We would sit in the many chairs lining the walls, and in the middle a couple of fiddlers would play, along with someone on the guitar. Everyone would clap their hands and stomp their feet along with the music. We had a really nice time just talking and spending time with one another.

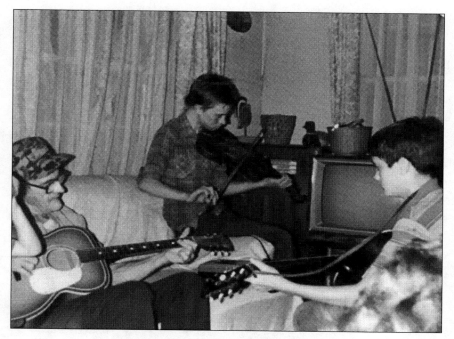
Granddad and my boys making mountain music

Although eventually I appreciated these simple enjoyments — activities that had been phased out in the workaholic culture I was reared in — I missed intellectual stimulation. Day in and day out, I spent all my time with the same people. I remember the first time I traveled to the public library and brought back a large stack of books for everyone. They just looked at me in surprise, without any sign of interest.

I soon discovered that the people in the mountains were not very educated. Many were barely literate, and only a few had actually completed their high school education. I hardly ever remember meeting anyone who had a college education!

That's why Granddad came to the attention of the circuit preacher. Granddad was fond of recalling the time back in the '40s, when he was sitting on his porch and he looked up to see an old Model-T Ford coming up the dusty path through the pine trees. As he watched, a little old man got out and introduced himself as Preacher McMicken.

The preacher addressed Granddad: "I was at the store and I asked, 'Is there anyone in these parts that reads the Bible a lot?' The man behind the counter spit out his wad of tobacco, looked up to the ceiling, and said, 'Ya know, thar shor is. Up thar on that mountain thar's Joe Massey. Him studies the Bible all the time. Ain't never seen nobody study the Bible like that man!'"

From that point on, the circuit preacher took Joe Massey under his wing and taught him the doctrines of our religion. He convinced him to become a Sabbath-observer and avoid "unclean" meats. Granddad never wavered from the teachings of Preacher McMicken.

What was even more unusual was that Granddad went out to the woods to pray and request that his sons would grow up to serve G-d. He also spent time discussing the Bible with his sons. Although they were passionate about their beliefs, the Massey men were able

Granddad and Granny with my daughter, baby Jenny

to debate logically, without becoming overly defensive and agitated if one of their arguments was threatened by someone else's position. Granny was the daughter of a fiery preacher and was rock solid in her beliefs as well. Over time, I realized that my in-laws were truly heroes for raising such moral children and sticking to their beliefs despite the low-class society they lived in.

Looking back, I believe that they were so successful because they had such a warm home. Their children knew they were loved and accepted. They had no need to look outside the home for fulfillment. In this way, Granny and Granddad managed to keep their children away from inappropriate influences.

Along with the slower-paced lifestyle was also a sense of simplicity, of being satisfied with little, and a deeply rooted reliance on G-d to provide. The mountaineers did not water their gardens; instead, they relied on the rain and G-d to help their crops flourish. I, a product of the 20th century, had the hardest time understanding why no one ever thought of buying a hose to water their crops during times of drought. They just waited passively for the rain to come.

And it was the rain that determined when Granddad and his sons would go out to work. The Masseys had been in the logging and sawmilling business for generations. Logging entailed purchasing a tract of timber and felling the trees with chain saws. First they'd determine in which direction they wanted the tree to fall. Then they would notch it and begin sawing on the opposite side. After the tree fell, the branches were cut off. In earlier days Granddad and the menfolk had used mules to drag the logs out of the woods, but now they had machines resembling huge tractors, called skidders. A strong metal cable was hooked onto the log and dragged it out to a clearing. There, the loader would grab each log, lifting it up onto the loading truck, which transported the timber to the sawmill.

The logs were unloaded and rolled, one by one, onto the sawmill, where they'd be thrown onto the carriage and strapped down

The boys with their father at the sawmill

tightly. First the bark would be trimmed off to be used for firewood. The sawyer would then decide how to cut the log. He could make railroad ties, two-by-fours, four-by-fours, or a combination of different sizes. Processing lumber was lucrative yet dangerous work, done outside in the heat of the day.

It's easy to understand why the men appreciated taking time off from work during inclement weather. During Georgia's heavy downpours, the forest became too muddy for the men to work. For Granddad, that was just as well. After breakfast, he'd look out the window, and if it was overcast and rainy he'd take the day off. Even during the rainy season he wasn't disturbed by a continuous loss of income. "More rain, more rest," he would declare, and return to the comfort of the couch.

This laid-back attitude toward business was the norm. I recall the time Granny's brother came to visit. He was warmly welcomed and served a delicious meal, and then he sat and spoke with the family for about three hours or so. After that he finally inquired if perhaps the Masseys were interested in selling a plot of land nearby. Money matters were obviously the last thing on the agenda. This certainly wasn't the kind of business inquiry I had been used to!

Here there were no Californian rat races where everyone rushed to accomplish, gather things, and run to the next pleasure. I had left behind a people who sometimes hardly knew even their own child, let alone their next-door neighbor. Here for the first time I was encountering a family who slowly savored the moments of each day of their life and enjoyed the simple pleasures of one another.

Despite my rocky beginnings, I gleaned many gifts from my time living on the mountain. As my fantasy of a glorified wife in a leadership role living in a little white house with a white picket fence faded, it was quietly replaced with the thought that *I know G-d has placed me here. He has not forgotten the prayers of my youth. I don't know why, but it looks like He wants me to start at the bottom.*

And so for the first time in my life I walked willingly into a kitchen, rolled up my sleeves, and learned to follow Granny's recipes exactly. And after many, many days I too could make her ultimate breakfast of browned biscuits, fried sweet potatoes, beefy gravy.

CHAPTER 5

Truant Officers and Cadillacs

Days turned slowly into weeks, and little by little I adjusted to my new lifestyle. My frustration and loneliness lifted somewhat when I realized that I was expecting a baby. The new life that I was soon to welcome into my heart was a great source of encouragement and joy to me.

Thankfully, my pregnancy proceeded without any problems. I gave birth to a healthy baby boy at the county clinic. Holding little Joey in my arms was an incredible experience. I remember lying on my bed with my warm little bundle fast asleep on me. Feeling the beat of his little heart against my own and his soft breath tickle my neck filled me with a deep sense of contentment. I was alone no longer. This child was flesh of my flesh, a most precious part of me that I would cherish and protect with every fiber of my being. This small, helpless person managed to transform a frustrated young wife into a fulfilled woman.

Motherhood brought much meaning to my married life. Although I had invested much effort in adjusting and acclimating to the new culture I found myself in, I still didn't fit in. Now that I was a mother I could channel my energies into nurturing my child. Following my parents' example, I saw to it that my baby was circumcised. I observed this practice with my eldest three sons until we finally gave it up due to family pressure, since my husband's family did not have this custom.

I was given nine-dozen cloth diapers as a baby gift, and it wasn't long before those diapers needed to be laundered. Granddad took it upon himself to show me how it was done. He brought out a large, three-legged, cast-iron pot and showed me how to build a fire beneath it. I had to haul up the water from the well outside, add soap, and get the fire going. I found a stick to stir the contents of the pot as it boiled. Next I rinsed them and hung them out to dry on the bushes. This cleaning process was very effective, and the diapers came out freshly whitened and clean. Granddad was right proud of me, and I was proud of my accomplishment, as well.

When little Joey was about a year old, a cousin offered us the use of one of his properties: an uninhabited, ramshackle old

A classic potbellied stove

house. I would have preferred something homier, but the old house was free and so it became our home. A family in our area was moving into a furnished trailer and offered to sell us some of their furniture and appliances. Everything was in good working order and the price was right, and so we became the owners of a lovely mahogany dining-room set and an avocado-colored stove.

We finally had a home of our own. The tin roof leaked

during the frequent Georgia rains, and it wasn't much to look at, but it was ours. In that rickety shack, I happily built a warm little nest for our family. There, I first began to formulate and put into practice my educational goals for my offspring.

I first analyzed the typical methods that the parents I knew in California had used to raise their children. I began to examine the major influences on a child, basing my research on actual statistics available at that time. They were startling. From birth until age 20, the average American child was watching 36,000–50,000 hours of television, which included at least 20,000 acts of violence. He would have 13,000–17,000 hours of public education, would spend hundreds of hours with friends and babysitters, and more time listening to secular music. If he was lucky he would get 1,000 hours of religious education. And time spent studying with his parents? Probably not even that much. No wonder there was such a generation gap, I concluded: parents weren't raising their own children! After leaving them to so many outside influences, they were shocked in the teenage years at this stranger-of-a-kid living in their home.

If a recipe is not turning out the way you want, if a chocolate cake turns out bitter every time, you change the recipe. That's what I decided to do.

What would happen if, as I raised my children, I eliminated the major influences of the outside world such as TV and public education? What if I gave them instead massive inputs of religious and parental influence?

At that moment a fiery resolve began burning within me: "I will raise my sons to be leaders, righteous moral men who will someday influence countries; I will teach them Bible principles, languages, all that they must know."

I began teaching my oldest son the alphabet before he even turned 2. By 3, he was reading primary books. My basic guide was the Scripture that states, "Teach … your sons … when you sit in your house, and when you walk on your way, when you lie down and when you get up... Teach them thoroughly to your children!" Whatever I was doing — when I first sat down with them in the morning, hanging out clothes, or walking on the trail to the folks — I would review stories from the Bible and share my own thoughts and experiences. The knowledge that I was doing G-d's Will was a tremendous source of comfort that served as a buffer from the loneliness of mountain living. My sense of satisfaction and the joy I took in my beautiful children gave me the strength I needed to persevere.

When Joey was 2½, we were blessed with another wonderful little boy. Nate was born in the dead of winter, and when he was two weeks old my husband decided that we ought to go spend the night in his parents' warm home. One night turned into two and then three; it stretched into one week and then another. A month later, we returned to our house. As we approached it, I saw a 12-year-old girl coming toward us smiling, wearing my favorite dress. Many of our wedding gifts and cookbooks lay out in the yard, waterlogged. Another family had moved into our home.

It was hard to see my things being used and abused without our permission. Before my negative feelings had a chance to register, though, I was able to see the situation through the innocent eyes of the girl and her younger siblings. They reminded me of my own brothers and sisters, whom I sorely missed, and I felt an immediate affinity for them. These children were completely faultless and weren't to be blamed for the absurd situation. The cousin who had let us move into his house for free had now given it to another family. Thank G-d we managed to recover most of our possessions.

We packed up the rest of our belongings and moved back in with the folks. Thus began a pattern that repeated itself over and over through the years. We would move out on our own for months and sometimes years at a time. Inevitably, we would lose our home or business and move back into my in-laws' house or on the back of their 10-acre lot.

Granny quietly accepted things that didn't quite turn out right.

Her favorite saying seemed to be, "Well, they say, poor people have poor ways." I often wondered: Did this mountain saying mean that poor people are always making the same mistakes over and over? Maybe we had a mental block and we just couldn't break through the barriers? For it surely seemed true that over and over we tried and we failed again and again.

We were sometimes given unbelievable business opportunities. Once, we moved to a little Alabama town just across the Georgia/Alabama state line. John was handed a glorious opportunity: a fully equipped sawmill to run. As he was a highly skilled sawyer and a hard worker, and had hired a full crew, we were hopeful that this time the business would take off. We rented a nice house and I prayed again that my husband's efforts in this sawmill business would become successful.

I was excited to find a library nearby, but every time I went in with my young sons the librarian gave us a lecture. "You transients never return your books," she would say with disgust as she looked down upon us. My young sons just looked back up at her with appealing eyes, hoping she would stamp their books. I kept my thoughts to myself: *A transient? A gypsy? Is that what she thinks I am? I have a track record of always returning my books .... She really doesn't know who I am.*

About this time my husband was invited to a meeting where an insurance salesman dangled before his audience an amazing incentive. "If anyone makes 15 sales this month I'll rent you a new Cadillac." The next day John went back to the sawmill and persuaded all 15 of his men to take out a much-needed insurance policy. So we became the recipients of the latest model, ultra-luxurious, silver Cadillac for one month!

We didn't have a refrigerator or other basics, and we were barely getting by as we struggled to pay off the sawmill crew each week. But I covered the plush velvet seats of our lengthy limousine with sheets and we carried the boys out one by one so they wouldn't step in the mud and dirty up the car. As we cruised around in this luxury car, we had to watch that our boys didn't push the wrong buttons or the trunk might fly up in midstreet or the antenna start whizzing up and down, maybe scaring some little old ladies.

Oh my! What interesting reactions we encountered as we drove around and when we went back to the mountain. Meandering up Mill Creek Road toward the folks, we passed neighbors whose heads whizzed around so fast their vertebras must have popped out of place!

Later, when we drove back to the library, *SHE* was slowly picking up the freshly delivered newspaper off the grass before opening up. Looking up, she spotted our fancy car driving up and ran to open the door, holding it open to greet us, drivers of the Cadillac! After we exchanged pleasantries, she thanked us for bringing back the books and pleaded, "Please come back anytime!"

I didn't understand. I was still the same person, wasn't I?

The day soon came that the Cadillac went back, the business fizzled, and Granddad came to pick us up and take us back to the mountain to spend the night. And again I wondered, *Are we just poor people with poor ways? Are we destined to forever be going around and around in a rut that's just getting deeper? I keep asking G-d to bless our businesses. Why doesn't He answer my prayers?*

It would be many, many years before I would begin to understand that the One Above had a greater master plan for our family.

People often asked me how I managed to keep myself together and my family functioning despite all the setbacks. I had no choice. When I woke up in the morning, my family needed me. Looking back, I do see that I wasn't very in tune with my feelings; emotional awareness was not a concept I was raised with. People back then weren't focused on feelings, and so when something went wrong I would swallow it down and move on. Somehow, especially in the beginning, I associated roughing it with the adventure of camping. Sure, it was inconvenient. At times, it was downright hard. But I kept my focus on what was within my control. I constantly asked myself, *What does G-d ask of me? How can I become a better wife and mother? What should I do today?* And I could focus on two things I was always thankful for: healthy children and a clear mind.

Never was there a dull moment while raising my growing family. I certainly felt very fulfilled. There was no shortage of tasks demanding my attention. However, it was my great passion for educating my children that gave me the exciting vitality to get up each morning.

When we were engaged, John and I, in one five-minute conversation, decided to homeschool our children. I knew that I could do a better job than the local public school. The public school system in our area was particularly bad; a full 40 percent of Walker County, Georgia, was illiterate.

By the time Joey was 2 years old, our little school was officially in session. I developed a syllabus and lesson plans and structured my day around our official school hours. Joey was an eager pupil, and he was soon joined by his younger brothers Nate, Samuel, and Elijah. Unfortunately, the homeschooling concept was not yet well known, making it very difficult for me to acquire the necessary materials. At that time, only four states in the United States officially recognized homeschooling, and Georgia was not one of them. Not only did Georgia not legally recognize homeschooling, but it was also considered to be a form of neglect, so we came under the jurisdiction of two groups: the school system and the social service system.

When Joey turned 7, we were called to task by the Department of Education. I remember one visit in particular. I had just put the baby to sleep in a laundry basket (we had just lost all of our furniture) behind a thick rocking chair (to protect him from his bouncy brothers) when Mr. Hayes, the truant officer, popped in. He sat in the rocker and began:

"I want to persuade you to volunteer to send your child to school freely of your own will —"

Bang, bang, bang.

My three lively sons, ages 2, 4, and 7, ran in, slamming the screen door loudly behind them.

"Problems that a child not attending school might have are: daydreaming excessively, being shy or withdrawn, lacking dependability, and lacking motivation."

Bang, bang, bang, slam! The boys raced out.

I had as usual tuned out the noise and was only focusing on my rebuttals for our truant officer. Suddenly the baby woke up screaming in the laundry basket behind him. Startled, he whirled around, glared at the basket and the baby, and barked at me, "How many children do you have anyway?"

Later the Social Services got involved and threatened to take action against us. John and his brother-in-law put up a four-by-four room with a roof on the back of his folks' tract of land. We moved in and cut holes in the sides of the walls for windows. Now if a visitor appeared down the trail, our boys quickly scampered out into the Appalachian wilderness, to hide from those who might want to take them away.

Their threats frightened us, and yet we were determined not to send our children to public school. My husband and I drew strength from a recording we once had heard where a homeschooling zealot from Utah said, "If homeschooling is just a preference for you, you will eventually give in when the pressure mounts. If it's your conviction, you will not give up!"

Months later, as Joey had turned 8, those working on our case demanded that we put him in school or they would take him away! John made an agreement with them that they should give us two weeks to leave the state of Georgia. We wanted to give our children much more than public school's offerings. How would we raise them to become responsible and moral while exposing them to the ills of the public school system? Our entire future was at stake. Heartbroken, I knew that I must fast and pray for G-d's salvation.

In the past I had fasted for three days at a time, refraining from

JOEL E. COOK
CHAIRMAN

FRANCES JOHNSTON
SUPERVISOR

Chattooga County Board of Education

JOHN W. KING, JR., SUPERINTENDENT

SUMMERVILLE, GEORGIA

The teachers of our schools want our children to develop into self-supporting, law-abiding, well adjusted, contributing members of adult society. problems that a child not attending school might have are the following:

1.) day dreaming excessively
2.) Being shy or withdrawn
3.) lacking dependability - in a group inter-action situation
4.) lacking exciting motivation (Rewards-and-success)

All four of these problems can be helped with your cooperation. Your child's future rests in your hands. please be fair to him.

Sincerely yours,

John W. Hayes,
VISITING TEACHER
CHATTOOGA COUNTY......

A stern warning from the local truant officer

everything but water. But this time, I was expecting my fifth child, and I felt it wouldn't be wise to fast for more than one day. Sunday was my day off from homeschooling, and so I picked this day for my fast.

That day I was down in the woods, praying, while my husband was out with the boys. My quiet concentration was pierced by Joey's excited cries. I looked up and saw him running over the bridge that spanned the creek. "Mother! Mother! Guess what?" At that moment I knew on some instinctive level that my prayers had been answered.

My dear friend Jewell had come to visit, along with her husband and family. We had remained in touch ever since she'd been my teacher in missionary college, even though she lived quite far away in the Midwest. This was the first time they had ever come down south, and since we had no phone, she hadn't informed me of her intended visit.

Somehow, I knew that Jewell would be instrumental in helping us. The fear I was dealing with, that soon they might come to take our precious son away, was unbearable. As my old friend appeared, the anxiety bursting inside of me came gushing out. "I only want with all my heart to raise my children right. Why are they chasing us like criminals? How can it be that this country, which stands for freedom, won't let a parent teach his own child? Jewell, they want to take our children away!" She listened, and cried with me as I told her all that was in my heart. It was hard to part, so seldom did I have a friend, but now how sweet to have shared. I waved and stood watching her car until it disappeared from view.

About a week later, Jewell called me at my in-laws' home. "We have it all worked out. All of you can come and live near us here in Tahlequah, Oklahoma. John can work in my husband's company, you can live in my grandfather's empty house, not so far from us. Homeschooling is not officially recognized in the state of Oklahoma, but my brother is the principal of the local elementary school, and he has agreed to overlook your family's truancy!"

We loaded our four sons into the car, packed up whatever housewares and clothing we could squeeze in, and drove out to Oklahoma. Just outside of the town of Tahlequah we came to rolling hills adorned with dogwood trees, whose dainty pink and white blossoms took my breath away. We felt right at home, as the Ozarks Mountain country had a culture very similar to that of the Appalachian Mountains we had just left.

We were given a quaint little home to live in. There were two bedrooms, a living room, and a kitchen. Before our arrival, Jewell and her family had lovingly furnished the house. We had a refrigerator and stove and everything we needed — except for one thing. Our new home did not have indoor plumbing.

I was very thankful that G-d had provided us this place of refuge. We had a comfortable home and my husband had a steady job moving houses. Most importantly, I was safe to continue home-schooling my boys! So what if we had to use an outhouse and drive down to the spring to draw water?

I actually learned to enjoy our daily trips to the spring. I would pack the boys and our large plastic cans into the car and drive two miles to this beautiful little oasis. Huge oak trees rose high above the spring, the green leaves rustling softly in the summertime. Near the brook, watercress grew in wild abundance, free for the taking, and there, in the center, bubbled a spring of refreshingly cool, clean water. As we arrived, my boys would jump out of the car and bend down on the stones around the spring to gulp it down.

With our water supply so far away, water was a precious commodity. I used clean water for drinking, cooking, and dishwashing, and the dirty water was used to scrub the floor. I managed to get hold of an ice chest, which worked well as a makeshift bathtub for the boys.

At first, I used to make regular trips to the laundromat, where I spent the afternoon keeping my four boys out of trouble as I did my 15 to 20 loads of laundry. One of our challenges was that if we appeared outside of our home during school hours people asked inquisitive questions. This was awkward and a bit scary for my sons. So I coached them to respond by looking at those who asked questions straight in the eye and saying, "I attend Oklahoma Technological School of Scientific Studies and Liberal Arts for Exceptional Children."

Unfortunately, I was unable to make the trip often enough to keep the laundry from piling up. I had to find a way to get the washing done more often, and so I was quite grateful when someone gave me a wringer washing machine. Jewell was horrified when I told her; she was concerned that I would overexert myself and that the hard, physical work could be dangerous to my pregnancy. I guess that I was blessed with greater physical stamina than most women, since I really didn't find the new laundering method to be too taxing.

First I, or a neighbor, would haul water from the spring. After filling up the basin I would add the soap and the dirty clothes and let it agitate for a while. When I felt they were clean enough, I would run each article of clothing through the wringer, squeezing out most of the water, which fell back into the basin. I would repeat the whole process with the next load, refilling the water as necessary. Once all the clothes were clean, I would attach a hose to the bottom of the tub to drain away the dirty water, and then refill the basin with clean water to begin the rinsing process. Once again I put the clothes

An old-fashioned wringer washing machine that I learned to use

in to agitate and wrung them out again. After everything was rinsed clean, I hung the clothes up to dry on ropes strung across the yard.

Although washing my clothes this way did save me the trouble of spending all afternoon in the laundromat, it was actually quite dangerous. The basin had no cover and I had to watch that my 2-year-old didn't fall in as the clothes agitated. I heard horror stories of people getting caught in the wringer.

My fears were not in vain. One day, I was ill with flu and trying valiantly to complete my tasks, despite my weakness. As I did the laundry, leaning over the wringer to support myself, my son decided to help me pass the clothes through the wringer. All of a sudden, his small arm became entangled in the contraption. Thank G-d I summoned the strength to hit the emergency button and his arm was released before any serious injury occurred.

I began my day bright and early every morning and set about fixing a proper breakfast. Now we often had "Okie food": eggs fried with wild onions, served with homemade biscuits and chocolate gravy. Sometimes I would prepare a stack of Southern banana-mayo sandwiches for my husband to take with him to work. After breakfast was served and cleared away and the boys were finishing up their chores, I put up a pot of our mainstay, pinto beans, to cook for our lunch, which was served at exactly noon.

Our school day began at 9 a.m. Whatever tasks I hadn't yet gotten to by that time I pushed off for the afternoon. I knew that I had to be organized and disciplined if my boys were to learn properly. My children's education was my top priority, and I invested much thought as I designed my lesson plans and teaching materials.

Before the start of each school year I would create a syllabus of all the material I intended to cover with each one of my children. When my efforts in procuring teaching materials were successful, it was much easier to create my lesson plans. When the publishing companies refused to sell me schoolbooks, I was forced to rely on my own creativity and design my own lessons.

I worked hard on refining my classes, always looking to make my lessons more interesting for my little pupils. Not a big believer in "busy work," I came up with creative ways to teach my children as much information as possible in the least amount of time. For example, I would have the children write letters to their grandparents, aunts, and uncles. This got them to practice writing, spelling, and English grammar as well as new vocabulary words, while simultaneously connecting them with their family.

Between teaching my boys, watching the toddler, preparing lunch, and keeping the fire going under my potbellied stove, my mornings flew by. I looked forward to my daily teaching sessions. Shaping the minds of my developing children and teaching them to be G-d-fearing people was my calling in life. For me, there was simply no greater joy than partnering with G-d in developing my precious children.

Precisely at noon, school was over for the day. After a nourishing lunch I would turn the boys loose outdoors. They spent their afternoons playing games such as Cowboys and Indians or collecting firewood. They would choose a tree they knew they could handle, and, using their bucksaw, two of them would cut it down together. Afterward they'd chop it into smaller logs, load up their wagon, tie it down, and push the whole load home.

Some of the people in our community were notoriously heavy drinkers. We had a little 4-year-old Native-American neighbor who once came over at breakfast time clutching a can of beer, insisting that that was what his mom normally served him in the morning. From the young age of 5 or 6, the little boys in our area sported their own tins of chewing tobacco. Despite my best intentions, there was no way to completely shelter my children from the ills of society. Instead, I constantly challenged them to be leaders and thinkers, not followers.

My lessons included a lot more than the standard curriculum of reading, writing, arithmetic, language, phonics, spelling, science, history, and social studies. I also made sure to incorporate many life lessons into our classroom discussions. In this way I was able to instill in my children the attitudes and values that their father and I had cultivated over the years. I also read to them from translations of the Jewish Bible. I explained the widely held theory of evolution and showed them where Darwin erred. We discussed topics such as the path of the wise versus that of the fool, from the Book of Proverbs; self-improvement, and the value of having large families. My personal favorite was dubbed "successful men," which I developed into a tool to get my sons to think beyond society's desire for instant gratification. I wanted them to have a chance at a brighter future, to grow to become men of vision who would build a life for themselves beyond the squalor that mired our society of hillbillies.

When we moved to Oklahoma, my husband was originally employed in the home-moving business. Not furniture moving: John actually moved homes. Home moving was a delicate procedure that involved carefully lifting a home off of its foundations and placing it on special girders that supported it as it was moved slowly through the streets. Special permits were procured and streets were closed to traffic. Even the telephone wires needed to be lifted as homes in transport inched down the street.

We spent two years in Oklahoma and found much satisfaction there. Not only were we blessed with a sufficient income, but in addition our fifth son was born during our stay there.

Jesse's birth was remarkable in its own way. As I began to feel his approaching birth, a severe thunderstorm was headed our way. There was a fear of flash flooding. Not wanting to get stranded at home, we decided to get to the hospital ahead of the rain. We had no one to watch the boys, so we loaded all four of them into the car and set out for the hospital. That night, the hospital parking lot became our home.

Realizing that the birth was imminent, my husband and I hurriedly entered the hospital. When we got to the floor of the maternity ward, we were shocked to see that it was completely deserted. No doctors, no nurses, no patients. Evidently the baby business that day was "kinda slow." Thankfully, after a few minutes staff members were summoned by our doctor.

Finally, Jesse was born. The pain and exhaustion of the day faded as I held my tender infant close to my heart. Soon my room began to fill with doctors and nurses eager for a look at the baby and a chance to offer their congratulations. It was quite obvious that birth in that hospital was not a very common occurrence.

Top left to right: Nate, Joey, Samuel   Bottom: Elijah and Jesse

After just a few hours' rest, I was discharged. I returned home to my lively brood of boys.

That evening friends and neighbors and of course my friend, Jewell, dropped by to get a look at the baby. And my mother arrived to take over for a few weeks.

During my stay in Oklahoma I made the acquaintance of a woman who would become a dear friend, Fay Flourney. I met her on one of my trips to the laundromat. While I was busy working my way through my own umpteen loads of laundry, she showed up with a truckload of her own. Sacks upon sacks of dirty washing filled the back of her pickup truck. Intrigued by this woman who was weighed down with even more laundry than I was, I quickly became acquainted with her. Was I ever surprised to find how much we had in common.

The Flourneys are devout Sabbath-observers. Not only was Fay blessed with six children, but she and her husband had also sponsored a family of refugees from Laos. I was impressed with her sincerity and devotion to her religious beliefs. The Flourneys maintain very high moral standards. Long before, they had thrown out their television. "One day," as her husband told the story, "I was angry by what had just appeared on my TV. I took a sledgehammer, bashed the whole thing up, and threw it into the trash."

At sixth grade they took their children out of school, before they entered their teenage years. Unlike everyone around them, the Flourney family also adhered to a strict interpretation of "resting on the Sabbath," not using electricity, shopping, or engaging in any form of business transaction on the Sabbath.

I continue to pray for Jewell and the Flourneys. I consider them to be righteous gentiles, or perhaps lost Jewish souls awaiting the day when the earth will be filled with knowledge of G-d, and all lost souls will return to the Land of Israel.

CHAPTER 6

Missouri

Once again, our family was on the move. After my father's death, my widowed mother rented a home in Joplin, Missouri. My youngest sisters and brothers were in their early teens at the time of my father's passing. They still needed the firm guidance of a father figure. My mother decided to live near my father's brother, Ray, so he would be able to help her raise her orphaned children. At some point she decided to buy a farm that boasted a lovely home at the top of a hill. It was 17 miles from the city, a truly peaceful setting for a grieving widow. She soon realized, though, that it was too far from the local school to make it a practical location. Lovely as it was, she would have to sell it, but meanwhile she offered to rent it to us.

We jumped at the idea. I was excited at the opportunity to live near my family. How I had missed my younger siblings all these years! I was unusually attached to them; nurturing my little brothers and sisters had become a surrogate source of love for me during my childhood. I am a true child of the 1950s, reared on Dr. Spock's firm, four-hour feeding schedule. My mother forced herself to override her maternal instincts to hold and feed her crying infant, picking me up once every four hours, as Dr. Spock had dictated. I know that it was hard for her to listen to my cries, and yet she felt compelled to withhold the nurturing I so needed in order to raise me by the book! Looking back, I believe that this parenting style is to be blamed for some of the deep feeling of disconnect I harbored toward my parents all throughout my childhood. As a child, my first feelings of love and connection developed through caring for animals. This spread into deep feelings of attachment to my younger siblings.

My new life in Missouri held much promise. Not only would I now live near my mother and my little sisters, but our new home also boasted all the comforts that indoor plumbing and electricity had to offer. After years of making do with an outhouse, I finally had a sparkling clean bathroom, as well as a bathtub and shower! What luxury!

As in Oklahoma, my husband held a steady job during our stay in Missouri. Yet, in spite of all the material comfort, our time spent in Missouri did not turn out quite the way I had anticipated. It was in Missouri that the longstanding conflict that had developed between my husband's and my own religious views finally came to a head.

Nearly seven years earlier, my husband's in-depth analysis of the Bible brought him to what I firmly believed was a blasphemous realization. John had become convinced that one of the basic tenets of Christianity was in fact nothing more than a myth.

I was devastated. My husband had forsaken the very basis of our religion. I exhausted every argument I could think of in trying to convince him that he was in error. Once or twice I had consulted with pastors and Bible scholars, looking for new angles in our ongoing debate, but they couldn't answer the problems he had brought up any better than I could. Their parting advice, as they closed their Bibles, usually went something like this: "Just go home and be a good wife and he'll come around." So it was the same old story: no matter how hard I or anyone else tried, it was not possible to out-debate John. His knowledge of the Bible was seamless, his logic sharp and clear. No one was able to offer a proof that John was unable to tear apart.

This ongoing conflict ate away at the fabric of our family life. Despite the fact that I was an independent thinker, I was still a good Christian. I was afraid to even consider that my husband might be correct, I think mainly because I had hope of an afterlife and I didn't want to give this up. There was simply no way that I was willing to turn my back on this religion. And yet, I was terrified of losing my marriage.

Missouri was my last hope. I knew that if anyone would be able to set my husband straight, it would be my uncle and his learned friend, the two scholars whom I most admired.

I looked forward to the big debate. The two scholars were all set to take on my husband, sure that they knew enough to convince John. I eagerly prepared our little house for our important visitors, and then brought my little ones to the back room, where I settled them down for the night.

The debate lasted perhaps 15 minutes. Hearing raised voices, I ran in to see what was going on. These two learned men were on the edges of their chairs, red in the face, shouting personal accusations at John. Their beliefs couldn't withstand John's critical analysis, and so all logic went out the window. I watched the discomfiture of these respectable members of the clergy and felt a sinking feeling of despair. If they couldn't get through to John, the problem was more hopeless than I had realized.

Our religious differences threatened the very foundations of our home. There didn't seem to be anything I could do to bring my wayward husband back. I was expecting my sixth child and I couldn't bear the thought of divorce. The next day, I fell down upon my bed and prayed to my Maker. For an hour, I cried and prayed, begging Him to return my husband to our religion. When my weeping subsided, a new prayer arose from the depths of my soul. It made its way to my lips. I was surprised by the words my mouth formed: "…and if my husband is right, please help me to see the truth."

Two weeks later, I was reading a religious commentary when suddenly I understood a foundational verse that John had tried for years to explain to me. *He is so right!* I marveled. I read the next verse and the next, and suddenly I could see every line exactly as he had tried to teach me for so many years. He was absolutely right; the Christians had distorted the Bible! Instead of reading the verses in order — as Jews do — and understanding the words within their context, they take excerpts from all over to prove their point, thereby distorting the original meaning of the text.

I shared my startling new understanding with John. After ascertaining that I did finally see his points, he was immensely relieved. After years of tension, we were finally able to move forward together in our studies.

With a clarity that I had never before experienced, I was able to see gaping holes in the veracity of the Christian Bible. Realizing the truth was a tremendously uplifting experience. I was euphoric! I developed an entirely new sense of clarity and was finally free to think out of the box that had contained me for so long. I was no longer afraid to give this Bible a serious study. When I did, I found it sorely lacking. It isn't even good journalism! The Christian Bible makes frequent references to the Jewish Bible, and yet not once did I find even a single verse quoted accurately!

My entire life, I had been bothered by the way the clergy had made me feel very ignorant. Often, sermons were prefaced by the words, "I know you haven't heard this before…" and then the pastor would go on to share the same old ideas he had relayed over the week before. I realized that we had always been discouraged from thinking. Now I was finally free to use the mind that G-d had endowed me with.

I had fought with myself for decades as I tried to make sense of the contradictions between my religion and my own relationship with the Creator. One of the hardest parts of belonging to this religion was the suffocating feeling that there was nothing else to learn. As a thinking individual, I had formed my own impressions of the world. I looked up to the heavens and saw an endless sky spread out above me. The dark expanse of the evening sky, studded with multitudes of stars, shining pinpricks of light coalescing into giant galaxies, all bore proof of the vastness of the universe and beyond. In contrast to the mind-boggling endlessness of the world, I found the complexity inherent in the DNA of the microscopic cells in even my littlest toe to be just as great a proof of an Intelligence so endless and so infinite that I was awed.

After witnessing firsthand the greatness of the physical world, I had been left wondering how the spiritual world could possibly be so simplistic and narrow. If the physical world is infused with a sense of infinity, why would the spiritual world be so limited, comprising just a few beliefs and practices? Shouldn't religion be at least as intricate as the physical world?

I had broken out of the confines of Christianity, and now I was finally free to learn. This was a tremendous breakthrough in our marriage, but I didn't do it for my husband, I did it for myself. Whereas we had once been locked in fierce theological debate, we now became study partners. I went back to my lifelong companion, the Bible, and looked at it with new eyes. John and I devoted the day of rest to in-depth Bible study; we sifted through the teachings of our youth and plucked out the inconsistencies and distortions. Slowly, we began to absorb the truth.

After seven years of tension, my husband and I were finally on the same page about our religious beliefs. The relief this afforded me was profound. Now, however, as I grew closer to my husband, a great chasm opened up in my relationship with my family.

We did not believe in the Christian beliefs, and so we no longer felt it appropriate to attend services. After generations of allegiance, I turned my back on the beliefs I had absorbed since I was a child. This was a huge blow to my pious mother. In fact, she often fasted for the turnaround of her wayward daughter.

There was something very significant about our home in Missouri. I had just come from Oklahoma, where I had to drive two miles to the spring to collect enough water for our family's daily needs. Our home in Missouri sat on top of an underground lake. How we reveled in the luxury of our endless water source. Even though the Massey home in Georgia had running water in the kitchen, their sink was fed by a shallow well. We had always been cognizant of the fact that the well could suddenly go dry, necessitating a wait of a few hours until it would refill. In Missouri we had no such worries; we had so much water I was even able to let my children play in it!

The prophet Jeremiah teaches that water is an allegory for Torah. All my life I had been studying the life-giving waters of the Bible, but I had been very far away from the source. It was in Missouri that I was finally able to leave the circuitous path of Christianity behind and begin to drink the pure, sweet waters of the Torah, untainted by the religion of my youth.

My life had been a series of painful struggles that culminated in our family breaking away from the religion of my youth. As the mother of a large family and a diehard homeschooler, I had certainly gotten used to being different. Yet, as different as I was, I had still been a faithful member of our congregation, and therefore part of a greater community. Now it was my husband and me united against the world. We were on our own.

When I look back on those days, I realize that I felt as isolated then as our forefather Abraham must have been when he discovered Hashem. He was called Avraham *Halvri*, literally, "on the other side." The whole world had a set of beliefs which he had exposed as false. So, too, did I keenly feel that our understanding of G-d set us apart from the rest of our surrounding society. However, the knowledge that we were living as G-d wanted us to gave me an inner peace. I was not bothered that our friends and neighbors thought us odd. My family's disapproval, however, hurt me deeply.

Although I was finally living near my family, spiritually and ideologically we were far apart. We were only a short car ride away, and yet we didn't get together with my mother on our day of rest. According to my folks, our departure from their religion was a tragedy. Our divergent views became a great source of tension that ruled out the possibility of our spending enjoyable family time together.

That year, my mother, my family, and the Flourneys wanted to join us out at the farm for Thanksgiving, but when they remembered that John would not pray to their savior at the holiday table, they were dismayed. Our holiday plans disintegrated into a family feud. Eventually, Fay Flourney proposed a compromise: John wouldn't say a prayer, but whoever else wanted to could quietly do so. Her suggestion saved the holiday, but didn't resolve the tension.

The rift between me and my family convinced John that, once again, the time had come to move. Just around the time that he decided to move, Granddad contacted us. "Granny's not doing well at all. I think you need to come back home to Georgia — I don't know if she's going to make it through the surgery."

After three years of relative financial security in the Midwest, we were heading back to the Appalachian Mountains.

CHAPTER 7

Return to
Lookout Mountain

I t wouldn't be the first time that I'd be packing up house and home and traveling hundreds of miles. This time, though, I viewed the upcoming move with ambivalence. On the one hand, it symbolized the fact that the rift between me and my mother and family was too strong to be easily resolved. At the same time, I looked forward to using my newfound spiritual freedom to lead me to a life built on truth.

In the meantime, we were left with the very practical problem of how to move our possessions. Our good friends the Flourneys came to the rescue and helped us transport our cow and her calf to our new home. One of the Flourney boys drove up from Oklahoma with his pickup truck, loaded Lucinda and her babe inside, and traveled down to Georgia with our livestock. Aside from our cow, the only other possessions that traveled with us were whatever clothing and housewares we were able to cram into the trunk of our car and squeeze between our precious human cargo. Materially, we had very little to show for our three years in the Midwest. On a spiritual level, however, we were light-years

My sons playing on the swings that Granddad built

beyond our starting point. The obscuring film of Christianity was finally removed, and brilliant rays of G-d's Light now penetrated my heart. My newfound clarity would stand me in good stead during the trials that still lay ahead.

With warm smiles, Granddad and Granny came out to welcome us as we returned to Lookout Mountain.

Gently Granddad urged, "Y'all come on in, Granny's got a big breakfast cooked up for everyone."

It seemed like a rich privilege for my children again to be indulged by grandparents, a relationship I never really had. Granny, as always, poured all her love into her meals: the fluffiest buttermilk biscuits, homemade fruit preserves, fried sweet potatoes sliced exactly lengthwise with brown sugar, and hominy grits and gravy.

Granddad spent hours telling stories, listening to his grandsons, working on projects, helping them with math, and patiently, with his storehouse of wisdom of life, directing them. As one of my sons said, "He never said, 'No, don't do that,' when we shared our plans with him. Instead, he might say, after contemplating a bit, 'I don't know if I would do that.'"

A few days after our return, we moved again to the back of John's parents' property, into the small, one-room shack that John had built for us a few years earlier. Our cabin had no plumbing or electricity. During the day it was illuminated by a few small windows John had cut out of its side; by night, part of the time we had a small, battery-powered lightbulb. We had no well, no pump, not even a spring to provide us with water. Each day my boys loaded their wagon with empty jugs and trekked up the trail to their grandparents' house, where they would fill them with drinking water.

They didn't always come back very soon, and I found that children like to be where the best food is. While we, the parents, were busy sorting out our spiritual spaghetti, one strand at a time, it seemed our boys needed the physical basics more. Most of their spare time was spent at John's folks' home, where they could get Granny's hot, yummy food: crunchy, skillet-baked cornbread, mounds of mashed potatoes, thick hamburgers, Southern country-fried chicken, chicken and dumplings, roasted steaks, green beans cooked down to perfection, coconut and chocolate cakes, golden fried apple pies.

When we had left Georgia three years before, we had entrusted our ducks to Granddad and Granny's care. During the three years in Missouri, we had all but forgotten about the ducks, left behind in their wire cage. How surprised we were to find them in good health upon our return. Excitedly, we brought them down to our part of the woods and let them out of their cage, thinking they'd flourish in their newfound freedom. Yet a curious thing happened. Having been cooped up since birth, our ducks didn't know they could walk, let alone fly.

The ducks spent the first few days of their freedom standing first on one leg and then another, making no attempt to explore their new vistas. Slowly, as my boys prodded them, they learned they could walk, and later as they found their freedom they foraged for food in the woods. My children delighted in running with the ducks. Then came the day when my 5-year-old son raced across the clearing, a duck flying gracefully above him. We laughed at the sight. We knew all along that ducks could fly, but we had grown accustomed to the land-hugging habits of our potentially airborne pets. Yet there came the day when our ducks fluttered their unused wings and lifted themselves up into the air.

How I identified with those ducks! For decades I had been bound by the limiting dogma of the religion I was reared upon. I had spent my whole life yearning for the wide expanse of the heavens above, but alas I was born a human and had had my wings clipped. Deep within me burned the knowledge that I could not live my life earthbound, caged in by a confining religion that stifled thinking. Now I had finally been set free. Just like those ducks, I would have to find my wings.

Our life was like an extended camping experience that lasted over a year. I cooked over a campfire, moving around the skillet with one hand, keeping the toddler away with the other, trying to avoid the smoke while the flames blackened some of the sliced potatoes and left others hardly cooked.

This was survival mode, with no personal privacy and no books, other than a small box of *Prevention* magazines someone had given me, which I eagerly devoured. Almost no one appeared from the outer world, except for a sister who lived close by and a relative named Lulu, who both popped in periodically to bring us "care packages." Here I was set down in some of the most beautiful scenery of the world, and yet the days were long and the nights were longer. Going to sleep shortly after sundown, as there wasn't really anything to do in the thick of the forest at night, I couldn't wait for the first rays of light; I longed for the dawn. Maybe the sun's rays would bring a change in our situation.

It always helped to try to look on the bright side; there were so many things to be thankful for. I had beautiful, healthy children and a clear mind. During the winter our first baby girl had joined us after five boys. Surely many people would have given their life savings for such gifts! We had plenty of food, the overflow of living in a wealthy country. Often in this wintery weather we joined Granddad's and Granny's heavily laden table. Yes, I was very thankful but, I wondered, wasn't there more to life than just eating good food all of the time?

I continued to strengthen myself. *Remember the families you saw in Tijuana,* I said to myself, *the crowds of families cramming in together to live along a dry creek bed, beside the town's trash pile?* One particular family of eight lived on the edge of a dump in a one-room, makeshift hut made of cardboard and ripped pieces of plastic. I remembered how our youth group tore down their house and removed all their possessions in assembly-line fashion, handing them from hand to hand. In about an hour we were done. Then our fathers stepped in to put up a quick prefab house for them. I resolved then as a wealthier American to never complain. How could I, knowing my situation was still far better than the normal lot of millions in the third-world countries?

But, I argued with myself, *even so, it is so cold, even with the wood stove,* and the snow had blown in on us as we slept and I had to constantly struggle to keep my newborn warm. *I can't stand to be so cold!* On the other hand, there was a stubbornness inside me that would never mouth the words, "It's too hard." As a teenager I had thrived on mountain climbing and breaking horses, but I realized that there was an even more exhilarating pleasure, far beyond the most physical challenges: when the Master of the Universe puts a person through His ultimate, multilayered obstacle course — emotional and spiritual challenges!

It is interesting that the same rugged lifestyle that I found to be quite challenging is remembered so fondly by my children. Joey once told me, "People often worry about the long-term effects of poverty on developing children. I can honestly say that I had a very happy and fulfilling childhood, full of warm memories of growing up in the loving embrace of my warm and loving family."

And for all the discomfort, we have fond memories of our time living on the edge of this vast wilderness. Joey's favorite childhood memories are of those times we lived deep in these woods. To this day he reminisces about digging a well with his father and brothers beside the little creek near our shack. First they dug a wide hole, using shovels and post-hole diggers. They kept going until they reached clay, and then the sand rock beneath that. Finally, they hit water. It wasn't a deep well, but it was good enough to provide us with water for washing. We continued to use Granddad's well for drinking water. My husband covered the mouth of the well with an old car hood to make sure that none of the children accidentally fell in. My boys were quite proud of their own well and also of the outhouse they constructed with their father. John brought some nice lumber down from his sawmill, and he and the boys set about digging an outhouse and erecting walls around it. It certainly was a very welcome improvement.

Later on, I directed my boys to gather railroad ties from the sawmill up by Granddad's. They loaded them onto their wagon and transported them home. With the wood, we built a bridge over the knee-deep creek on our property. By crossing over our homemade bridge, we were able to avoid the muddy banks. We built the bridge at the most beautiful point along our little brook, where mossy fern grew and the water burbled. Here on the edge of this vast wilderness there was a tranquility I just loved: the quiet rustles as a graceful deer slipped through the thick carpet of old leaves; the whistle of the quail and the call of the blue jay adding a soft melody all their own to our little oasis beneath towering pine and oak trees.

As a 12-year-old, I had sat on the quiet rocks surrounded by my grazing goats crunching happily on dry desert bushes. I tuned out the noises of the four-lane Foothill Boulevard that ran in front of our house and inspired myself with the lemon groves close by and Mount Baldy on the other side, far above. As I studied G-d's creations I was awestruck; subtly, I was tuning into my Creator and discovering the pure joy of just thinking about Him.

Later, as a teenager, when my parents took us on camping trips,

I hiked upward to hide away in the forests of Southern California, seeking to find the most untainted spot along a gurgling brook. Gently I placed myself into the serenity of aloneness, in a place where it was only G-d and me. I locked my eyes upward as if searching for His eyes, and I tried to understand more about this Creator. It was then that I called out with all my emotions and tears. I very much wanted a relationship with Him, and it seemed that G-d responded with all His sweetness.

How I missed those days! I wondered: *As a youth, I raced to find such beautiful places to spend even a few moments. Now I'm living in such an awesome, permanent retreat, but something is missing. What is it? I'm totally locked into this situation, completely disconnected and unplugged from the outside world. Every day I awake only to teach my children and to survive. What happened to my youthful prayers? I know He heard me then. No, my G-d has not abandoned me!*

Looking back it seems to me that the big signal Hashem was giving me at that time was: Don't be superficial in your search for Me. All our water sources at this time were shallow or polluted. The creek was a small flow, the well was murky, and later on we were to find our drinking water was also polluted. The well my family had dug as a new water source turned out to be muddy. If we wanted the flow of pure knowledge and the ultimate connection of spiritual bliss, we would have to dig deeper!

How many times had I seen people who passed through our California circles searching for truth? They seemed very sincere, they looked and found a few truths from the Bible, but after trying on their own to find the whole recipe for life, they more or less gave up. Like the sureness of the law of gravity — if the apple falls, it will land on your head — the spiritual principle is: "You will find Him, if you search for Him with all your heart and all your soul."[1]

---

1 *Deuteronomy* 4:29.

As our second summer back in Georgia was ending, still wary of the authorities, we were reluctant to think of putting down roots, and so we just watched and waited. A report had been filed that a family with six children lived in deprivation down in the woods. Once again, we had been picked up by the radar of the social services. As the school year approached, we were again visited by the truant officers.

Our shack was located right on the county lines, and so we came under the jurisdiction of two different counties. We were now subjected to even more frequent visits by the authorities. I remember the day when John and I had just finished meeting with a group of officials up at my in-laws' house and eaten lunch there. As we prepared to head back down to our shack, we were accosted by a second carload from the other county!

As the threats became more serious, we were again told we would have to leave the state or they would take our school-age children away from us. For the second time we were preparing to leave the state of Georgia. Our sons now had their own game plan and quickly flew out the windows and disappeared into the forest at the first sign of intruders, using bird and animal sounds to signal to one another.

One day, as I sat preparing supper at the card table in front of our cabin, John came hurriedly down the trail, breathlessly exclaiming, "Guess what? I just called the truant officer. He said the State of Georgia just passed a homeschooling law, making it legal for parents to teach their children at home. Now there's nothing else they can do against us; we are free to stay!"

I was stunned; this was totally unexpected!

The fact that homeschooling was now legal in Georgia led us to realize that there was a whole network of people out there who felt as strongly as we did about homeschooling. Here was a group of lobbyists who had gone to the trouble of proposing the new legislation and seeing it through to the end. This made us feel far less isolated. We began to subscribe to *Growing Without Schooling*, a homeschooling magazine put out by John Holt. The intrusive attention of the social workers and the truant officers immediately ceased. Once again, G-d had come to our aid!

CHAPTER 8

On Husky Farm

The threat of truant officers and social workers had abated. We no longer had to think about fleeing the authorities. It was time to settle down.

Once again, G-d sent us what we needed just when we needed it. Someone came by to tell us that Mr. Husky, our neighbor across the road from Granddad's, had just finished fixing up a two-bedroom home on his farm to retire on. His wife had refused to move in there, and, afraid of hunters and vandals, he didn't want to leave the 100-acre farm unattended. If we would take care of his property for him, he was more than happy to have us move in rent-free.

Before our move we were told by some of the country folk, speaking in dramatic whispers, their eyes darting back and forth: "We've heared straaaaange noises in that there Husky house—I shuuuuure wouldn' go near thaaaat place..." We, who had spent so many years studying and rooting out our superstitious beliefs, had no fear. We just laughed and told them, "We don't believe in such things."

So we moved in and didn't let the interesting noises scare us off, but what a racket in the attic above! We used to imagine "they" were playing like a group of clowns entertaining, as they rolled barrels and jumped and tumbled around. As the attic was sealed off, we could only guess what was really up there. Years went by, and one of our children one day found a little critter with large brown eyes called a flying squirrel at the bottom of the huge oak tree right outside the front of our house. Now the pieces of the puzzle came together. Apparently, a whole family of these gliding squirrels lived up in the top of our ancient oak trees, and they swooped down into our attic to play!

Although in our new place we were blessed with running water, which came from our well, my in-laws had warned us not to use our tap water for drinking. Our well had not been used for many years, and they were concerned that its waters had become stagnant. For a long time we used our water for cleaning, and we

Our family in front of our tin-roofed house on Husky Farm

trekked to my in-laws' home to collect our drinking water. That is, until the day that we had our water tested by the county Health Department. Were we ever surprised by the results! We were given the go-ahead to use our own water, since it was found to be of superior quality. My in-laws' water, though, was found to be heavily polluted with bacteria, and condemned!

As had often been the case in the past, I felt that G-d was talking to me through the powerful metaphors He sent into my life. Could it be that our water situation was a message for us that we were correct in relying upon the spirituality that bubbled up from the wellspring of our own souls? Time and again I had learned that others didn't really have better to offer than the religious ideas my husband and I were discovering on our own.

The area we lived in was exceptionally fertile and known for producing bountiful crops. In its subtropical climate we got more than our fair share of thunderstorms. The storms were particularly frightening on Husky Farm. Our roof was a thin rusty tin, which greatly amplified the sounds; the pounding rains came down with such force that one had to holler to make himself heard. We were located in a clearing in the woods, with the massive old oak trees right by our house, and lightning often struck nearby. Even though the lightning rod on the corner of our roof was supposed to carry the enormous electrical current safely away from our structure to the ground when lightning hit, no protection system can ever guarantee absolute safety. We still often heard such enormous pops that even the jumpiest children became good little boys who, with no prompting, fearfully went to sit quietly on the couch.

We respected greatly the power of the bolt from the sky. A few years before, when we resided in Missouri, we had taken the children out for a short drive and passed a herd of enormous, fatted, white-faced beef cattle. Only moments later we turned around to head back home and were shocked to see half the herd lying inert on the ground. Apparently, they had been standing in water

A run in our front yard

as they fed in their metal feeders, and with one flash from the sky 20 cows now lay dead.

My sons actually experienced a number of close calls as they walked through the fields in the rain. The air around them became so charged that the hair on their heads stood on end. They immediately dropped to the ground. A blinding bolt of lightning would split the sky above as the thunder boomed!

Like John and me, my boys grew up to be real nature lovers. The scenic beauty of the lush mountain and the rushing creeks afforded my boys the perfect opportunity to explore and understand G-d's majestic world. As they reached adolescence and young adulthood, the idyllic setting provided the perfect backdrop for solitude and meditation.

These were good years as we were to be blessed with three more children, another boy and two more girls. My sons recall the years we spent on Husky Farm as some of the best years of their childhood. Not only did we have electricity, but we also had acres upon acres of land for them to run about and explore. After they spent their mornings learning, they were free to care for our animals, cut logs for firewood, pick huckleberries and gooseberries, swing on muscadine vines back in the woods, whittle whistles out of hickory, make nests for bluebirds, dig up sassafras root for tea, or just play baseball. In the dead of winter they whittled piles of shavings around the wood stove or played hours of chess. There weren't any other kids on the mountain for them to play with, so their games were adapted to accommodate all their siblings. They loved to race across the clearing in front of the house, and to give everyone a fair chance of winning, they staggered the starting points. Each child's starting point took his size and ability into account.

Now we completely complied with the State of Georgia and their new laws for homeschoolers. Each month I sent in a report of our school attendance. Every three years the state tested our children to see that they were up to par. The ones who arrived now to knock on our door were helpful folks, called visiting teachers.

I had been educated in the very atheistic schools of California, where they were careful not to ever mention that we had a Creator. But lo and behold in ninth grade in a business law course, out of the blue we were taught that most insurance companies would not cover expenses for destructive events called "acts of G-d." I found this to be astounding. For all those 10 years of schooling they had never once introduced us to "G-d," and now we are supposed to know who they are talking about? Even more unbelievable: not one classmate raised a hand to ask, "Who?"

I was determined that my children should have a foundation of truth that would cause them to completely acknowledge the Creator of our world. I taught them points that had strengthened me. I spoke to them about the creation of the universe. There are people who say it just happened, I told them. I challenged them: Take this ball that I am holding in my hand and make it stay in the middle of this room. Our world is suspended in space, how does it stay there? We studied astronomy and the layout of the skies. In August we got up very early to lay blankets out on the grass, study the dark, starry skies, and watch the spectacular annual August meteorite shower of falling stars.

I felt very grateful to have a secluded country setting in which to raise our children, but we still had our challenges. Granny and I both waged our personal wars against immorality. One would often open a magazine in her house that had pages missing, as she had gotten to them first, passionately ripping out inappropriate pictures, wadding them up, and throwing them into the fire. We were together on this battlefront; she dealt with it in her home and I in mine. As much as we tried to shelter our families from the corruptness of our era, it still had to be dealt with.

John and I were now coming to believe in a bigger G-d, one who wasn't "handicapped." We had been told that the Creator of the universe was so great that He couldn't hear our prayers without someone else helping Him, which is kind of like saying that someone is the greatest ballplayer in the world, but he can't lean down and tie his shoes. I had almost made a major mistake in my life as I had read over and over a passage that said that if one really wanted to serve G-d "it's better not to get married." I had very seriously considered this teaching when I was in college in the Midwest. Now I felt such anger at a book that taught such a concept. It had almost ruined my life. What if I had taken this vow and lost out on having my beautiful family? Thank G-d He had heard my plea as a youth: "Help me not make mistakes."

For the most part we were mostly only finding from our studies what we didn't believe. Once, we became very excited when John discovered a new bit of truth: the new moon. The question we then pursued was: What is the significance of this new moon business? I had never encountered or been taught such a concept that the moon had cycles and that it began with a new moon. I was surprised that in all of my reading I had never known the signs of the moon and never in my whole life had even noticed that it had a sequence of going from smaller to larger!

Husky Farm was a haven for us, and it also became home to many animals. Our cows were soon joined by a horse, and our chickens and ducks had the lively companionship of dozens of birds. It seemed that each time my boys went to the county trade day they came home with yet another species of fowl. They became the proud owners of different varieties of chicken, turkeys, white ducks, mallards, and guineas.

Samuel and our horse, Buckshot

Once at Granddad's place we had a cute little chicken family of one rooster and one hen, who each day laid one egg in the bottom of an old dresser drawer. She sat on those eggs for about three weeks. How proud they both were when Mama Hen came off her nest with all of her little chickies. Papa Rooster strutted right by her side and every so often would peck a little cutie sharply on the head, sending it scurrying back to Mama. We were a bit upset with Papa Rooster's behavior: How could he be so mean to his own chickies? But most of these chicks survived because they had a Papa Rooster that taught them to be afraid. When Mama Hen clucked, they ran quickly to her, and when she screamed even louder they scurried to dive under her wings, listening so well that she was able to save them from the hawks and snakes.

Hatching chicks was a little project of ours on Husky Farm. John converted an old refrigerator into a makeshift incubator for our eggs. I soon discovered that baby chicks cared for by a surrogate hen fared better than those on their own. After experimenting, I realized that the little bantam hens made the best moms. If I placed a chick under a hen's wings as she slept, come morning, she'd adopt the new arrival as one of her own. I made good use of this knowledge, placing my fledglings under the hen's care. I realized that I had gotten a bit carried away when I saw my little hen struggling to spread her wings over a host of chicks. As she stretched her wings as far as they would possibly go, the heads of her overgrown babes nearly lifted her off the ground!

It wasn't long before we noticed that our little hatchlings were very vulnerable. Nearly every day one would be missing, having fallen prey to a hungry raccoon or possum, a slithering snake, or a passing hawk. So my sons built separate pens for the mother hens with new chicks who had no father rooster. My boys learned to gather in each and every one of their hundred birds before going to sleep at night. They climbed up trees and through bushes until all were accounted for. Only once their precious birds were safely enclosed in the large, wire-mesh pen they had lovingly built for the birds' protection did they turn in for the night.

Every so often a child would come in downcast or teary-eyed with a wet chick half-dead in his hand. I would take out my old hairdryer and blow-dry it. In a few minutes the fluffed-up chick and child were all smiles, and together they would disappear back outside.

Each morning, as they opened up the door to the pen and released their birds for the day, the turkeys would come a-running and gobbling. Chickens squawked on their heels and beautiful mallards flew up in an arc, going up above the pines trees to spend the day in our large creek below. It was an unbelievable sight.

Once in the early spring as I sat with a baby on my lap, teaching two boys at a time, two others doing workbooks, and the toddler running about, suddenly my whole classroom emptied out. Without warning, every last boy took off as if a shot had been fired. Later when they returned and I asked them what happened, it went something like this, "Didn't you hear that hen hollering? She was cackling out by the barn and we ran out to find her nest." Later on in the summer, as all of our fine-feathered friends were now laying and the hens were cackling to the world, "I laid an egg, I laid an egg, puck-puck, puck-puck," no one paid any attention anymore.

The children also got to try their hand at gardening. They'd lovingly plant their little seeds, and water and care for the first shoots with devotion. How excited they were when their plants bloomed! No matter what I was busy with, I'd have to come out. "Mother, come and see." When their vegetables were fully grown, even my pickiest eaters proudly tasted the vegetables they normally avoided.

My boys often set out with their fishing rods and bamboo poles to fish in one of the many ponds, lakes, or creeks in the area. They'd proudly come back home weighed down with fresh bass or blue gill, which had the requisite fins and scales that marked them as "clean" and fit for consumption according to the dictates of the Bible. Even after leaving our congregation, we still made sure never to eat "unclean" meats.

Fishing on the mountain

One of our family's favorite fishing memories is of the time when, years later, my youngest son Benton hooked a whopper of a catfish. Although we would not have eaten the catfish ourselves, but given it to a neighbor, the excitement of such a large catch thrilled all the children. My boys stood around cheering Benton on as he tried to reel it in. The fish was so heavy it bent the pole way down. Benton's brothers ran over to help, but my strong-willed toddler refused to relinquish his pole. "Let me do it! Let me do it!" he cried. Suddenly, the fish slipped off the hook. Joey jumped into the water to catch it in his arms. Although he managed to touch it, the fish got away, leaving our family with nothing more than a rich "fish story" to tell and retell over the years.

When they were still small, my boys would spend hours outdoors, running across the meadows and playing under the sky. Sweaty and dirty, they'd return home toward evening and in pure, little-boy innocence present me with a wilted bouquet of dandelions and wildflowers. "To me this is the most beautiful bouquet in the world," I used to tell them as I accepted their gift. My heart melted each time anew as I thought of my little boy clutching his precious bunch of flowers throughout his afternoon of play, carefully guarding them so that he'd have a gift for his mother. The boundless love that this little boy's heart wasn't capable of expressing in words was captured in all its beauty in those little bouquets of wilted wildflowers.

Of course, the outdoors also presented my boys with many opportunities to develop the tougher side of their masculine natures. At one time my boys came up with the pastime of throwing rocks at hornet nests hanging in the trees or digging up a nest of yellow jackets. Inevitably they came home with numerous stings, hobbling into the house moaning and groaning and boasting of their many wounds. John and I figured that the painful stings would teach them to leave the nests alone. We were wrong. They kept up their dangerous pastime until we finally had to stop them.

Although for the most part we loved both nature and animals, I lived in fear of one creature: the venomous snake. Man's oldest enemy was a frequent trespasser at Husky Farm. Our first months at the farm were interspersed with numerous rattlesnake, copperhead, and cottonmouth sightings. Interestingly enough, we had been spared many of the injuries and illnesses that often keep mothers of large families on their toes. Aside from a few stitches now and then, none of my children ever suffered a serious illness or injury. No one ever broke a bone, and we were spared the strain of emergency-room visits, a blessing, considering the 17 miles that lay between us and the hospital. Still, I was terrified of the snakes. I felt that it was beyond my capabilities to protect my precious children from those dreaded vipers.

I remember lying in bed one night, the moon peeking in on the infant cradled on my arm and a toddler nestling against my other side. From outside the window, I heard the croak of bullfrogs and the gulping creek. Nearby, the roosters crowed spasmodically and a lonely fox yapped.

Gently extricating myself, I crawled to the end of my bed, propped up my saggy pillow, and lay peering out the window toward the silhouetted berry bushes and apple trees. Beyond, the woods were dark and silent. Only once in a blue moon did I, a frazzled mother, writhe with insomnia.

But considering the day's events, it wasn't surprising. That afternoon, two of my smaller boys had been playing in the cow pasture beside the house. A large frog hopped into view, and it entertained my sons as they hopped after it. The frog hopped toward a huge decaying log. Suddenly, a coiled copperhead snake reared up and struck the frog. Our crawling sons had been just a few seconds behind it. It could have been them. The panic was still there, inside me, refusing to let me rest.

Yes, I'd never heard of anyone dying from copperhead bites, but Husky Farm seemed to be unreasonably infested. I pencil-marked every sighting of a venomous snake that first summer, and was more unsettled when the number climbed to an alarming 50. We realized that we were smack in the middle of a snake crossing! The snakes made their way from the woods to the creek below in search of water. There were many penciled slashes beside *rattle-snakes*, and I'd heard enough horror stories to know they could be deadly. One of our old-time mountain men had killed so many deadly snakes that he'd lost his fear of them. The last day of his life, he'd tackled a snake using a tire tool, instead of a longer weapon. The rattler had nipped him on his thumb. There are no ambulances on the mountains. He lasted all of 15 minutes.

If, G-d forbid, one of the children was bitten, the scattered houses sitting along our long, crooked, and nameless roads would make it very difficult for the emergency services to find us. We had a hot-rodder-of-a-hero neighbor who'd once zoomed an old lady who'd been bitten down our steep mountain passes. She'd received antivenin 10 minutes after the bite — and survived!

As I lay in bed, I wondered where my youthful conviction of solid-steel faith had vanished. When I was a girl, I had worked in my aunt and uncle's mint and alfalfa fields in Washington State, where the fields were infested with rattlesnakes. If I got bitten, I planned I wouldn't tell anyone. G-d would protect me. I mostly based my attitude on my legendary Grandpa Dugger, who once claimed he'd been bitten by a rattler and never skipped a beat. When those around him expressed concern, he brushed it off: "I'm doing G-d's work and He'll take care of me." But now, staring out the window, I wondered if it had been a rattler after all.

My parents themselves wrestled with the proper balance of medical intervention versus faith healing. Once they testified that I had pneumonia as a baby, and as they cared for me at home I had turned blue. They had prayed, and I had recovered. But years later, Daddy changed on the concept of "faith only" as my little baby brother lay day after day being treated around the clock by my mother for pneumonia. Daddy came home from work one day and announced, "We are taking him to the hospital now!" That night, as my little brother's lungs collapsed, my parents realized they'd had a very close call. (Ultimately, he did recover.)

On this mountain we had a cousin who'd lost his only baby boy, born at six months at home. Their religious leader forbade them to go to a doctor, insisting they should just have faith. How could it be that a person who seemed to have so much more faith than others who went to "mere men" for healing, should be so let down? It just didn't make sense. *If only,* I wished, *there was some wise man with a long white beard whom I could ask these questions to.*

Whatever level of faith I had myself, I certainly wouldn't rely on a miracle for my children's safety. So in the morning for the next few days, I rose to check for snakes around the massive oak trees overlooking our house, the bushes around the yard, and the children's toys.

Eventually, we happened on another solution: turkeys. As we began to collect turkeys, we found our fine-feathered friends did an excellent job of weeding out the smaller snakes. A few times I looked out just in time to see a turkey flapping through our property with a snake dangling from each side of its beak.

One afternoon, when Joey was about 11, my boys were digging a trench through the embankment of the creek to give our cows access to the water. Suddenly, Joey spotted a huge cottonmouth curled up on a beaver dam over the creek. He ran back to the house, grabbed his father's rifle, raced back to the creek, lifted the rifle to his shoulder, and aimed. With his first shot, he blew off the snake's head. Impressed by his bravery and aim, John decided that Joey was ready for a rifle of his own.

Thankfully, the number of snake sightings dwindled, and slowly I began to learn how to avoid snake encounters. I tried not to leave things lying around near the house that might serve as camouflage for snakes: we were wary of lifting up rocks, and during the summer we avoided going out at dusk. Snakes hibernate during the winter, but in the summer, they avoid heat. At dusk as it cools down they begin to move; thus it's a prime time for snake sightings.

Snakes aside, daily life in the mountains brought many challenges. Even feeding my family didn't come easily. Despite the fact that we lived very simply, at times our income wasn't enough to meet the needs of our large and growing family. Over the years I learned that the cheapest way to keep my family fed was to rely heavily on a particular inexpensive and filling food. Those of Eastern European descent will most surely nod their heads in familiar appreciation when they hear that the staple of our diet was potatoes. Without this humble tuber, it would have been impossible to feed a double-digit family on sixty dollars or so a week.

I remember the time I made my weekly 20-mile drive to the market with only $30 in my wallet. I consulted my shopping list and chose only the cheapest products that I just could not do without. I picked up a few packages of pinto beans and some bags of cornmeal and reverently placed them in my shopping cart beside the box of powdered milk and a single bottle of oil. I was grateful that at least I had enough money for these purchases.

It wasn't long before the $30 were pretty well used up. I realized that I wouldn't have enough money to get everything on my list. I decided to forgo the potatoes for now. I didn't quite know how I was going to buy them, but I wasn't too worried. I knew G-d would provide; He always had.

Later that week, someone knocked at my door. It wasn't unusual for one of the neighbors to drop by with a bag of outgrown clothes or some other unwanted item. It was well known that we were the poorest family around, since we certainly had the most mouths to feed. In fact, we received so many hand-me-downs that I never had to buy any clothes for my family.

I put down my knife and the tomato I was peeling, spilled a little water from the bucket beside me over my hands, and quickly wiped them dry. I opened the door for Clifford, our neighbor from down the road. "I was wonderin' if y'all could use some 'taters. Ya see, a truck was coming down the mountain and overturned. The road was covered in 'taters and I wasn't gonna let 'em go to waste. Real good spuds they were, I tell ya. So I gathered 'em up and loaded 'em into my pickup to bring home. Thing is, I already had a good load of them 'taters of my own, so I was wonderin' if perhaps y'all wanted mine?"

As usual, G-d was looking out for our welfare. Even though at times things got tough, and it seemed weekly we went from bare cupboard to bare cupboard, I learned not to worry; G-d always provided. We never went hungry.

While Ethiopia and Ecuador might have had trouble clothing their children, we in the American backwoods had the reverse challenge of too many clothes. A car would pull up in the yard and some neighbor would drive up with 10 garbage bags of clothes, or an unknown fellow would pull up with a whole pickup truck of blue jeans and give the standard line: "I just didn't know what to do with all these clothes and I didn't want to throw them away, and I thought of you." So we almost had disposable clothes. If the thought ever passed my mind that this child needed a hat or pants, the next time someone dropped off a bag there was sure to be just what we needed.

Our big social event was our weekly trip to our little town 20 miles away to buy groceries. Once, as I came down the first aisle with my children, a lady looked us up and down with a condescending glare. In the second aisle she asked, "Are these all yours?" The third time our paths crossed, she attacked. "Don't you know the world is overpopulated?"

I always figured this question really meant she felt she would have to have fewer hamburgers and potato chips if I kept having children. So I just smiled. She had her mindset and so did I. I was child-rich and I knew it was no big deal for the One Above to feed all of His children.

After years on the farm, I began to see our stark realities more clearly. The daily demands of caring for my family and running my home under such primitive conditions built up my stamina and faith in G-d. Still, I reached some interesting conclusions. I had grown up in a middle-class home in Southern California at a time of relative prosperity. I was still struck by the culture of material indulgence that flourished all around me. Against this backdrop of indulgence I was schooled in Christian doctrine, which frowns upon all forms of material indulgence.

As a child of the '60s, I was also somewhat influenced by the hippie generation. In contrast to the superficial culture of materialism they had been reared upon, the hippies declared that there was more to life than money and possessions. But in their attempt to rebel against society's superficiality, instead of moving to live more wholesome lives, they broke down many of the moral barriers of modern society. Although I was repelled by their immorality, I did relate to their antimaterialistic views. I made do with very little. Even when my few paltry possessions were lost or damaged, I didn't complain. I was proud of myself for roughing it in the wilderness on a permanent basis.

Yet, as I struggled to keep my children warm, safe, and well fed day after day and year after year, I slowly came to a troubling realization. Living a life of privation and austerity was not quite the road to spiritual liberation that I had imagined. My daily life was a great struggle, it was just about impossible to keep clean or organize even one step in household management. I began to realize that there were benefits to modernity and to the G-d-given knowledge of how to improve our physical circumstances, live better, save time, keep warm, and lead more productive lives.

As the years went on, I began to regret the time lost in the struggle of meeting my family's basic survival needs under such harsh conditions. Even though I was with my children 24 hours a day, seven days a week, I still felt guilty about not really being there for them. I yearned for more time to teach my children, to feel and to reevaluate my relationships and the direction my life had taken. I began to realize that while there is more to life than material comfort, I needed to have my basic needs met in order to live a more spiritual life.

Occasionally I considered joining the workforce to augment my family's income. Most of the country folk in my area worked in nearby factories. Yet the idea of investing my time and energy into someone else's business instead of building up my own dynasty didn't sit well with me. I knew that there was nothing as important or as precious as my own family, and certainly no better use of my talents than educating my children. Even if I were to do something important such as social work, I realized that my time would be better spent molding the psyches of my children than untangling other people's thorny problems. I was devoting my life to providing my children with the best upbringing possible, even if that meant making do with very little in the way of materialism.

There was something of a new vision taking hold all over America. A popular magazine called *Mother Earth News* fueled a movement for independence and self-reliance. People would move away from an interdependent city life, back toward reliance on nature and the sweat of one's brow. Since we were already in the situation anyway, we envisioned a setup where we could live totally independently, providing all of our needs on our own farm.

Our hundred acres of farmland had provided us with the perfect opportunity to experiment with independent living. We figured that, with Lucinda's second calf, we could begin milking her. That way, we would have as much milk as we could possibly want, and even butter and cheese as well. We did manage to make some homemade butter every now and then, but that was as far as it went. The milk itself tasted so awful we weren't able to drink it; unfortunately, it wasn't until later that we learned that the taste of the milk was ruined because of the bitter weed Lucinda grazed on in the pasture.

It seemed that everything relating to Lucinda was more trouble that it was worth. We should have known when we bought her that she was a real case. A dairy farmer who has 2 to 300 cows — and this is the one he wants to sell!

Here was this very large red-and-white mama cow that had acres and acres of the greenest grass to munch on, but who delighted in finding a weakness in the fence. We sometimes got a call from neighbors a mile away, "Your cow is in my garden!" As I raced toward her with my stick, she would head back home, trotting along between trees, always keeping just a little out of reach of my stick until she ran back under the fence into the pasture.

One year we decided to buy her a huge bale of hay. We had probably passed hundreds of cows in our travels and enjoyed this tranquil scene: gentle cows surrounding the hay quietly chomping on the side of the bale. Not Lucinda. Two days after we brought in this huge bale of hay as big as a room, she hadn't stopped eating; by day three, now as wide as she was long, this 1,500-pound cow was standing on top of the bale looking ridiculous, crushing the hay that was underneath her.

Early every morning she came up to the fence right outside of our windows and started mooing for me to milk her. She started at daylight, and even though I usually tried to get to her early, it wasn't always as early as she would have liked, and her bellowing got more intense until sometimes she would moo herself hoarse urging me to come. Milking her meant contending with a tail that constantly slapped me in the face as she pretended to swat a fly. I kept my left arm up as I milked so as to keep a swift kick from knocking the bucket over. Sometimes the foot would go right in the bucket, meaning I had to vie with her almost two tons of pure stubbornness when she would then pretend she couldn't move her foot. With Lucinda everything was a battle of wills.

During one of our last years at the Husky Farm we decided instead of the usual summer garden to make the most of our land and plant a large number of acres. John purchased a tractor, and he and the boys began cutting down young saplings that had sprouted in the fields in the years they had lain fallow. They cleared out the larger rocks, made furrows, dropped the fertilizer, and knocked dirt on top before putting in the seeds and covering them with earth.

We loved running out in the morning to behold the miraculous growth that had taken root in our fields. We planted squash, okra, beans, potatoes, onions, tomatoes, and corn. We certainly managed to plant more than usual, but we should have recalled the old Indian law: "Plant three — one for the rabbit, one for the coon, and one for me." First came a torrential downpour that washed away a lot of seed. Then, when the little seedlings sprouted, the rabbits began picking at them.

Later on, we set about hilling up our rows in preparation for planting watermelon seedlings. Our entire family got in on the action, and we looked on in pride at the beautiful row of seedlings we had planted. Unfortunately, the next morning, the proud green line had wilted — casualties of cutworms that had paid our farm a nocturnal visit.

Thankfully we still had a half-grown field of corn. This gave us some comfort, until a herd of deer came by for a midnight feast. All that was left was a dirt field littered with chewed and crushed stalks. Our potatoes and onions were still safe within the soil, and we were very happy to be left with our staples. We spent the rest of that summer tending those plants in anticipation of a bountiful yield.

Come autumn, the tops of "them 'taters" and onions dried up and turned yellow. The time had come to harvest our crop. The boys spent a day or two digging, and we tied the onions in bunches and hung them up to dry from the rafters of our front porch. Underneath, we spread out our potatoes to dry.

The next morning, we got up to see that both cows had gotten out during the night. The cows balanced on the potatoes to eat the onions, and in the words of 11-year-old Samuel as he told it to a cousin, "What potatoes and onions they didn't eat, they messed on!"

I think this was the straw that broke the camel's back. One week when I went shopping, after buying only absolutely the bare essentials, I realized I had spent $17 on the animals' food and $16 on food for the children. I realized that I, who had been such an animal lover, was now extremely resentful of our whole farm full of animals. I was seeing our animals as nuisances, hindrances to my most important priority: my children. The cow that got out in the neighbors' garden so I had to leave the children and their books to bring her back, the horse that we never used, the bee swarms that flew away, the chickens that hid their eggs, the hunting dogs that mostly stayed tied to the trees barking...

We were not prioritizing right; we had gotten distracted. This "Mother Earth" dream was keeping our noses down to the earth instead of turning our eyes up to that which was above us. It was inspiring to admire the creation, but it wasn't leading us to a Creator.

One day, when Joey was 16, I glimpsed my eldest son riding his bicycle over the packed sand under the oak trees. My heart swelled with maternal pride. Joey was almost grown, and I was so proud of the way he was turning out.

All at once, I was struck by a very troubling thought. My children were thriving under the love and care we had invested in them. They were growing up to be moral, responsible people. And yet, if we continued living in isolation, whom would they marry? I was horrified by the thought that they would make their way out into the world as they became adults and marry the first woman they came across! What then would happen to all that I had invested in them?

Doesn't G-d have a people? I wondered. *Is it really possible that no one else in the whole wide world shares our beliefs?* If that would be so, then everything — every second of every day that I'd invested into them — would all be for naught! The possibility was overwhelming. We had G-d. We had the Jewish Bible. Was there more?

I pulled out the *World Book Encyclopedia* and flipped to the entries under *World Religions.* I read through the list, and again, as I had done years before, I mentally discounted each one. I knew that the answer couldn't be Buddhism, Confucianism, Christianity, Islam, Taoism, or Judaism.

G-d has no people, I thought.
We are really alone.

CHAPTER 9

What Jews Eat
for Breakfast

"**W**hy don't we go to the Jews?"

I looked up from the dishes I was washing. My husband's expression was unusually pensive. "Jews also don't believe in the books added by the Christian Bible."

Why had I not thought of that before? "That's a good idea," I found myself saying.

Until this day I am surprised that I agreed to go along with him. Growing up in a Christian society, I had a lot of bias against the Jews' religion. I had never even considered the possibility that Judaism might contain the answers I sought.

At the time we were living in the shadow of Lookout Mountain, a flattened hill 90 miles long that curved like a snake from Alabama through the corner of Georgia, finally ending at Tennessee. Battles had been fought there as long ago as the Revolutionary War, and during the Civil War soldiers had climbed it and used it as a lookout point to scan the panorama of seven states that lay below its rocky cliffs.

Once again, my harsh surroundings served as a metaphor for my search. We too had disconnected from the security of our friendly forces, climbing treacherous cliffs to scout out new territory, not knowing what we would see beyond.

My husband looked up the closest Jewish community in the phone book. Right below the lookout point of our mountain sat the town of Chattanooga, Tennessee. It was here that we descended to start our search.

Our family's first foray into the world of Judaism brought us to a small Conservative congregation in Chattanooga. I was thrilled with the charming Friday-night service held in the basement of the synagogue. The congregation was led by a polished Harvard graduate, and I was deeply inspired by my first exposure to the *Kiddush* ceremony.

We attended services weekly, until the fateful Sabbath when we attended our first *bris*. A most immodestly attired woman came to the synagogue for her son's circumcision. As she carried him on a white pillow and then stood during the ceremony, it deeply offended our moral standards. To top it off, the rabbi had invited a priest to speak. My daughter still remembers how upset we were, and as we drove home, John decided to look for a new congregation.

Our next stop was a Reform temple in Rome, Georgia. I do not remember much about it, except that the young rabbinical student told a story of the Jews from Chelm who thought they pushed a mountain. No inspiration there.

Finally, my husband decided that the time had come for us to look into Orthodox Judaism. He searched through the Yellow Pages until he came up with the name of an Orthodox rabbi in Chattanooga. That's how he first met Rabbi Michael Katz, the South African son-in-law of Rabbi Nachman Bulman, *zt"l*.

Until this day, my children still remember John's announcement after their initial meeting. "For the first time in my life, I met a man who could answer my questions!" He was excited and inspired. However, in keeping with the Torah's directive to turn away prospective converts, Rabbi Katz recommended that we join a Unitarian Universalist congregation.

My brief exposure to Judaism had aroused within me an interest in Jewish things, and I had no interest whatsoever in investigating another religion. My husband, however, did attend the Unitarian service, and he brought home a bulletin to show me. As soon as I saw that this congregation had objectionable moral standards, I absolutely refused to pursue Unitarian Universalism any further.

We spent another year on the mountain going about our lives without making any further effort to discover if G-d had a People. I honestly felt that finding a People who would be compatible with my beliefs was a lost cause. Besides, the only image I had of an Orthodox Jew was a huge photo on the front page of a Los Angeles newspaper showing a man with long sidelocks throwing rocks at cars in Jerusalem. He looked rather barbaric to me. So I really didn't give it much more thought.

Eventually, my husband decided to return to Rabbi Katz. This time he took along an impressive photo of our large family. Looking the rabbi squarely in the eye, my husband showed him the picture and asked, "Don't you feel kinda sorry for a family who's all alone on the mountain?"

This time Rabbi Katz again tried to put him off by insisting that services at his synagogue were conducted in Hebrew and would be difficult for us to follow. When he saw that my husband would not be deterred, he invited him to come to the synagogue with our two oldest boys. Later he invited our entire family to come to the synagogue on Sunday, so he could meet with us. It was at this meeting that he delivered a bombshell: Jews don't hunt. Shooting an animal can result in a wounded animal and cause pain and suffering.

We lived our lives in a strongly hunting-oriented culture. A rifle was a necessary tool of day-to-day life, found in every home in the vicinity, much as city dwellers have Scotch-tape dispensers and staplers, hammers and screwdrivers. John trained our sons to become good hunters from a young age. Our family did not hunt for the sport of it, and certainly not because we enjoyed killing animals. In fact, my husband and the boys had a reverence for nature and all that lived in it. Hunting was a necessity. Knowing how to properly use a gun was a survival skill, much as learning how to safely cross the street and avoid talking to strangers is a must for children reared in the city. They were skilled marksmen, a skill that kept them safe from venomous snakes and wild dogs.

My boys loved hunting primarily because they loved spending time out in the woods exploring. When our food supplies ran low, my husband would take the boys out to the woods to hunt deer. He would bring the deer back home, tie it upside down on a tree, clean it, and skin it. I would do the butchering on our kitchen table, splitting the carcass, sawing through the bone joints, and cutting it into large hunks before slicing it into smaller pieces to store in water in our refrigerator. Usually some of the first servings of the tender pieces I fried and served between biscuits.

And yet, with all that, I felt Rabbi Katz was right. Years later I found out that one of my sons actually took this pronouncement very hard, but openly no one objected to this requirement.

Finally, Rabbi Katz invited our family to his home for a Shabbos meal. Rebbetzin Toby Katz had a new baby at home, and in an effort not to burden her the rabbi asked us to bring only half of our family the first week, and the second half the next.

I sat at the Shabbos table that evening just soaking up the beautiful atmosphere. I loved the way Rabbi Katz interacted with my sons. He asked them questions, explained the Jewish rituals as he went along, and played chess with them after the meal.

In an effort to protect my sons from becoming caught up in the culture of heavy drinking so prevalent in our culture, I taught them to abstain from alcohol. A look of utter confusion and discomfiture appeared on their faces when Rabbi Katz poured them each a taste of the *Kiddush* wine. Not wanting to appear rude, yet uncertain about how to proceed, one of my sons began diluting his small serving of wine with a large quantity of Coke. It was rather comical, but Rabbi Katz took it all in stride.

During my first Shabbos meal at the Katzes' home, I instantaneously and yet concretely realized that I wanted to be a Jew. I was smitten by the beauty of the Shabbos table and the warmth of Jewish family life. For the first time I had encountered a people who actually cherished children as much as I did! My heart longed to join them.

Still, my head held me back. I had a number of questions about Judaism. Before I could be sure that it was the truth, I needed answers.

I followed Toby back into the kitchen between courses, and I privately asked her questions that had been troubling me. I wanted to know why Jews had such liberal ideas regarding so many issues that the Bible clearly forbids. Toby patiently explained the difference between secular Jewish philosophies and Torah-true Judaism. Once those serious issues had been resolved, I had just two more questions left for the Rebbetzin: must all Jewish women shave their heads, and are Jews really cheats? Quietly this tremendously intellectual woman just said simply, "No, it's not true."

As a family we were very impressed by our first Shabbos experience at the Katzes. Since breakfast was such a feast in the South, one of my children wondered on the way home, "If this is what they eat for supper, I wonder what Jews eat for breakfast!"

One Sunday John came home from meeting with Rabbi Katz and asked all of our children to come in, as he had something to tell them. I, who hardly ever sat down, was busy in the kitchen, but I was all ears. As they sat on the couches, he gave them a whole salesman's pitch on why they should join the Jewish people. As he paced back and forth, punctuating his strongest reasons by waving a fist in the air, I was slightly horrified to hear him say, "And not only should all of you become Jewish, but I want all of you to become rabbis!"

Oh, my goodness, I thought, *this is way too strong for teenag-*

Rabbi Michael Katz (left) with his daughter and my oldest son

ers. It's only going to backfire. We found the Jewish people too late for our older boys. Teenagers are so notorious for rebelling against their parents, we'll be lucky if one or two decide to make this journey with us.

Was I ever wrong! With those words, every one of our children began throwing off their mountain garb to race toward the Jewish people!

John and our two oldest boys, Joey and Nate, soon began to drive up to Chattanooga every Sunday to join Rabbi Katz's *shiur* in *Derech Hashem*, which they found to be interesting and inspiring. On Shabbos we would cram all nine of our children into our little blue Pinto and drive the 35 miles to services in Rabbi Katz's *shul*. It was not a comfortable ride, but it was certainly worth it! I soon found out that married women were supposed to cover their hair, so I started doing this. I thought, only half-humorously, *G-d really knows the lot of busy mothers. It will be one less thing I'll have to worry about. You just cover your hair and you don't have to worry about combing it every few hours.*

How I enjoyed our weekly excursions to the synagogue! Toby Katz dug up an old musty blue *siddur* with English translation for me and directed me through the prayers. I had been praying all my life, yet it was she who taught me to *daven*.

Rabbi Katz had a Friday-afternoon radio program that we made sure to tune into. The theme song was Abie Rotenberg's "It's Time to Say Good Shabbos."

"So throw away your hammer, there's nothing left to do. Go on home and find the gift that's waiting there for you..."

The song echoed through our little tin-roofed house, and each time I heard it, I was literally moved to tears. All alone in the mountains, with no one for miles around who shared our ideals, it seemed as if the radio program had been established for the sole benefit of our family, offering us our first opportunity to connect to the Jewish people through the most beautiful music I had ever encountered in my life.

Soon John, speaking on behalf of all of us, told Rabbi Katz, "We want to convert to Judaism." Rabbi Katz, who had experience working with converts in South Africa, replied, "Um, so things will start happening." We thought that was an interesting reaction but didn't know what he meant.

We had now lived on the farm for about seven years. One night a few weeks later, we were sleeping when suddenly someone was standing in the doorway of our bedroom giving us orders. I pretended to be asleep and burrowed my head further into my pillow.

Now, everyone on the mountain stayed prepared for these moments by having plenty of weapons stored in strategic places. Even the elderly aunts carried pistols in their purses. We had 20 to 30 guns in a few places, including about 10 in the corner of our bedroom, but they were out of reach.

The huge man almost filled our whole doorway. "Ah, man, I just brought mah boat."

John, now wide awake, asked, "What do you want?"

"I wrote you a paper about it on your table. I brought you a boat; it's out in the yard to keep for awhile. I'll come back next week."

And he disappeared, closing the door behind him.

We called the sheriff, and it turned out the man had stolen the boat and for some reason had decided to store it in our front yard. That very strange incident marked the end of still another mountain myth of ours: that guns protect you.

One week later the intruder's parents just walked into our house, stomping around from room to room, ranting and raving and screaming, "Get out right now!" They were angry because we had called the police on their son, and they had arranged with the landlord to have us kicked out.

That night we ended up again on the back of John's folks' land across the dirt road, on the edge of the vast wilderness. This time the little cabin had rotted down, so we slept in the forest under tarps.

We had already started getting rid of our animals. I was very happy the day they came to take our cow, Lucinda. Of course, she stubbornly refused to climb into her new owner's trailer, and he was about to back out of the deal. All my years of contending with her strengthened my determination to get rid of her now! It was 120 pounds of me against her nearly 1,500 pounds, but in the end I won.

About a week later I was sitting in the dentist's office engrossed in my own thoughts and not really listening to the conversation around me when I heard a woman say, "My husband used to be a priest, but now he's an atheist." I'd found that people who make such claims were often searchers. Intrigued, I entered the conversation. The woman eventually asked me where I lived. When I told her, she gasped, jumped up, and ran to call her husband. "These people are living in the woods. They just got kicked out of their home. We have to do something to help them," she declared.

We created something of an uproar as the dentist and his wife came out and joined the discussion as to what should be done. On the spot, the atheist wrote us out a check. And the dentist and his family later came out to the mountain and brought us a tent.

We built a small platform and staked our tent upon it. For the next five months, we had torrential downpours. It seemed that it rained every day, almost all day long. At night the blankets would suck up water off the tent bottom, getting our feet wet. Many of the possessions we had accumulated got ruined. But with all these conditions, I continued to homeschool. Holding my newborn infant in my arms, as there was no place to put her down, I taught my boys their lessons while they bounced on the bed. And no matter what, I took my little old blue *siddur* out to *daven* every day.

I hungrily soaked up every opportunity for connection with the Jewish people. I hadn't even realized how much I longed for sustenance. My hunger was not physical; it was a deep spiritual yearning for truth, as well as social contact.

Though I had interacted with other women on the mountain, somehow I never quite fit in. In the winter all they seemed to talk of was quilt-making, and in the summer the subject was canning. Every self-respecting woman would keep herself busy sweating away in her kitchen, surrounded by fresh homegrown produce and canning jars. There was fierce competition. "And so far I've canned 100 quarts of green beans, 200 quarts of soup, and 50 pints of pickles," a neighbor would drone on. Another woman would vie for admiration: "Really, my cellar is already full, but I still hope to lay away 500 more quarts of blackberries, okra, tomatoes."

I was always wistfully hoping that the conversations would take a deeper turn. While holding yet another baby on my lap, I'd wonder how much of this activity was done out of necessity and how much was merely a cultural habit. Granny's sister, Aunt Vera, had raised a family of 11 children, and even after her children had grown and left the nest she never slowed down. She slaved over her wooden stove all summer to lay away a few more jars of goodies to

Elijah and Jesse blackberrry
picking with Aunt Vera

keep on hand for her visiting children and grandchildren. Her huge
cellar was always bursting with jars and jars of plums, applesauce,
soup, pickled okra, tomatoes, apple jam, pears, and the like. The
funny thing was that though the demand for her canned goods
never seemed to meet the vast supplies, she kept laying away. It
seemed as if canning had become a well-worn habit that she just
couldn't break! Other than talking about canning, I didn't have
much to discuss with the neighboring women.

The more involved I became with Judaism, the more I wanted
to share the beauty of Torah with my children. I got hold of a
Feldheim catalogue and ordered Jewish books and tapes in order to
incorporate Judaism into my children's lessons. Wanting to enrich
my repertoire of Jewish children's songs, I ordered a book of Jewish
songs that came with a tape. I played many of these songs over and
over until my children were able to sing along, their high-pitched
voices taking on a Brooklyn accent in place of a Southern drawl.

Many years later Toby Katz mentioned how surprised she had

been to hear my little kids, who knew nothing about *challah* or gefilte fish, singing a song about the *Parah Adumah* in a New York accent! I remember my children enthusiastically telling Rabbi Katz that we had a red heifer of our own back on the mountain. Yet the good rabbi insisted that our heifer wasn't completely red. "I want you to go back home and check the hairs on its neck. If you look carefully, you'll be sure to find a few different colors of hair."

As soon as we got home that Shabbos, my kids jumped out of the car and raced over to inspect our red heifer. Sure enough, they found some black and white hairs on its neck! My older sons worked on a ranch and thought they knew a lot about cattle, and yet the rabbi was right! We were amazed that a rabbi learning in the city knew more about cows than we did.

Our red heifer

CHAPTER 10

Noahide or Jew?

By the time Joey was 13, he had already begun to question some of the Church's teachings. In many Christian sects, violence in any form — even in the context of self-defense — is frowned upon. Joey was confused by this doctrine and spent much time thinking it through. *If an intruder came into the house and threatened little Benton with a knife, I should just stay passive?* he wondered, disturbed. He finally came to the conclusion that if he was capable of defending his family but refrained from doing so, it would be tantamount to harming them himself.

My boys were very firm in their beliefs, and John and I trusted their ability to hold their own during religious debates. For a number of years, our family was targeted by missionaries. Knowing that our boys could handle it and wanting them also to have an educated choice in this journey, we allowed them to enter into debates with the men who came to our door. After a while, the missionaries understood just whom they were up against. They stopped coming.

Joey had never laid eyes on a religious Jew. Granddad's eldest brother, who often came to sit in the cab of his truck and discuss religion with Granddad, once made a reference to the Israelites that for years lay dormant in Joey's memory. His words: "There is no place in the world that the earth isn't full of their bodies."

Having being trained from a young age to seek the truth, when Joey was exposed to the Torah, he immediately recognized its veracity. It wasn't long before he accepted Rabbi Katz as his mentor and frequently attended his classes on Torah thought. His new understanding of Torah led him to the realization that the central tenets of his family's religion, namely Shabbos and *kashrus*, actually belonged to the Jewish people.

Joey saw two distinct roads stretching before him, two divergent pathways to the authentic service of G-d. Both pathways were entirely legitimate, both true. As a G-d-fearing gentile, he was obligated to observe just seven Noahide Laws. Yet another option lay open to him as well: becoming a Jew.

Although we as a family were happy attending the little Orthodox synagogue in Chattanooga, Tennessee, we weren't completely accepted by all the congregants. Joey decided to follow through on Rabbi Katz's suggestion to begin attending services in Atlanta. During this period, Rabbi and Mrs. Katz also moved to Atlanta.

Joey's teenage drive and idealism didn't allow him to go along with the traditionally slow pace of change in the backwoods of Appalachia. He has always been very determined and driven. He was loath to leave the question of our family's relationship with Judaism up to his slow-moving parents. He decided to take things into his own hands.

Joey had worked on a local farm from the age of 15, and by the time he was 18 he had enough money saved up to buy a car of his own. He determined to buy a vehicle solid enough to navigate a daily four-hour round trip to Atlanta, so that he could properly investigate Orthodox Judaism. He first bought a 1964 Chevy Flatbed, which didn't quite do the job. Eventually he purchased a gently used, bright-red Ford Ranger pickup. This car became a common sight in Atlanta's *frum* neighborhood.

As he spent more and more time in the big city, Joey sensed some hesitation on the part of the locals at home. City life went against the grain of his ancestors and their simple, timeless life-style. What little exposure the mountain folk had of Atlanta came primarily from the evening news reports they followed on their outdated TV sets.

They had very poor reception up on the mountain. There were just three channels, which were notoriously full of static. My boys tell me that there were times that they were watching a program at their grandparents' home when suddenly they would lose all reception, and an annoying buzzing sound was all they would hear. Invariably one of them would have to go outside and turn the homemade TV antenna, which was an oven rack attached to a long strip of wood and connected by a wire to the TV. Patiently he would try out different positions until the shouts coming from the house let him know that the reception had been restored.

My in-laws' TV was their main source of connection with the outside world. The daily reports — which often included news of muggings or people held up at gunpoint — did little to ease their discomfort with Joey's excursions to the big city. Upon hear-ing about our family's foray into the teachings of Judaism, one of our relatives brought us a book criticizing the Talmud. Despite the naysayers and encouraged by my support, Joey continued on his quest to learn about Judaism.

Each Shabbos morning, he got up at about 3 a.m. to make it to Atlanta for *Shacharis*. Joey was very impressed with the synagogue in the big city. It offered a plethora of resources for newcomers to Judaism, from a well-stocked library of ArtScroll *sefarim* to Rabbi David Silverman's beginners' program, and, in addition, a warm and inviting community.

There was a well-meaning man in *shul* who often tried to dis-courage Joey and his brother Nate from taking the path of con-version. He suggested that they remain loyal Sons of Noach. Joey argued back. "*Davening* three times a day, laying *tefillin*, and affixing *mezuzos* on the doors of my home will bring me so much closer to Hashem. As a *ben Noach*, I'd be left out in the cold."

Still, it was a serious decision: Noahide or Jew?

Joey had grown up a Sabbath-observer and felt a deep connection to both the Jewish day of rest and the study of Torah, both of which were purely the domain of the Jew and not the *ben Noach*. He also loved learning *Sefer Yeshayahu* and reading about the wondrous future in store for G-d's Chosen People at the End of Days. He wanted to share that destiny.

His decision was partially influenced by his sense of community. Judaism has a much greater sense of community than had the fledgling Noahide movement. Continuing his family tradition, he strongly valued the idea of having a large family, a concept that resonated with the *frum* community as well.

Finally, when Joey's thoughts turned to the fate of his future children, he knew that he must become a Jew.

The time had come for him to move to Atlanta. For generations, the family had lived in isolation on the mountain, and everyone was very emotional at the thought of Joey leaving. Although I would miss Joey, I had no reservations, and I was very proud of this milestone in my son's life.

The decision to become a full-fledged member of the Jewish community was not easy for him. He'd be leaving a lot behind. Not only would he have to give up both hunting and the woods he so loved, but he also had a number of good job offers back on the mountain that didn't compare with the work available in the city. Joey was close to his grandparents. He liked the people he grew up with and their lifestyle. He missed the way that the country folk waved to passing cars and pedestrians, and found the city to be cold and unfriendly.

Most poignantly, Joey harbored a secret fear that he might cross the bridge over to Judaism alone. Although he knew that we were also interested in Judaism, he worried that we might not follow him.

A family alone on the mountain

And yet, in the very deepest recess of his soul, Joey knew that he must put everything on the line and become a Jew. Only Judaism could offer what he so keenly desired: a close relationship with G-d and a connection to His holy Torah, G-d's own guidebook.

Joey had spent most of his time on the mountain working on a beautiful ranch belonging to a man named Mr. Rollins. He enjoyed landscaping, gardening, and working with livestock and so began to look for a similar job on the outskirts of Atlanta. Once he realized that it just wasn't feasible to live 20 to 30 miles outside of Atlanta and still integrate into the *frum* community, Joey put his dream on hold and looked for work in the city. His former boss had a daughter in Atlanta, and Joey began to do her landscaping. Through word of mouth, he soon got some more landscaping jobs. Still, as he wasn't earning enough to support himself in the city, he looked for a permanent job.

Joey found a job laying pipe for new suburbs of Atlanta. Although the pay was better, he didn't enjoy the work or the atmosphere. Eventually, he found a well-paid job working for a landscaping company. It wasn't easy to adjust to living in the city, but he considered it a necessary stepping-stone to his biggest obsession: to become a Jew!

Every morning, Joey arrived at *shul* at least an hour or two before *Shacharis*, to learn and schmooze with his fellow congregants. His religious devotion was obvious. The community members jokingly blessed him that one day he'd be just like them and occasionally come late for services.

Meanwhile, back at the ranch (literally!), we had moved into a little house after spending five months in a tent. Houses were scarce on the mountain and people didn't want to rent to families with children, but since our boys had worked for years on this 15,000-acre ranch, the owners had agreed to rent to us.

Though we weren't forging ahead as quickly as Joey, we, too, were sailing into new spiritual waters. The Katzes loaned us *The Jew and His Home*, by Eliyahu Kitov. I will never forget the feeling: After reading thousands of books in my life, for the first time I was

Our children on a haystack – full of childhood joy!

going to open a book I could trust. I felt like a pirate who after years of searching and digging brings up the rusty treasure chest full of gold. My fingers actually trembled as I opened the book.

My family, too, was growing. Physically, we were blessed with the birth of our 10th child, a girl. And spiritually? My sons were learning more and more. One day I cooked up a big supper of beef liver and onions. That night my sons came in from working on the ranch and, seeing the repast in front of them, firmly declined.

I was upset. No one had told me that we couldn't eat liver, and now I would have to cook supper all over again. These were big working guys and it took a lot to fill them up. But they declared that since we were gentiles we had to abide by the laws given to Noah. We were not allowed to eat a limb from a living animal. Apparently this was a problem, as some animals are only stunned in the slaughterhouses and this organ could have been taken out before the animal died. I used all the arguments I could think of as to why they should go ahead and eat the delicious supper I had prepared, but it was useless; I was soon to learn that my sons were immovable in these matters.

Another day I was giving the children haircuts. My youngest son, Benton, in his turn climbed up into the chair and cupped his hands over his hair right in front of his ears. I didn't say anything, and neither did he. I was immensely proud of him but dumbfounded. I wondered, as I cut the hair around his hands, *Who told him about peyos?*

I now began to include Jewish studies in our school schedule, but though I tried to teach the children Hebrew I found I was just holding them back, so eventually I turned them loose to learn on their own. One of the books we liked to discuss was *Love Your Neighbor,* by Rabbi Zelig Pliskin. The definition of love I'd always heard was just feeling good toward someone, but here were a thousand ways to really be sensitive and give to another person.

As I learned more, I was astounded at the high pedestal a Jewish woman was placed upon. She was cherished as a person who could use every fiber of her brain and talents to build her home.

How grateful I was to go beyond studying the ways of the bees and the birds and being inspired by the beauty of the trees and the gardens. We were now learning about the Creator of these things. How incredible to be accumulating a higher knowledge and wisdom by the people who had been chosen by the Mastermind of the Universe! I felt like an eagle who all of his life thought he was a chicken and pecked around the barnyard. One day a wolf hiding behind the bushes jumped out after him, and, with a sudden flash, the eagle found his wings. What a thrill as he began to soar above the earth!

We began to take on Jewish Shabbos customs. I traveled the 20 miles to Summerville, Georgia, and looked all over for a long tablecloth, but there was not one to be found. I finally came home with an aqua-blue flat sheet. Now each week as we went to town, we also picked up a bottle of grape juice or Manischewitz wine. We bought our first set of nice dishes, white with green and flowered trim. It seemed so right and good to put some money and beauty into our home in honor of Shabbos.

I tried to present the options to the children and leave to them their own final decision. I once told them, "Judaism looks to me like it's not a religion for couch potatoes. It's a way of life for energetic people."

There just wasn't enough time to pack in all of the learning we wanted to do each day, especially with the boys working on the ranch. I had found an industrial-size muffin tin and I promised, "Whoever gets up at 4 o'clock to learn gets hot blueberry muffins!" It actually worked for a few weeks.

Books became my lifeline to the Jewish world. There was so much we needed to learn, and there were still so many questions to ask. I pored over the publisher's catalogs and carefully selected one or two books each time.

The children had a lot of lively discussions. They studied on

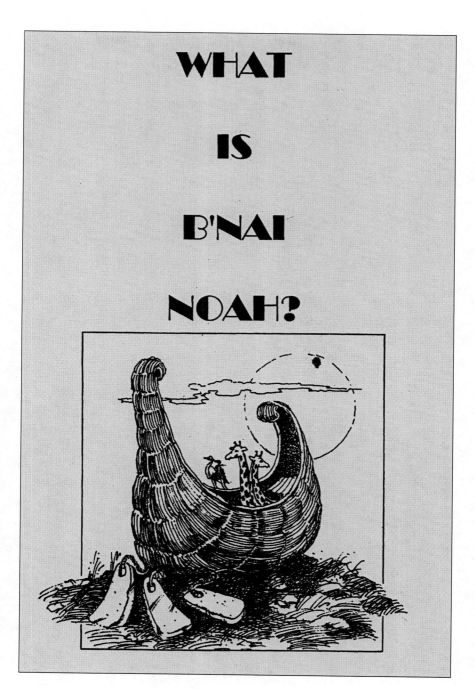

A pamphlet from the Noahide movement

their own and made their own decisions about taking on *mitzvos*. I would sometimes hear them aggressively trying to convince another sibling to take on something they were doing. When they pushed too hard, the defender would take all the fizz out of the argument by saying, "But I'm not Jewish yet. I don't have to."

John was still looking into the *b'nei Noach* and their "only seven laws," so we began to make longer trips up into the Tennessee Valley to visit the Noahide community of J. David Davis. We were privileged to hear a historical address given there by Rabbi Nachman Bulman, *zt"l*, Rabbi Katz's father-in-law, who came in from Israel. He spoke about how the peoples from the three sons of Noah each have a mission and that when all three synchronize their missions we will fulfill G-d's purpose for our world.

Later we were to attend another of these groups in Georgia, but I cried all the way there. I had encountered the Jewish people, and this was what I wanted with all my heart for my children. Each day I made my way up to our attic to *daven* out of my little blue

The little house on the mountain where we first lit our Chanukah candles

siddur and beg Hashem to take us to Atlanta to hover under the wings of His people.

Joey came from Atlanta the day before Chanukah bearing good news. Rabbi Katz had said that after we kept a year of Jewish holidays he would convert us. All that afternoon my boys whittled a *menorah* out of wood while Joey taught us about Chanukah. As the afternoon wore on and the *menorah* was still not ready, they abandoned it and fashioned an impromptu *menorah* from wire hangers.

That night we celebrated Chanukah for the first time. With awe and great excitement, Joey carefully pronounced the blessings and kindled the first light. For the first time ever, the light of Torah shone in our humble little home in the Appalachian Mountains.

We completed our celebration with delicious homemade doughnuts, dipped into bowls of chocolate, butterscotch, and cinnamon sugar. Those first doughnuts were made from my challah dough recipe, and have since become a family tradition.

After a wonderful Chanukah experience we looked forward to Purim. For months we talked about driving out to Atlanta for the *Megillah* reading. As we counted down the days to our family's first public celebration among the Jewish people, I realized that John had still not decided that he wanted to attend. I was worried and unsure of how to proceed. Would it be inappropriate to take the family all the way to Atlanta without him?

A clear act of Divine Providence smoothed our way to Atlanta. My husband's uncle passed away in Florida, and the funeral was to be held on *Taanis Esther*. John decided to drive down to Florida for the funeral, and I drove out to Atlanta with the kids on my own.

Each encounter I had with authentic Torah Judaism only fueled my desire for more. After our wonderful Purim experience, I was even more determined to move our family down to Atlanta. But though I was determined to make the move, it seemed impossible. We had recently moved to a new house on the mountain. Not only was rent in the big city prohibitively expensive, we didn't even have a car large enough to safely make the trip with all our kids. That

Dovid, right after conversion

problem was solved when I was presented with the opportunity to buy an old station wagon. Finally, I had a vehicle large enough to transport my entire family to Atlanta. Still, we had no way of paying rent.

Once Joey had been living in Atlanta for more than a year, a local congregant encouraged him to approach Rabbi Katz again and ask to be converted to Judaism. At that point the *rabbanim* of Atlanta realized that Joey was indeed ready to become a Jew. Just a few days after Shavuos of 1992, Joey became Dovid ben Avraham, a full-fledged member of the Jewish nation.

We were still in our semiparalyzed state on the mountain, with no way to communicate regularly with our rabbi or the Jewish community, as we hadn't had a phone in over a year. Making regular family trips to Atlanta was about as remote as saying, "Let's go to Alaska." As for joining Joey when he converted, we were clueless as to what we could and should do.

It was then that Nate, my second oldest, decided to move to Atlanta as well and study for conversion. Dovid was no longer alone on his journey to Jewish observance.

Eventually, Atlanta's community *kollel* convinced Dovid to continue his studies in Jerusalem at Yeshivas Ohr Somayach, under the tutelage of Rabbi Nachman Bulman. Just before Dovid flew off to Israel, he sat down to try to learn some Gemara with another recent convert: his brother Nate, who now went by the name Nosson. They opened up to *Maseches Shabbos* and tried to make sense of the first *mishnah*. After an hour they finally gave up. Dovid realized that he would have to wait until he got to yeshivah in order to learn how to learn Gemara.

Shortly thereafter we once again lost our home and had to temporarily move back in with my in-laws. By now my children were so committed to Judaism that they had begun to grow *peyos* and wear yarmulkes, and they no longer ate milk and meat together. Without any prompting on my part, they were determined to observe Jewish laws and customs even while living with their grandparents. Tensions soon began to build.

Eventually, it all became too much for poor Granddad. One day in the future, he would support our path, even telling Joey, "If I was only younger, I would join you." But that day was still far off. One day, Granddad just snapped and told John, "Take your family and leave now."

Coming back to our room, John urged, "Hurry, pack up, we're going to Atlanta." We gathered up our belongings and quickly shepherded the children into the car. For almost four years I had prayed for G-d to bring us to Atlanta. Now, in the blink of an eye we had been driven off Lookout Mountain, right into the Jewish community!

Stone Mountain

More than five miles around at its base,
this quartz dome of rock rises
to a summit of 1,686 feet.

"Here we encountered closed doors, strict justice ..."

"The Rock. Perfect is His work… and fair is He" (*Deuteronomy* 32:4).

CHAPTER 11

Atlanta

W e all piled into Dovid and Nosson's basement apartment that night, and we stayed for a few days until we were able to find better accommodations. Providence brought us to Atlanta shortly after a delegation of young *kollel* families from Baltimore's Yeshivah Ner Yisrael had been sent there to establish a community *kollel*. Dovid found us a house near the *kollel* families, and before long we established a warm relationship with a number of the young rabbis. The Deutsch, Goldberger, and Friedman families became our close friends. They invited us over for Shabbos meals and my teenagers became the neighborhood babysitters.

Through the initiative of the *kollel,* many people in the community hired my husband and sons to construct and assemble *succos* for them ahead of the coming holiday. This proved to be a nice source of income. Once again, it was evident that G-d was providing for us. We had made a leap of faith and moved to Atlanta without any means of support — or even the ability to pay the rent — and before long a new job market had opened for us.

Two weeks after our fateful move, we loaded our family into the station wagon and drove back up to Lookout Mountain to collect the rest of our belongings. The trip passed uneventfully. When I pulled into our driveway in Atlanta on our return, our trusty station wagon caught fire. It wasn't major, but just enough to put our car out of business. Thank G-d, my family was safe, but our car was finished.

That night, when I'd had time to calm down, I realized that G-d's providence had once again been at work. He had provided us with a vehicle large enough to transport our family to Atlanta, yet once we were finally settled in our new community we lost our car, and with it, the means to return to the mountain.

Back on the mountain, I had felt that my husband and I were the sole guardians of our family's spirituality. Here, we were a large and established family upon the threshold of an entirely new way of life. Not only were we moving from the backwoods to the city, but we were also changing course altogether. No longer would we live in isolation; we were actually going to become part of G-d's chosen nation!

It was an amazing experience for our entire family to finally become part of a community. Still, taking on 613 commandments when I was unfamiliar with the practical aspects of their observance was a daunting task. It seemed like turning the ocean liner that was our family 180 degrees into uncharted waters. I knew the job was too big for me alone, and so Hashem sent us to the wonderfully supportive community of Atlanta to steer us in the right direction.

In addition to all the new commandments we had to learn about, there was another, more subtle, challenge. On the mountain we had been very independent. We had thought, debated, discussed, and discerned right from wrong. We had chosen our own spiritual path in life. Would we now be able to seek out the knowledge of others and submit ourselves to their counsel? There is a hint of arrogance inherent in the feeling that "G-d singled *me* out to make a unique journey." For years, we had flown in the face of society. When we arrived in Atlanta, we felt very validated in all that we had done.

Our challenge now was to submit to the authority of limitless Torah wisdom. Here we were faced with a new experience; we had to learn to receive. To my joy, I found that when we did reach out and ask others, the experience was incredibly enlightening. In fact, I would never trade the clarity gained from tapping into Torah wisdom and consciousness. A Torah sage is able to tune into ageless Torah wisdom and dispel the choking darkness of confusion.

Rabbi Michoel Lipschutz, a member of the *kollel* who took on a guiding role in our lives, was adamant that we learn to access the community and all it had to offer. He stressed that the *mitzvos* were meant to be observed in a community setting, and that one Jew alone cannot fulfill all of G-d's commandments.

Our family was warmly accepted by the community in Atlanta. Not only were we frequently invited out for Shabbos meals, but an old friend from Chattanooga bought each of my sons a pair of *tefillin* when he converted. Others bought tickets for them as one by one they began flying off to study at Yeshivah Ohr Somayach in Israel.

I thrived during the time we spent in Atlanta. I had spent all my adult years living in isolation, with no one but simple country folk nearby. Even during my childhood years I hadn't been given the opportunity to enjoy female companionship, since the co-ed public schools I attended did little to foster an atmosphere of healthy relationships between girls. After all these years I had an entire community of women to befriend! During the first weekly Shabbos *Kiddush* I attended, I sat in the social hall, taking in the sight of my new community members. I looked at all the elegantly dressed and intelligent women and wondered who would become my new friends.

I was truly impressed by the serious and deep-thinking women and developed a number of close friendships. For the first time in my life I met individuals who shared my perspective on life. Here was a group of women who believed in One G-d, lived moral lives dedicated to fulfilling G-d's Will, and who were also devoted to their children's education.

Down my street lived a very kind woman who became a dear friend. Lisa Elon opened her home to us every Shabbos and hosted us for *shalosh seudos*. During these meals, she answered many of my questions. My oldest daughter, Jenny, had been pining for a Jewish girlfriend. When she met Lisa's daughter, her wish was finally fulfilled. Lisa was a true friend, at my side to ease my adjustment to Judaism and the Jewish holidays.

To be honest, I did have my share of surprises along the way. When I learned that one is not allowed to bathe on Shabbos I was secretly distressed. After so many years of making do without running water, I fully enjoyed the convenience of indoor plumbing. I just couldn't imagine giving up my Shabbos-morning shower. Once again, Providence intervened, and I received a vital tip no one had thought to give me.

One Friday afternoon, one of my children took ill and I found myself in desperate need of a vaporizer. I hurriedly made the rounds of a number of the families in the neighborhood in pursuit of a vaporizer to borrow. To my surprise, at each door, I was greeted with the exact same scenario. No one was able to come to the door since they were showering! That's when it dawned on me that *frum* families bathe on *Erev Shabbos*!

For the first year of our stay in Atlanta I continued to homeschool my younger children. My teenage sons attended classes at the *kollel*. It was amazing to see my previously isolated children begin to socialize and integrate within the community. Although they were shy, they soon made friends and naturally absorbed the particular social mores of our new community.

Since I was blessed with a large family, it wasn't long before the neighborhood children were drawn to our home. I loved helping out my neighbors and keeping an eye on their children when necessary. It was a surreal experience for me to observe real live descendants of Avraham, Yitzchak, and Yaakov playing in my back-yard!

After learning about religious Jews and experiencing firsthand their love for children as well as their emphasis on the family unit, I had expected to see many more large families. Finally, I asked one of my new friends about it. "Where are all the women with lots of kids?" I asked.

"You've got more than anyone else!" was the surprising answer.

I remember the first time we observed the Days of Awe. I took the concept of Rosh Hashanah as the Day of Judgment very seri-ously. Never before had I pictured all of humanity passing before G-d one by one, as sheep passing before a shepherd. Had I learned about Rosh Hashanah without being able to experience it as part of an authentic Jewish community I would have spent the whole day trembling in fear. After all, my earliest impressions of the A-mighty were highly influenced by the religion of my youth. I would never

Our first Purim in Atlanta

have thought to celebrate the Day of Judgment in happiness and joy. When I saw how the Jewish people gracefully managed to host guests for the *Yom Tov* meals despite the day's awesome significance, I gained an even greater appreciation for the Jew's ability to achieve a delicate balance between his relationship with G-d and his relationship with his fellow man.

Despite all the wonderful experiences I had acclimating to the Jewish community, there were still challenges. Clueless to the social norms, I had no idea that I needed to buy a seat in *shul* for the High Holy Days. When I arrived in *shul*, heavily pregnant with my 11th child, there was nowhere for me to sit. I spent the day moving around from one empty seat to another. Not only did I spend the entire *davening* playing musical chairs, but I also hadn't realized that I needed to bring along my own Rosh Hashanah prayer book.

I was feeling totally lost when finally I noticed a woman who was obviously not using her *machzor*. I asked her if I could borrow it. She must have gotten impatient waiting for me to complete the silent *Shemoneh Esrei*, since she came over to me and abruptly grabbed it out of my hands and walked out. I was left swallowing tears. Thank G-d, I quieted myself and didn't judge the entire Jewish people by one woman's thoughtless behavior. I managed to take my frustrating Rosh Hashanah experiences in stride and continue to focus on the positive.

As soon as we came to Atlanta, Samuel and Elijah asked if they could keep kosher. Toby Katz accompanied me to Kroger's, the local supermarket, and took me up and down the aisles, pointing out the products that were acceptable. We were both in the advanced stages of pregnancy at that time and had to stop and rest every so often.

For an entire year, my boys were willing to eat packaged goods such as cold cuts and crackers in our basement, since our kitchen was not yet kosher. I was very proud of their commitment to follow the *mitzvos*. I myself was biding my time and waiting for my husband to decide that he was ready to go ahead and convert. Not

My "what's kosher and what's not kosher" shopping lists. Toby Katz tutored me in the fundamentals of keeping kosher.

wanting to cause any tension by pushing him into a level of commitment he wasn't yet ready for, I decided to slow down and wait for him to go at his own pace. Still, I was excited about our family's imminent conversion.

My children were still racing on. Now they had taken on saying *berachos*, something that still seemed too complicated to me. But as I waited, I wondered.

When would we finally become Jews?

CHAPTER 12

Leah Rose

I was an ungainly seven months pregnant when I ran outside to wish my sons "good Shabbos" as they left for *shul*. As I ran, I lost my footing, slipped, and fell. Although I wasn't really worried that my baby had been injured in the fall, Sunday morning found me at my Jewish obstetrician, just as a precaution. Dr. Tate performed an ultrasound and was concerned that something wasn't quite right with my baby. He referred me to a specialist for a more detailed ultrasound.

Within a few days I found myself seated in the office of the specialist. The second ultrasound confirmed my obstetrician's concern. There was something seriously wrong with my baby. I was referred to yet another doctor, a neonatologist, for further evaluation. When I arrived at the office of the Muslim neonatologist, I was a bit taken aback to find that he had just stepped out for prayer. I found it quite bewildering that after so many years of searching for the truth, I was finally living in a Jewish community and seeing a Jewish obstetrician, yet for some reason G-d wanted me to be treated by both a Christian and a Muslim doctor as well.

I was not given a good report. My doctors weren't quite sure what was wrong, but it was obvious that the baby was terribly swollen. She was so bloated that I would be unable to have a natural birth. Gravely, the doctor issued his warning: "The baby you carry may not be compatible with life."

I refused to allow his prognosis to frighten me. G-d was surely on my side. Somehow my baby would survive. I had breezed through 10 pregnancies without any complications at all; surely this one couldn't be so different. I pushed all negative thoughts out of my mind and kept myself busy caring for my family.

A Caesarean section was recommended, and in the meantime I went for stress tests every other day to assess my baby's wellbeing. Thankfully, her heart rate was strong, and we didn't see any deterioration in her condition. Life continued pretty much as usual, until the day my baby was born.

As soon as my labor began, we raced to the hospital, where I underwent an emergency C-section. I delivered a little baby girl. While I was still in the operating theater, one of the nurses said, "Looks like a 21 to me." I was too disoriented to make sense of her words. A few hours later her comment finally registered. I remembered that "trisomy 21" was another term for a form of Down syndrome.

When my obstetrician came to examine me that afternoon, the first thing I asked was whether my baby had Down. "It's too soon to make a diagnosis," he told me. He was waiting for the test results to come back. The news wasn't long in coming. My little daughter did have Down syndrome. She also had a heart defect.

My emotions at that time were a confusing mess. For the duration of each of my 10 pregnancies I had worried about two things: the prospect of giving birth to a mentally deficient child and, G-d forbid, losing a baby to SIDS. Both scenarios terrified me. And now, after being blessed with 10 beautiful, healthy children, one of my worst fears was realized.

I spent the first few days after my baby's birth trying to make sense of my feelings. Why exactly was I so distraught? Until now my greatest joy had been educating my children and developing their minds. I wondered if my sadness was rooted in the fact that this child would not be as intelligent as her siblings. Or perhaps I was uncomfortable with the thought of how others would see my child? After all, back on the mountain, some simple country folk shunned retarded people. We were cautioned to avoid associating with a particular family that had three retarded sons.

I delved deeper into my memories. As I sifted through childhood stories, I came upon some reassuring points of hope. I remembered my mother's Aunt Winny, who cared for an entire home of sick and disabled children. When she grew older and had to retire, she turned the care of these special souls over to others. Nevertheless, she decided to adopt Kyler, a young man with Down syndrome. Kyler was a very likeable fellow, and my siblings and I loved playing tag with him when we visited.

While I was still in the hospital recovering from birth, a new friend, Jackie Lowenstein, came to visit me. She was very positive and upbeat about my baby. "We're going to dress her up and you'll see, she's going to be the life of the *shul*!" she said. She told me of a couple in Israel who had given birth to a daughter with Down syndrome. Amazingly, she went on to care for her parents in their old age.

Hearing these stories gave me a lot of encouragement, and I began to look forward to mothering this baby and fully loving her as my own. We named our new baby Leah Rose, after my husband's recently departed aunt and my sister: both very special people. Within a short time we opened our hearts and lives and welcomed her inside.

When Leah's doctors were unable to wean her off the ventilator, they decided to transfer her to Egleston Hospital for Children for further assessment. In Egleston, the full extent of Leah Rose's problems finally came to light. In addition to the problems we knew about — Down syndrome and the heart defect — Leah Rose was diagnosed with a very rare disorder called diffuse lymphangiectasia, a disorder of the lymphatic system. Our pediatrician, Dr.

Clark, explained that Leah Rose was unable to circulate fluids properly throughout her body. Instead of being expelled, excess bodily fluids and waste products were seeping into her tissues, causing extensive swelling throughout her body, as well as kidney damage.

In those first few days after Leah Rose's diagnosis, I wasn't able to absorb all the medical details of her condition. I could barely process what the doctors and nurses were trying to explain to me. All I wanted to know was if there was any hope that my baby would live. When I grew a little stronger, I started to read up on her condition. I learned that lymphangiectasia was so rare that there were only 100 documented cases. Of these cases, there were no survivors.

Often, when I was asked to step out into the hall so that the medical staff could work on my little Leah Rose, I would overhear other parents' animated conversations. I heard them tell of how doctors hadn't thought their baby would pull through, but they prayed and their baby rallied. I had a hard time with these stories. I couldn't understand why all these gentile parents needed to do was call out to G-d and they'd be answered. Here I was, deep in the process of conversion, having taken the giant step of moving to the Jewish community, and yet G-d wouldn't say yes to my prayers. I was deeply hurt.

My baby lived for a month; I spent most of the 30 days by her side. My responsible teenage sons managed to hold down the fort and help their younger siblings with their lessons, while I spent the better part of each day in the NICU. With the help of our amazing community, my children managed very well. The *chesed* the community showered upon our not-yet-Jewish family was unbelievable. Meals were sent to my home, and my kids were invited over to friends' houses. Sometimes my children were taken out for pizza. Every day, my friend Jackie came to the hospital to bring me lunch. What really was unbelievable to me was how the student body at Atlanta's Jewish high school eagerly volunteered to donate blood for my little baby. They didn't even know us.

Those weeks in the hospital became a precious bonding experience between our family and the Jewish community. I have no idea how I would have survived those painful weeks if not for the support of Atlanta's Jewish community.

One of Leah Rose's primary nurses was a wonderful woman named Eileen. She was a tremendous source of guidance and support for me, and she helped me navigate the tragedy of seeing my child struggle to survive. The doctors soon determined that they would need to create a port in Leah's chest to administer medications. Eileen sat with me at my baby's bedside as she recovered from her minor surgery. She showed me how to comfort my fragile infant by gently and lovingly massaging her with baby lotion. I was not allowed to hold my child; she was too sick and unstable to be lifted. Massaging her, one little swollen limb at a time, became my way of expressing the agonizing love I felt for my suffering child.

Eileen and Barbara, another primary nurse, bought me a small notebook and began a journal of my little baby's life. On the first page, they pasted in a photograph of my little one in her bed in the Neonatal Intensive Care Unit. They carefully wrote in little captions detailing the intimidating machines that kept little Leah Rose alive. The journal begins with a letter written on Leah's behalf to me and my husband, explaining her medical situation in a way that we could understand.

I found great comfort in writing in Leah Rose's journal. Not only was it a great way for me to keep track of all the special people who cared for and visited my precious little baby, but the journal also allowed me to give vent to my feelings of anguish. As I watched her fragile life slip away, I took up my pen and let the pain ooze out onto the accepting pages.

A week before Leah Rose's death, the doctors informed us that there was nothing they could do to save her. They encouraged us to consider taking her off of life support. The thought of pulling the plug on my own child was beyond something I could endure. The next morning my husband and I drove over to talk with Rabbi Katz and ask him for guidance. He made it very clear to us that the Torah never allows one to take away oxygen or water from the dying.

When I heard Rabbi Katz's words, I felt as if the weight of the world had been rolled off my shoulders. At this critical time, how thankful I was to have a rabbi and the Torah's guidance. I felt comforted knowing that G-d didn't allow me to hasten my baby's death.

Not long after, the doctors told me Leah Rose's kidneys were shutting down. We were told to bring in our children to say goodbye to their youngest sister. My sons and daughters gathered around the large hospital bed upon which their tiny little sister rested. Each one got a final chance to hold her little hand and stroke her soft head.

As the end drew near, I feared that I would be unable to bear the death of my child. Tearfully I turned to Eileen. "Am I going to be able to handle this?"

Eileen looked up and spoke softly. "You'll find you have the strength."

All the next day, I sat by my Leah Rose, crying. I hoped her nurse would go out and leave us alone. I soaked a roll of paper towels with my tears, and then moved on to toilet paper. Finally someone handed me a box of tissues.

My anguish found release in the following poem, which I showed my baby's doctor. She started to read it and then quickly left the room.

> *Today my baby is dying,*
> *My G-d, what do You want from me?*
> *A broken heart?*
> *Mine is broken in a jillion pieces.*
> *A million promises*
> *That in my humanness I know I can't keep?*
> *If You want more tears than there are raindrops,*
> *Give her more minutes and they will fall.*
> *If I could plead her case more eloquently*

Than the most brilliant lawyer,
Would You change Your mind?
If my love for my baby could surpass the expanse
     of the universe,
Would You change Your Divine decree?
Man has said no,
Only You can say yes,
My G-d, I'm this baby's mother!
What do You want from me?

My doctor entered again and suggested I put my arms underneath Leah Rose. This was the closest I had ever come to actually holding her, and I cherished the fading moments. And so I sat.

It was the first night of Chanukah. The numbers on the heart monitor began their slow countdown to death. After nightfall, Toby Katz came to the hospital, bearing tea and blankets. I slipped out for a few minutes, but as soon as I did, they called me right back.

Leah Rose had entered the world amid much pain and chaos. Sitting with her in the bustling NICU and keeping abreast of all her medical problems and procedures was like being surrounded by the commotion of a raging storm. At the moment of her death, I felt a great peace descend upon me.

In the very eye of the storm, there was nothing but silence — and G-d.

Then Toby helped me verbalize my thoughts in the most perfect way possible. In a hushed tone she whispered the age-old words: "Blessed are You, Hashem, the True Judge." Slowly, hesitantly, I repeated them after her.

And then they finally let me hold her. I picked up my baby and cradled her close. I sat for hours, holding my baby's lifeless body, my husband and Toby at my side.

CHAPTER 13

The Aftermath

I t was Granddad who made the funeral arrangements. My baby's casket was loaded on a covered wagon hitched to a team of mules that brought her to her final resting place in the family graveyard on Lookout Mountain. My friends from Atlanta rented a spacious van for us to drive out to the mountain, and members of the Jewish community joined in the procession. Rabbi Michoel Lipschutz led the ceremony and read a few chapters of *Psalms*, including Chapter 71, which really spoke to me. "…You, Who has shown me many grievous troubles; revive me again… Increase my greatness, and turn back to comfort me…" Although Leah Rose never did convert to Judaism, she merited a burial in the Jewish tradition.

I was devastated by the death of my baby, and although I wasn't really all that aware of my surroundings on that day, I have spent much time studying the photo of her funeral procession. This unusual photo is a study in contrasts, depicting modern vehicles against the backdrop of a rustic wagon and unpaved country roads. Our gentile relatives and friends, a *b'nei Noach* family, and our Jewish friends all joined the procession, and the misty, overcast day was brightened by a peculiar ray of light that broke through the cloudy heavens, bringing me a measure of hope and comfort in my time of intense pain.

I had expected a miracle. I had expected G-d to heal Leah Rose — a stamp of Divine approval of my family's journey. Upon learning that Leah Rose had Down syndrome, I had gone through the painful process of grief. Ultimately, I came to a place of true acceptance and love: I was ready to invest all my mind and my heart in raising my special-needs child. And then, as I reached this place, G-d took Leah Rose back.

I cried for three years after Leah Rose's death. It was as if part of my heart had been torn out, leaving only a gaping wound. Up until this point, my children had been the main source of joy in my difficult life. I had been so deprived and lonely that each new baby was an unusually important event. I found that the birth of each one of my children opened within me an increased capacity for love. Leah Rose's fragility and utter dependence aroused within me an unusually strong and deep love, such as I had never known before. Our bond had intensified during the long days and nights I had spent by her side in the hospital.

I was still a beginner when it came to Judaism and Torah thought. I hadn't learned or absorbed the Jewish attitude to death, tragedy, and that bulwark of Judaism: the truth of G-d's ultimate goodness. I had few spiritual resources to guide me through this crisis. I had always thought I was strong. I could pull up buckets of water and chop wood for kindling, but I'd never faced the stabbing pain of the death of one of my children.

Through this period, I suffered an additional blow. John and I shared a strong commitment to the concept of fulfilling G-d's command to "be fruitful and multiply," and for the most part we agreed on how to raise our children. Together, we had made a difficult and painful journey away from our parents' religion. Now here we were, upon the threshold of Judaism, and yet we were drifting apart. I was groping for solace through the searing pain of my loss,

Funeral of Leah Rose, the picture that captured my two lives

and I was unable to find any comfort. In an almost eerie premonition, during my days in the hospital a social worker told me that 60 percent of couples who lose a child divorce within a year.

It took me many months to work through my grief. Devastated, I didn't have the energy to manage the day-to-day needs of my home and family. It took me all morning just to get out of bed, wash my hands, and say the morning blessings. While I struggled to keep myself from sinking into despair, Samuel, Elijah, and Jesse cared for their younger siblings. In all my life, I had never received such a blow, and I had no idea that emotional pain could be so horrific.

I thirsted for information on what I was going through, and hungrily devoured anything that discussed either death or dying. I particularly appreciated Maurice Lamm's *The Jewish Way in Death and Mourning*. I was dumbfounded by the eloquence with which *halachah* addresses the needs of the mourner. In contrast to other religions, which cover the starkness of death with flowers in an effort to distract the mourner from his loss, the *shivah* period encourages the mourner to acknowledge his loss. It also provides him with the setting to speak about his departed loved one. It made beautiful sense that my Creator truly understood how I felt.

Some of my brothers and sisters came from out of state to be there for me. The wonderful women in the community were very supportive. Even though I didn't sit *shivah*, ladies came to cry with me over the loss of my baby. They shared my pain, and in doing so gave me comfort.

While still in the grips of horrendous grief, I was excruciatingly sensitive to the well-meant but tactless platitudes thrown my way. One person tried to jolly me out of my pain: "Don't take it so hard. Leah Rose was only a Down child." I was left breathless by his insensitivity. Another offering: "Perhaps she would have been too difficult to raise, so G-d took her away." These comments caused me terrible anguish.

During this time I was consumed with a need to understand the intense feelings that gripped me. The agony of the loss would wrench me from sleep. Searing questions pounded through my mind. *Why does it hurt so much? Why is it so hard to let go? How had I managed to bond with Leah Rose so deeply in the few short weeks I knew her?*

With my thoughts so occupied by my intense feelings, it wasn't long before my teaching sessions were distorted by concepts that were too heavy for the young minds of my children. After nearly two decades, I no longer felt capable of homeschooling my kids.

A close friend encouraged me to enroll the children in Atlanta's Torah Day School. I was skeptical; after all, we were still in the process of conversion. I was both surprised and jubilant to find out that we were accepted for the upcoming school year. My lesson plans and homeschooling methods must have been up to par, since my younger children went right into the grades they belonged in. Around that time, Samuel, 16, and Elijah, 14, converted and became Shaul and Eliyahu respectively. They headed to a yeshivah in upstate New York to learn for a year, while Dovid was arranging for them to join him in Yerushalayim's Ohr Somayach.

Shaul and Eliyahu at a celebration in honor of their conversion

One of the first times my boys laid *tefillin* after their conversion

My children were thrilled with their new school. It gave them the opportunity to learn more about Judaism, as well as to better integrate into the Jewish community. My eldest daughter, Jenny, was always very sociable, and she was very excited to finally go to school with the little girls she already knew from the neighborhood. She was well received by her new classmates and became the focus of much positive attention. In fact, her classmates even picked out the Jewish name they wanted her to take on after her conversion. The adult Estie now chuckles over the amusing antics of her fifth-grade classmates. One little girl warned the class that they had better behave so as not to make a *chillul Hashem* in front of Jenny! On the whole, the girls were very friendly and went out of their way to make Jenny feel welcome.

My children were as usual racing way ahead of me in Jewish observance. They were all taking a piece of fruit or a cracker in their hand and saying different lines of Hebrew over them, called *berachos*. I had no idea how they knew what to say for what. On Shabbos they extended their prayers after the meal for 10 or 15 minutes to thank the Creator for the food they had eaten.

One day as I was riding in the car with a friend, she very nonchalantly gave me a banana after taking one for herself. After we both peeled them, she said, "Repeat after me: *Baruch atah. . .borei pri ha'adamah.*" And so I began traveling down the path of making *berachos* because of the sweet concern of a friend.

One of our family's most amusing memories of our time in Atlanta is the story of the food drive. This was held by the school to benefit the needy of the community. The food drive must have taken place when I was at an all-time low, as I didn't even notice when one of my sons completely emptied our home of all our canned goods in his zeal to win the school's contest! He did, in fact, win a prize for bringing in the most cans. The very next day, the contest coordinators showed up at our house with boxes of groceries — and canned goods — because we had been picked to be the recipients of the community's generosity!

My children thrived on the organized education they now received. I am thoroughly grateful to the warm and supportive community of Atlanta for making our family's first foray into the Jewish community such a positive experience.

I, however, was still not functioning well. I had great difficulty concentrating and could barely eat. One day, I actually missed the same exit on the highway three times! Every so often, people would recommend that I see a psychologist. However, the mountain mentality of proud independence was still deeply ingrained in me, and I looked down on the concept of therapy or medication.

My mother decided to come out to Atlanta to help me get back on my feet. She pointed out that I was no longer feeding my family organized meals, and she helped me get them back on a normal schedule. Thinking it would afford me some succor, Mother accompanied me to Leah Rose's grave. The experience didn't have the intended effect. I knew that Leah Rose was in Heaven; visiting her gravesite didn't help me feel close to her.

Mother stayed a few weeks and helped me in the best way she knew. Finally I reached a point where I realized that I had to do something to help myself heal. If for nothing else, I had to become a healthy, functional mother. I began to make an effort to care for and nurture myself. I forced myself to sit down to a nourishing breakfast every morning, and I realized that I needed to get out of the house.

My obstetrician, Dr. Tate, suggested that I see a therapist to help me process my grief. Initially, I shrugged off his suggestion, but when I got to talking to Dr. Sharon Habif at the weekly Shabbos *Kiddush* his suggestion echoed in my mind. Sharon told me that she felt she could help me. For the next two years, I saw her weekly. During our sessions I learned about a previously uncharted world: that of my emotions.

While I delved deeply into my emotions, I also embarked on a spiritual-intellectual journey. The Book of *Job* became my support and guidance. I identified closely with Iyov's journey through pain and loss that ultimately ended with a closer connection to Hashem. After Iyov lost his riches, children, and health, he expresses many of the negative emotions common to those who suffer. As he sits in his hole of depression, scraping his boils, Iyov's three friends come and sit with him. For days they empathize and discuss why all of this has happened to him.

I was struck by Iyov's struggle with pain and spiritual meaning, aspects of grief not commonly mentioned in secular works. I also came to realize that the mourner craves the opportunity to experience his wide range of emotions at this time. The solid support of his friends as they share his darkest days makes a huge difference.

As a girl I had read many historical accounts of the American settlers moving out West. A common sentiment I had come across was encapsulated in the words, "And Ma never was the same after little Carrie died." I began to see that a person could either shrivel up from tragedies or see suffering as a G-d-given opportunity for accelerated growth, yielding a deeper bond with others and G-d.

Iyov's questions are answered. His friends and acquaintances come to him to sympathize and he is comforted. This seemed to be an old-time remedy not commonly practiced in the Western world. The time would come, later in my life, when I would experience the Jewish practice of sitting *shivah* and receive emotional validation and words of inspiration from my community. In many ways this echoed the empathy of Iyov's friends in Biblical times.

I began training as a nursing assistant. Back in the days when I had worked in a nursing home in California, we didn't really concern ourselves with the particular wants and needs of the residents. It was the caretakers who made all the decisions. Old Mr. Jones wasn't able to decide whether or not he wanted a bath; the nursing staff made that decision for him. Likewise, we told him when to eat dinner, and helped him to bed at our predetermined bedtime. He had almost no independence; control was entirely in our hands.

Now I was trained to think of the patient's emotional needs. We were taught to feel compassion for all that a new resident has lost upon his placement in a nursing home. Very often, this vulnerable population has lost spouse, home, and independence as well as the ability to care for themselves on a day-to-day basis.

I soaked up my lessons and felt as if a whole new world had opened to me: that of acknowledging and appreciating emotion. I put my newfound knowledge to good use and began to explore the uncharted territory of my own emotional world.

I began to attend each and every support group I thought would be beneficial. One particular session of the Compassionate Friends, a support group for grieving parents, has seared itself into my memory. At a special gathering of local grief groups they brought in a keynote speaker, a tall, broadly built army colonel. He cleared his throat before he began. "When my daughter passed away, it was as if someone had taken a machete and chopped all the superficiality out of me," he said. "From time to time, I lock my office door and just sit and cry." To hear such an imposing man reveal his human frailty was a powerfully validating experience. It also verified to me that the grief process is an opportunity for accelerated life growth.

I also joined a class given by Rebbetzin Miriam Feldman, based on Miriam Adahan's *It's All a Gift*. The underlying premise — that every challenge in life is an opportunity for growth — was deeply meaningful, and I found myself looking back at my life and reframing the stages and incidents that had brought me to my present situation. It was actually Rebbetzin Feldman who suggested that my intense sadness was not only due to the loss of my baby. She felt that for years I had battled through life without allowing myself to acknowledge the pain and frustration. It was as if I had stored all my negative emotions inside like a balloon, and the loss of my baby finally punctured the repository of my hidden feelings. Now it was all spilling out.

My husband and I were both suffering intensely, and we were unable to support each other. The distance between us developed into a gaping chasm that threatened to swallow both of us alive. We sought rabbinical advice. Ultimately, we decided to divorce.

Rabbi Katz and his family had left Atlanta to settle in Florida, and now that I was single I approached the community rabbi regarding my conversion and that of my younger children. The rabbi told me that with Leah Rose's death, it was as if a bomb had gone off in our family. He felt that I needed to wait for the dust to settle. He recommended that we take the necessary time to properly find our bearings in our new reality. He also said that he personally wouldn't be able to convert us, as he didn't do conversions.

Although we did stay in Atlanta for another year, I began to set my sights on joining the community in Baltimore. I never once had second thoughts about my burning desire to become a Jew, and I thought that the larger Torah community in Baltimore would have more to offer me.

By this time, Jesse was 14, and he keenly felt the absence of his brothers and his father from our home. We decided to send

With my girls at Stone Mountain

him off to Jerusalem to be reunited with his older brothers. There, Jesse underwent his conversion, taking on the name *Yishai*. Since he was too young to learn at Ohr Somayach, Rabbi Katz's brother-in-law, Rabbi Daniel Belsky, took him into his yeshivah and under his wing.

During our stay in Atlanta, I had the privilege of participating in a number of special *mitzvos*. One day in my nursing assistant class I overheard a recent Russian immigrant bemoaning the fact that he was unable to get his sons — aged 6 and 8 — circumcised. During all the years of his Russian exile, a *bris milah* was something he could only dream about. Now that he lived in America, he wanted to make those dreams a reality. In the meantime, though, he was stymied. Where could he find a Jewish community?

I excitedly offered to put him in contact with some rabbis who I knew would be able to help him. Sure enough, they arranged a *bris milah* for the man's two sons. My grateful classmate invited my family to an informal reception in his home after the *bris*. This placed us in an awkward — and paradoxical — position: we had already begun to keep kosher and we wondered whether or not to sample the homemade delicacies. I was amazed that I had been given the great *zechus* of playing a significant role in bringing two Jewish boys into the *bris* of Avraham Avinu!

My background and gentile status gave me the opportunity to help other Jews in unique ways. One day a *rav* approached me and said, "We've heard reports that a church right on the outskirts of our community is targeting Jewish immigrants from the Soviet Union." Since I wasn't yet a Jew and therefore was able to enter the church, the rabbi continued, "We would like for you to attend their services one Sunday night and tell us what's going on."

The next Sunday night I passed busloads of Russians unloading in the parking lot of this enormous church. I made my way down into their luxurious basement, scanning the premises for the most strategic spot. Then I sat off to the side, watching the smiling old men in the front row as they were entertained by attractive young women singers. That was all. There were no eloquent, intellectual-spiritual speakers — none at all. It was the old Midianite-Moabite scheme. Afterward they handed out lavish bags of food and bused them back to their pick-up points. I relayed my observations to those who had sent me.

Then there was Katie. She was a young Jewish woman who had fallen prey to a messianic cult. I was approached by a *Chabad shaliach* in Atlanta to help deprogram her. Katie and I met every Sunday. With my children out visiting their father, Katie and I settled on either end of my couch and went at it, fiercely discussing and debating Scripture. After a year, Katie admitted that she had never encountered anyone who knew the Bible as well as I did. Unfortunately, she was so emotionally ensnared that she was unable to break free.

Through these experiences I was able to see that the emotional fog that had obscured my mind as I searched for truth might never have been lifted if G-d hadn't sent me my ex-husband, John, a very tough messenger. For seven years he had not given up until at last the fog lifted and I was able to see the light!

Of course, we also took on the traditional role of Shabbos *goy*. As gentiles, we weren't permitted to fully observe the Shabbos. Each of us was supposed to perform at least one forbidden act each Shabbos, such as shutting off or turning on a light or striking a match. There were times when I was asked to drive a woman in labor to the hospital. We felt very privileged to help the Jewish community in this way.

One of my most meaningful memories from Atlanta is of the first time our family merited to give *tzedakah*. Since we were not yet Jewish, we did not appear on the community list, and we were not yet privileged to have *meshulachim* knocking on our door. That is, until an English-speaking charity collector from Yerushalayim showed up at our home, seeking money to pay for medical treatment for his sick child. We enthusiastically invited him in, happy to be given our first opportunity to give back to the Jewish people!

My kids ran to empty their piggy banks, pooled their resources, and graciously presented the rabbi with a heavy little bag containing their precious savings.

We sat and talked with our visitor for a while. We learned that he was a *chassid* of Toldos Aharon from Meah Shearim. When he heard that I had two Jewish sons learning in Yerushalayim, he decided to contact them.

Upon his return to Israel, the *chassid* called Ohr Somayach to invite Dovid and Nosson over to his home. Dovid was ill at the time, and it was my shy son Nosson who came to the phone. The rabbi invited him for a meal, but Nosson quickly declined; without his more gregarious sidekick he wasn't about to visit the home of a stranger. Undeterred, the good rabbi packed up a basket of fruit and made his way over to the yeshivah to perform the double *mitzvah* of visiting the sick and loving the convert. A very warm and supportive relationship developed between our two families. To this day, we attend their family *simchos*. Nosson even named a son after this special man, who sadly fell ill and passed away a number of years ago.

After years of struggling to find one gem of truth at a time, it was so precious now to sit at the feet of G-d's people and soak in their wisdom. And it was easy to fall in love with this people that showed such loving-kindness: we, the perfect strangers in their midst!

Once, when I was a child, an aunt and uncle had taken our family on a tour up into the Rocky Mountains. We passed through an eerie ghost town. Its empty houses had once been attractive, but now their paint was peeling and their windows were broken, because the mining and the money the town had flourished on had long since run out. As we climbed up a steep incline, my uncle said, "Look, that's where Tin-Can Charlie lives."

Up on the mountainside, "Charlie" had picked out a cabin with a spectacular view and just one window. Perhaps his answer to soured relationships was just to decide one day that the easiest way to deal with people was to run away from them all. Living all by himself was so much easier; he could now beat the system called life.

With no gas and no electricity and no rent or taxes, Charlie didn't have to work except when he wanted to. There were no paper plates to buy and no dishes to wash. He'd simplified life down to a crude art. As soon as he finished eating he tossed the can out the window, where it clanked noisily onto the mountainous pile of decades of rusty cans!

Now, as I blossomed in the warmth of the Atlanta Jewish community it was as if Hashem had, in one day, led me, the ascetic loner mooning over a pile of rusty cans, down off the mountain and into a rich and vibrant world, to revel in real life!

To me, "Tin-Can Annie," this banquet of life was like a long table laden with every kind of exotic fruit and delicacy. I hardly knew where to start feasting. You taste a little here and a little there, one frosted grape, one bite of smoked salmon, but it was incredibly rich. I had come to the spiritual giants, to many wise men, and I was surrounded by countless opportunities for the kind of friendships I had so often longed for. I hardly knew where to start.

I began to work for an Iranian family who ran the Jewish bookstore in Atlanta. Each morning as I got dressed for work, I looked into the mirror and asked myself, *This is really me?* My outer transformation was mirroring the inner.

After Leah Rose's death, my inner world had become a crater of grief that couldn't be filled, a black hole of breathtaking magnitude. Only my Creator could know how to fill this cavity, and He, in all His brilliance, had given this task to "community." I felt I would never have made it back up, if not for the deep, heartfelt connections of His people.

With the dust of our lives finally settling, I began to muster up the emotional stamina to think about moving on. We had arrived in Atlanta as mountain folk, ignorant in the ways of Judaism and its outlook. Now, three years later, five of my children had converted. We were making progress, but six years after encountering the Jewish people, I was still a gentile.

CHAPTER 14

From Sheryl to Tzirel

I had set out on the path of conversion nearly seven years earlier, but it seemed my sincerity was still being tested. Early in the winter, I flew to Baltimore to meet with a rabbi regarding my conversion. My plane made a quick stopover in Carolina to pick up some passengers en route to Maryland. There, we encountered a heavy drizzle. By the time we landed in Baltimore, the city was in the throes of a full-fledged blizzard. At first I hardly noticed the weather because inside I was soaring, as I was encountering Rabbi Dessler's *Strive for Truth* for the first time.

But now, in the airport, I had a major problem. A friend had planned to pick me up from the airport, but she was unable to drive in the snow. Having grown up in suburbia and then spending nearly a quarter-century on the mountain, I had no idea how to navigate the public transport system. It didn't even occur to me to flag down a cab. I was stranded at the airport, with no idea how I was going to get to my friend's house. Then I spotted two modestly dressed young women standing in the airport. *They must be religious Jews*, I thought. I approached them.

They had come out to the airport to collect their brother and had just found out that his flight out of Chicago had been canceled due to the inclement weather. They were only too happy to give me a ride into the Jewish community. As I sat in the back of the car watching the flurry of white, I felt warm and secure in my newfound sense of belonging.

As we drove through the snow, the story of the Beckners, who lived higher up on Lookout Mountain, came to my mind. They were Seventh Day Adventists who drove out West with their six children. Somehow, on their way back to Georgia, they ran out of money. Joe Beckner was a plumber, and he had no choice but to sell off his plumbing tools, piece by piece. He went from city to city, selling only as much as he needed to get money for gas to get to the next town. What a secure thought to now know that I was becoming part of a Jewish family that would help me anywhere I went in the world!

The following morning I met with a rabbi, who wanted to make sure that I was sincere in my desire to convert. No ulterior motives were allowed to taint my yearning to become a fully practicing Jew. The rabbi was later to warn me not to come up to Baltimore expecting to be supported by the *frum* community. I knew that I wouldn't feel comfortable asking my brothers to help fund my conversion either, and of course leaving Atlanta's warm community would sever the generous assistance the community there had provided me with. This one, I had to figure out on my own.

I returned to Atlanta, confident that eventually something would work out. I decided to spend the coming school year in Atlanta. Later, I drove up to Baltimore with my youngest daughter in order to speak with Rabbi Mendel Feldman about my conversion. By this time I was beginning to feel desperately uncomfortable with my non-Jewish status. Neither Jew nor gentile, I lived alone in no-man's land.

Rabbi Feldman's *shul* was reached via a set of curved stone steps. As I waited outside, I noticed a gaping hole where one of the stones should have been. When I spotted the forlorn stone, cast off to the side, I immediately identified with that missing piece. I belonged with the Jewish people, just as that stone belonged to the stairs. And yet, after so many years of searching for the truth, I was still all alone, struggling to find my way home.

I took the small hand of my 4-year-old Debra firmly within my own and entered the old *shul*. Rabbi Feldman offered us seats across the table from him. I felt his eyes bore through me. "Well?"

He waited for me to begin speaking, but I didn't know where to start or how to begin. As I desperately thought of what to say, I remembered a letter I'd received from Rabbi Yehuda Samet of Ohr Somayach. It was in my U-Haul truck. I excused myself to retrieve the letter.

Upon my return, I handed Rabbi Feldman the cherished piece of paper.

> *Dear Mrs. Massey,*
>
> *You have just become the proud mother of the fifth Massey tzaddik! We know that the souls of all the geirim were at Har Sinai, but for one father and mother to be privileged to bring so many of these souls into the world is unusual.*
>
> *How many tears have Jewish mothers shed throughout the ages to be worthy of sons like your boys. Each one of them is a jewel in his own right.*
>
> *I have been very close with them since they came. They have found favor in the eyes of many, so that you as a concerned mother don't have to worry about their spiritual and material welfare.*
>
> *I am sure that with Hashem's help they will all find good shidduchim. Dovid once pointed out to me that one of their virtues is that they were never exposed to the impurities of the modern world.*
>
> *I hope that things will work out for you soon in Baltimore with your geirus, as well as the other children.*
>
> *May the time soon come that your whole family as*

well as the entire Jewish people will be together here in
Eretz Yisrael with the coming of the Mashiach, speedily
in our times.
  Sincerely,
  Rabbi Yehuda Samet

Rabbi Feldman read the letter through and then looked up once or twice as he paced back and forth. "Did you solicit this letter?"

"No."

Finally he said, "Okay, I'll convert you."

I continued to state my case.

"Did you hear what I said? I said I would convert you."

Finally it started to sink in. I hardly heard much of what he continued to say. I was both elated and guarded, as we had thought we were so close a few times before.

All I had to do was move my family to Baltimore and then we would be allowed to convert.

I spent every moment of spare time that year planning the move. I decided that the best time was in June, when school was out. That way I'd have the entire summer to enroll my children in schools in Baltimore. I earmarked my child support from the month of May for the moving expenses, and dedicated the first week in June as moving week.

I spent all day Wednesday, Thursday, and Friday packing, and my good friend Jackie hired a man to load all my furniture and appliances into the U-Haul I'd rented. Although I was sure Hashem would somehow provide me with gas money for my trip on *Motza'ei Shabbos*, by Friday morning the funds had not yet materialized. Still, I was not at all surprised when a friend stopped by before Shabbos and presented me with money for gas.

The plan was to send my children — four girls and my 10-year-old son — off to friends and neighbors after Shabbos. Then I would get into the U-Haul and drive through the night to Baltimore. I would spend Sunday unpacking our belongings in the home I had rented, and Monday would see me in the airport, boarding a flight back to Atlanta. I would pick up the kids and the rest of our stuff and drive back up to Baltimore. En route, we'd take the time to stop over and give the kids a nice little family trip. We'd still have our new home up and running before Shabbos.

That was the plan. But in Heaven, this was deemed the perfect time to introduce me to the old Yiddish saying: "Man plans and G-d laughs."

I drove up to Baltimore on *Motza'ei Shabbos* and arrived Sunday afternoon, exhausted, in front of the home I had rented. As arranged, the landlord was there to meet me, but without the key. "We decided we are not renting the place to a family with children," he pronounced. I had heard this line a few times before.

Not sure I had heard right, since we had had an agreement, I asked him to repeat himself. "We don't want to rent to families with children."

I got back into the U-Haul blinking back tears, utterly at a loss as to what I should do. I drove around town, asking if anyone knew of a place to rent and trying to compose myself. By evening, I was utterly drained. I stopped over at a friend's in order to get some sleep.

On Monday morning, I had no choice but to put my things in storage and head out to the airport to catch my flight. I had been so used to relying on my family's substantial manpower that I hadn't given much thought to logistics; I just figured I would somehow manage to unload the U-Haul at Baltimore's ezStorage. I started the overwhelming task on my own, until the manager felt sorry for me and told his workers to give me a hand. Thank G-d, we managed to get it all unloaded and into storage with time to spare.

Finally, I returned the empty U-Haul and entered the airport. The place was in utter chaos. ValuJet had gone bankrupt overnight. All their flights were canceled and thousands of passengers were stranded. I had no credit card, no cash, and absolutely no one to turn to for help. I lost my composure and burst into bitter tears. My distress was not lost upon the reporters from the local news station. They pounced on me and pressured me into agreeing to say a few words for the camera. That evening, all of Baltimore was privy to my misfortune. I appeared on the news in tears saying, "I don't know anything at all about ValuJet, all I know is now I can't go down to Atlanta to get my kids!"

I had no idea how to get back to Atlanta and felt bereft of inner resources. I called Rabbi Lipschutz. "I'm stuck in Baltimore, with no home and no means of getting back to Atlanta," I told him tearfully. After consulting his wife, he calmly encouraged me to leave my children in Atlanta while I made the necessary arrangements.

Rabbi Shlomo Porter, dean of Baltimore's Etz Chaim Center, found a place for me in the comfortable home of another woman. Although it was June, torrential rain battered the city. I braved the elements each day, canvassing the streets on foot as I searched for a job and a home to rent. At the week's end, I was still no further in my search, and my hostess said she could no longer host me.

I tried the office of the Jewish Family Services to see if they would help me. When I told them that I was in the process of conversion and had no money and no home, they shrugged me off. "We aren't equipped to handle people as needy as you," they told me.

I walked out of the office onto the gray, wet street. I was alone. My family was miles away. I had no support system in Baltimore. I had no money. No place to stay. No way to get back home. I was at rock bottom.

I walked through the wet streets, blind to everything but my own desperation. And then I remembered an old *shul*, Glen Avenue Shearith Israel. I entered and climbed up to the women's section to *daven*. No one could help me but G-d. I sat down on an ancient bench and breathed in the musty smell of hard wood. I picked up a *Sefer Tehillim* and resolved for the first time to say the whole book. I sat there the entire day. I read *perek* after *perek* and cried my heart out to my Maker. Every so often, exhaustion overcame me and I dozed off on the hard benches. Each time I jolted awake, I turned once again to the pages of the *Tehillim*.

The next day I returned to Rabbi Feldman. I told him that I had been in a state of limbo for seven years and could no longer continue. I just couldn't do it anymore. He had to tell me when he could convert us. He said he would convert me the week after I brought my children up to Baltimore. I was flooded with feelings of relief; at last someone was offering me some sort of a commitment!

I took the community phone book and looked up an organization that provided support for divorced women. When I asked the woman who answered the phone to help me find a place to stay, she invited me to come stay with her. I was fortunate to spend the next few weeks in the home of a true *tzadekes*. Her loving hospitality was the perfect balm for my broken spirit. I spent much of my time just crying and saying *Tehillim*, treasuring the opportunity to seclude myself with Hashem. Finally, refreshed and fortified, I continued my quest for home and employment.

Each time I saw a suitable home, I was asked for a reference. I still owed my landlord in Atlanta the last month's rent, so again and again I was turned down. I wondered, *Maybe Hashem wants me to stay in Atlanta. Maybe I should test the waters.* I began making calls back to Atlanta to see if there was anything to rent. The answer was a resounding no! This was the summer of '96, and with the city gearing up for the Olympics every available rental in the area was snatched up. So with the doors closed like steel in Atlanta too, I felt Hashem did want me here.

Then I remembered a home I had seen on my last trip to Baltimore. It was a comfortable and affordable townhouse, situated on a predominantly African-American street with a few *frum* neighbors. The owners were holding out for Jewish tenants and were very happy to rent their home to me. I was delighted to find that a warm Jewish family lived across the street. Dr. and Mrs. Michael Ring had a bunch of daughters about the same age as my girls. Behind us was a block full of lively boys in the same age bracket as my son Benton. With much joy and tremendous relief, I signed the rental contract. An airline ticket was somehow generously presented to me, and I finally flew back to Atlanta to get my children.

After a separation of more than two weeks, I was reunited with my beloved children. Excitedly, we went about making our final preparations, while taking leave of some of the many special people who had touched our lives during our years in Atlanta.

I tearfully bid farewell to my dear friends Lisa and Jackie, piled my kids into the car, and drove out of the city. During our drive up north I reminded my children that we would be converting about a week after our arrival in Baltimore. They were very excited to finally become part of the Jewish people. I told them that they had to come to a decision on their choice of names. For years, they had been enthusiastically choosing and discarding Jewish names. I deliberately left the choice of their Jewish names up to them, as a symbolic statement of their own personal acceptance of Judaism.

As we drove into Maryland, the kids announced their final decisions. Jenny would become Estie, Benton chose Binyamin, Suzy would be Shira, Lynn chose Leora, and little Debra would be Devora. My own name, Tzirel, was Estie's suggestion.

When we arrived in Baltimore, we met up with my son Nosson, who had flown in from Israel to help us move and settle in. The next week was a flurry of unpacking. Still, our imminent conversion was at the forefront of my mind. As the day drew near, I wondered how my little girls would manage in the *mikveh* by themselves, since they didn't know how to swim. That's when I remembered that Mrs. Dena Deutsch in Atlanta had told me her mother, Rebbetzin Edith Neuberger, would be glad to help us out. Rebbetzin Neuberger graciously agreed to accompany us to the *mikveh* on our special day. She would supervise my little ones while I was occupied with my own conversion.

Morning dawned on my long-awaited day. I awoke as Sheryl, daughter of Pastor and Orabelle Youngs. Before nightfall I would become Tzirel bas Sarah Imeinu, a Jewess. And yet I couldn't stop crying. These weren't the soul-stirring tears of happiness that well up during life's most joyous occasions. I cried pain-filled tears of grief. I was bewildered. Why, on this momentous and festive day, was I overcome with sadness?

I called Toby Katz, the woman who had been by my side from the first day of my journey. I shared my emotions with Toby, and she helped me understand. "Today you finally realize the steep price you have paid to become a Jew. You distanced your mother and siblings. You lost a precious baby. You went through a divorce. You sent five of your children overseas. You had to uproot yourself from your support system in Atlanta and start over on your own in Baltimore. You have gone through much agony and suffering to get to where you are today, and now finally you are able to see just how painful was your path." With Toby's understanding and support, I was able to pull myself together and head off with my family to the *mivkeh*.

We were met there by Rebbetzin Neuberger. She presented my children with little shower slippers she had bought them. With her help and support, my children were spared any stressful or scary experiences. She ensured that our special day would be remembered with joy and happiness.

I was asked, "Do you promise to keep the 613 mitzvos?" and then I immersed in the holy and purifying waters of the *mikveh*. I was a Jew! With barely a few seconds to feel that inner jubilation, I was soon surrounded by my five smiling children.

A festive *seudah* was prepared for us at the home of Yitzchak and Rochel Strauss, a new friend of mine. In attendance were my son Nosson, the three rabbis who converted me — Rabbi Shlomo Porter, Rabbi Mendel Feldman, and Rabbi Moshe Rappaport — as well as the Rings and Rebbetzin Neuberger.

Rabbi Porter spoke of how Moshe Rabbeinu prayed 500 times before Hashem told him to stop. He connected this outpouring of prayer to my own journey: "So too, this woman before us had to pray a multitude of prayers in order to receive all she received today."

The message resonated: the fact that I converted along with 10 children was a manifestation of prayer and Divine assistance. It was clear to us all that my rebirth as a Jewess — and mother of 10 holy Jewish children — was nothing short of miraculous. And bursting into a lively *niggun,* he began singing: *"She'hechiyanu v'kiyimanu v'higi'anu la'zeman hazeh."*

The day of our conversion was saturated with emotion. Some of my children remember they couldn't stop smiling. One recalls feeling so clean and purified, but growing disappointed as she went through the day realizing that she had done an *aveirah.* I was exhausted by the time I dropped into bed that night. The next morning, though, I awoke early and marveled at the sun streaming through my bedroom window. I washed, dressed, and opened my *siddur.* And then, with a heart full of gratitude, for the first time I said the morning blessings as a Jew.

CHAPTER 15

My First Year as a Jew

Now that my soul was Jewish, my kitchen had to be, too. About a week after my conversion, Rabbi Porter came to *kasher* my kitchen. Until then, we had been living on cold cereal, and I was excited to return to cooking for my family. He asked me to take out my largest pot, which he filled with water and put up to boil. Then he asked my kids to bring him a rock to put in the pot. We excitedly watched the water boil over the sides and *kasher* the pot. One by one, Rabbi Porter lowered my other pots and silverware into the boiling water and rendered them fit for use in a kosher kitchen.

Before we converted, there wasn't much clarity about which Jewish practices we should take on. According to Torah law, as gentiles we could not keep Shabbos, and thus we had to do at least one *melachah*. Shabbos is an exclusive gift to the Jewish people, and until we converted we were forbidden to fully observe the holy day. Other than that, there was really nothing we were obligated to do — although we had "practiced" everything from *negel vasser* to *Havdalah*. Now that we were finally Jewish and we *had* to keep kosher, my children were thrilled!

A friend had warned me that I would be unable to *kasher* such things as dishes and cutlery, so I set aside a large box of housewares to give to my sister Lesa. When Rabbi Porter *kashered* my pots, he asked if I would like him to look through my boxes and see if there was anything inside that might be salvageable. I assured him that my friend had already given me the rundown on what could and could not be *kashered*. "Is your friend a rabbi?" Rabbi Porter asked.

I stubbornly chose to refuse his help and, in my ignorance, gave away an expensive set of stainless steel dishes that could have been *kashered*. I learned a valuable lesson from this experience: though good friends are a very precious asset, their counsel should never be substituted for rabbinical guidance.

After the *kashering*, we packed up our pots and silverware and immersed them in the *mikveh*. Now we were really keeping kosher!

My next priority was to enroll my children in appropriate schools. Rabbi Porter placed my son Binyamin in Torah Academy and Shira, Leora, and Devora were enrolled in the Bais Yaakov elementary school. Estie was to attend the middle school. I paid rent with my child-support check, but I desperately needed a job to pay my children's tuition.

Not long after my conversion I began having second thoughts about my name. Tzirel had a familiar ring to it, as it sounded a lot like Sheryl. Still, I couldn't really identify with it since I didn't know what it meant. I decided I wanted to add the name *Ruth* in honor of the Moabite princess who sacrificed everything to become a Jewess. Rabbi Feldman told me I could choose a name and just begin calling myself by it, and so I became Tzirel Ruth Massey.

Rabbi Porter was like a father figure. He took an interest in guiding me in many areas of my life, and suggested that I attend *shiurim* and look for a mentor. It was he who told me that the time had come for me to stop crying in front of my kids. He recommended that I buy a tape recorder and fill my home with music, a wonderful idea that I made sure to put into practice. From then on the uplifting strains of the best of contemporary Jewish music filled our home in Baltimore.

It was 10-year-old Binyamin who found me my first job. He spent a lot of time playing at the home of the family who lived behind us. Not only was Simy a great neighbor and dear friend, but she also agreed to employ me to clean the KinderKademy preschool that she ran. I arranged for her to deposit my paycheck directly into Bais Yaakov's account to pay the tuition of my three youngest children. Rabbi Porter encouraged me to learn a trade so that I could support my family more easily, so at the same time I enrolled in Baltimore Community College to train as an emergency medical technician.

I began my day at 3 a.m., when I woke up and drove over to the preschool to clean. I was finished and home by 6, to get my children up and ready for school. On carpool days, I would drop off all the kids before driving half an hour to my classes at BCC. In the afternoon, I headed out to my second job: helping cancer patients through the local *bikur cholim* organization. When my kids came home from school we sat down to dinner that I had put up the night before in my Crock-Pot.

Early one morning, while cleaning one of the classrooms in KinderKademy, I saw on each table a beautiful representation of the *kohen gadol* and his holy garments. It was the first time I had ever seen a picture of the high priest's colorful breastplate, and I was moved to tears.

How many years had I spent trying to understand the Bible! I read and reread a number of difficult segments, trying in vain to gain clarity. For the life of me I could not understand just what Abraham was doing when he was waving around those birds, or what Jacob was doing with the rods. I puzzled over the passage in *Deuteronomy* 13:2 that reads, "If there should stand up in your midst a prophet or a dreamer of a dream, and he will produce to you a sign or a wonder, and the sign or the wonder comes about, of which he spoke to you, saying, 'Let us follow gods of others that you did not know and we shall worship them!' — do not hearken to the words of that prophet."* I just could not understand any of this. *Why shouldn't we listen to a prophet who actually performed a miracle?!* Without the Oral Torah, there were no answers to these questions.

How I had struggled with this! I very badly wanted to understand the word of G-d. The knowledge that is the birthright of the smallest Jewish child was locked away from me.

Finally I sat down and put pen to paper. This is the letter I left for the teacher who was busy making *Kohanim Gedolim* with her students.

> *5:00 a.m.*
>
> *Your Kohen Gadol projects are so beautiful. I've cried the whole time I've cleaned your room this morning. Even the smallest of your children know so much more Torah than I was ever taught. It's a privilege I'll probably never have much time for anymore. I found the teachers of the Torah too late in life.*
>
> *Even with all my creativity in homeschooling my children, I could never, as one person on my own, come up with all the projects, lesson plans, etc., that you teachers come up with together.*
>
> *You morahs are so blessed. Never underestimate the impact you are making on these children and the privilege you have.*
>
> *I'm sure Hashem's face is shining on you as you teach His precious children.*

I've often wondered if that teacher ever really knew how deeply she touched me through her little *Kohen Gadol* project.

Although I had a grueling daily schedule in Baltimore, we were still very excited by our new community and all it had to offer. We were frequently invited out for Shabbos, which helped us to

---

* Translation from the ArtScroll Stone edition.

develop relationships and integrate into the community. However, my children were naturally shy, and it wasn't long before our weekly social outings became too much for them. At that point I decided we would stay home and make the Shabbos *seudos* ourselves.

My sons living in Israel were very happy, and tried to convince me to move the whole family there. I was preoccupied with settling into my new community in Baltimore and was hesitant to make such a drastic move at that time.

I made a number of good friends during the time I lived in Baltimore. I have fond memories of our neighbors, the Rings, and the warm support that they extended to me and my family. One Friday night, the cold winter air caused my car horn to go off in the middle of the night. The noise would wake up the entire block! I had no idea what I was allowed to do in order to remedy the situation. Distraught, I knocked hesitantly on the Rings' door to consult with them about my options.

Dr. Ring's response was that I couldn't "personally" turn off the horn, but I could hint to a non-Jewish neighbor that I needed help. I was terribly uncomfortable with the thought of disturbing all my neighbors, and yet if *halachah* forbade me from stopping the racket, then living with the noise was my personal challenge. The horn was still blaring away. I went back to stand by the car, freezing. I hated to be in this situation, but there was no way I could just go back to bed, crawl under my covers, and pretend that it wasn't my horn rudely disturbing the predawn stillness. Finally, I spotted one of my non-Jewish neighbors in his doorway. I apologetically told him that my car's battery cable had to be disconnected, and that I couldn't do it right now. He got the hint. Peace and quiet finally returned to my block—and my heart. I had passed my test.

One day shortly before Succos, I drove home from school trying to figure out how I could possibly get everything done before the holiday. We had our *succah* up, but we still had no *schach* and absolutely no idea how to go about getting some. I was exhausted and still needed to get the groceries before I could even think about cooking. As I rounded the corner and drove up to my home, I was feeling quite overwhelmed. An unbelievable sight greeted me. Dr. Ring was gathering branches from my non-Jewish neighbor's tree and placing them atop my *succah*!

Flooded with relief and gratitude, I ran over to find out how Dr. Ring had persuaded Mr. Jackson to prune every branch off his tree. He laughingly explained, "We saw your family had built your *succah* near the front wall of the house. I walked over to help. It was immediately apparent that the walls, while makeshift, would do. It was also apparent that there was not a single piece of *schach* on top. I knew you could not purchase anything. This put me in a dilemma. What was my responsibility? Should I make another purchase that I could not really afford? How else would you be able to complete this *succah*?

"I remember that moment like it was yesterday. While I was standing there trying to decide what to do, the sound of a power saw came from nowhere. I turned around and there was your neighbor cutting down this large leafy tree. I asked him if he wanted the cut branches. No, not at all, he answered. Would he mind if I took them? Also not at all. This was your *schach*. The *hashgachah pratis* of that moment was very clear!"

There were many things that I learned in Baltimore, and of all of them it may just have been the carpool experience that gave me the most insight into the inner workings of Jewish community life. With my five children attending three different schools, all located in different areas of Baltimore — north, east, and west — it would have been a logistical nightmare to drop them all off and pick them up by myself on a daily basis. Joining a carpool is a must for the parents of Baltimore's day school children. I was very fortunate to find a carpool so close to the opening of the school year; many parents actually begin working on their carpools for the coming year as early as January. I was very impressed by the cooperation and organizational skills that kept carpools functioning efficiently.

My six-month training course at Baltimore Community College

came to an end during the midwinter break. Before I received my certificate, I had to get some hands-on training and complete the coursework. I had been interested in learning to become an ambulance driver for a number of years. When I enrolled in the EMT course in Baltimore, I hadn't really known just what I was getting myself into. First of all, I was the only woman in my course. This didn't really faze me, since I enjoyed being back in school and found the coursework very interesting. However, I was uncomfortable with the loose mixing between genders and the disturbing lack of respect for human suffering that I sensed while volunteering in such places as Baltimore's Shock Trauma.

When Dovid got engaged and married in Israel shortly before my final exam, I can't say that I was too disappointed at the thought of messing up my certification process. I had begun to realize that this wasn't what I wanted to spend my time doing. Besides, I was already in my mid-40s and no longer had the physical strength and stamina that would be necessary to carry a 300-pound drug addict down four flights of stairs to a waiting ambulance. I came to the conclusion that I did not want to be an EMT after all. But my time wasn't wasted: although I couldn't have known it then, my background in emergency medicine proved invaluable during my second marriage.

Dovid's upcoming marriage was the source of great joy and excitement to our family. *Shidduchim* hadn't come easy. In fact, despite meeting with a number of matchmakers, he had gone a year and a half without a date!

When Rabbi Bulman got up in Ohr Somayach after *Kol Nidrei* that Yom Kippur, he became very emotional. He broke down in tears as he spoke of a family of 10 children that sacrificed so much in order to keep the Torah. Later, he asked my sons for forgiveness for having spoken about them in public, albeit without mentioning their names. He explained that he had felt the need to shake things up a bit and arouse the Mercy of Heaven on behalf our family. Not long after, Dovid finally found his intended and got engaged.

Dovid with Rav and Rebbetzin Bulman

We were thrilled, and I excitedly began planning my first trip to Israel to attend the wedding. My neighbors kindly offered to host my children for the duration of my trip, and Rebbetzin Neuberger saw to it that I was appropriately attired for the happy occasion. Seven years had already passed since I first began to cover my hair. I had gone through a number of different kinds of hair coverings, from bandanas to wide-brimmed, fancy Shabbos hats that a sudden gust of wind could lift, to more everyday hats. In honor of Dovid's wedding, I was presented with my first *sheitel*.

With laden suitcases and a heart bursting with gratitude, I made my way to the airport. I couldn't help but think of my devastating experience just six months earlier. The contrast was astounding. Now I was a Jewess, mother of a large Jewish family, flying to Eretz Yisrael to escort my son to his *chuppah*. I was thrilled that one of my progeny would finally be privileged to build his own Jewish home among G-d's Chosen Nation.

While on the plane, I remember thinking about the upcoming wedding and how I had absolutely nothing to do with any of it. I hadn't met the bride or attended the engagement party. I hadn't picked the hall, hired a band, or chosen a photographer. I didn't even send out any invitations. The *kallah's* friends at She'arim had raised the necessary funds, while the staff at both Ohr Somayach and She'arim had made the arrangements. I was to be more of a guest than mother of the groom at the upcoming *simchah*, and I was thankful that others had filled in for me to make my son's wedding as happy as possible.

After 12 hours in the air, my plane began its descent over the glistening blue of the Mediterranean. I sat buckled into my cushioned seat, thousands of feet above the Holy Land, and thought about the Shabbos candles I kindled each week. The glowing match in my hand moved above my candles, setting one after the other aglow. Only when the last candle burst into flame was the home enveloped in the palpable holiness of Shabbos. So too, I was speeding ever closer to my encounter with the holiest of all lands. My excitement built, and when we finally touched down in Israel's Ben-Gurion Airport, I felt as if I had entered another dimension.

My sons met me at the airport and accompanied me to Yerushalayim. There, I was warmly received by my hosts, the revered Rabbi Yehuda and Rebbetzin Yehudis Samet of Mattersdorf. I woke each morning to Rabbi Samet's melodious recitation of the *Birchos HaShachar*. I enjoyed speaking with the sweet Samet girls about their pure and holy life in Yerushalayim. In turn, they loved asking me about my colorful background.

And then came Shabbos, the highlight of the week. That Friday night, the Samets hosted all five of my sons. As Rabbi Samet lovingly placed his hands upon the head of his son, I was seized by a great desire to bless my sons as well. I stood before Dovid, my firstborn, placed my hands upon his head, and slowly blessed him with the ancient words: "*Yesimcha Elokim k'Efraim u'k'Menasheh ....*" Nosson bent his head before me and I blessed him as well. When

Shaul approached, I could no longer hold back the tears. When I moved on to Eliyahu and Yishai, I noticed that the Samets had tactfully disappeared into the kitchen. This was the first time that I had all five of my Jewish *bachurim* together and was able to bless them as a Jewish mother.

After the *seudah* my sons invited me to a *tisch* in Meah Shearim. We set out on the half-hour trek through the *Shabbosdik* streets of Yerushalayim. I was flanked by my five grown sons, each sporting black hats and jackets. Brimming with excitement and eager to share their impressions of life in the Holy City, they all seemed to talk at once. There was so much to see and so much to hear, but I was deeply engrossed in thoughts of my own. Here I was, a Jewish mother walking with five of my Jewish sons. It was now that I was introduced to yet another Jewish concept, that of *Yiddishe nachas*!

As we neared our destination, I saw white-kerchiefed women and swarms of girls in braids. I followed them through a door into a darkened room. The room was filled with women and girls standing on bleachers and peering down through small holes in the latticework atop the *mechitzah*.

Carefully, I climbed up and found my own perch. I stood on tiptoe and grasped the pole above to steady myself. I looked down and glimpsed a sea of *shtreimel*-crowned heads all swaying and singing together. It was Friday night and the *chassidim* must have been tired, yet they left their cozy homes to come together and sing Shabbos *zemiros*. This swaying mass of humanity had joined together in sublime service of G-d, and the energy was palpable. Something within my soul was touched deeply. *How Hashem must love these people!* I whispered as I watched.

The following morning I awoke to the powerful peace of Shabbos in Jerusalem. It was the absence of sound that screamed out at me: no barking dogs, no motors, no airplanes. Just the serenity of the Holy Day spent in the Holy City. Ever since I landed, I'd felt a very special connection to this Land, a filling up of a void I had carried with me all my life, a special closeness to Hashem. I didn't know how I would ever be able to tear myself away and return to the Diaspora.

Later on, I stood in the women's section of Yeshivas Ohr Somayach and picked out the forms of my sons down below. I spotted Dovid and recalled with pride the strength and leadership he showed our family. I remembered my little tow-haired Joey and marveled at how the same piercing blue eyes still shone from his face. Yet how different was that little boy from the tall figure with the full red beard, standing on the threshold of marriage.

I had met Dovid's bride before Shabbos, and I was very impressed by her refinement and beautiful character. Finally, Dovid had found someone with whom to share his life. After Shabbos Dovid and I went out for pizza, our last opportunity for a little chat before his big day. Earlier he had discussed with me some of the formalities of his upcoming wedding and asked for my opinion on whom I felt should accompany him and his bride to their *chuppah*. I appreciated his sensitivity to my feelings and told him to go ahead and make whatever arrangements he felt would work best for both sides. I had no desire to get in the way. In fact, being relatively unfamiliar with the customs of Jewish weddings, I felt more comfortable with the informal role of observer.

The big night finally arrived. I stood by the *kallah's* chair at the veiling ceremony and watched as my son slowly approached to draw the veil over the face of his bride. I was perplexed by the solemnity of the ritual and the stark contrast with the gaiety of non-Jewish weddings. I snatched a few moments to confer with Rebbetzin Samet before someone led me and the mother of the bride outside into the cool Jerusalem night. We were given a place of honor under the wedding canopy.

We stood there, waiting, until we heard a low hum. The men were approaching. Soon we caught sight of them: my son in a white robe, flanked by burning torches. The scene was eerie, and for me it conjured up a fearful image of the Ku Klux Klan in the Deep South. I grabbed hold of my *mechutenista,* who hails from

Rav Nachman Bulman *zt'l* at Dovid's *chuppah*

South Carolina, and asked her what was happening, but she didn't know either. In the meantime, the photographer snapped a picture of the two of us clutching each other. To this day, my family still enjoys a good laugh whenever they see the photo.

Confusion soon turned to joy. The ceremony took place, the glass was smashed, and music and shouts of *"Mazel tov!"* exploded from all present. My son and his glowing bride were accompanied by a lively crowd of dancing men to a private room off to the side. I was smothered by the congratulatory embraces of the women. We then entered the hall where we were served an elegant meal, until Dovid and his bride were danced back into the center of the festivities.

The joy of my children's friends and well-wishers was an electric current pulsing through the room. I had never seen such dancing before and was unfamiliar with the dance steps; still, I was soon swept up in the exuberant tide.

The students of She'arim included me in all their antics, tossing tennis balls back and forth with me over the heads of the dancing

The spirited dancing of Dovid and his friends

crowd. I felt at one with the merry throng as we celebrated together. When I was subsequently asked to speak for the young women at their school about my own journey to Judaism I didn't hesitate to accept, for I felt a deep affinity and connection to my daughter-in-law's exuberant friends, who had made her wedding such a smashing success.

Each night, I was invited to a festive *sheva berachos* at the home of a friend or acquaintance of my children. I had expected that the families who offered to host one of the nightly celebrations would have large comfortable homes that could easily accommodate a crowd. I was mistaken.

I spent night after night crowded around a tiny kitchen table, marveling at the great lengths to which our hostess had gone in order to gladden the hearts of the bride and groom. I watched as young women pulled out pan after pan of steaming hot chicken and kugel and set them down on chairs for lack of counter space. I deeply admired how happy they were to work so hard.

Before I left Israel, one more important milestone awaited me:

my first trip to the *Kosel*. My son Shaul picked me up at the Samet home and together we boarded the number 2 bus to the *Kosel*. I enjoyed the 40-minute ride through the winding Jerusalem streets, and I gazed out the window, absorbing the sights and sounds of my people going about their daily lives. Slowly, the scenery changed. Streets filled with the *peyos*-framed faces of black-clad Yerushalmim morphed into the crowded centers of the swarthy-complexioned and kaffiyeh-crowned Muslims. Finally, we alighted at the bus stop and headed to the Kosel Plaza.

My son Shaul, ever at my side, cautioned me not to look at the Wall until I tore *keriah*. I grabbed hold of the scissors and made a small cut in my blouse. I grasped the two parts of the fabric and ripped. The sound of ripping fabric shuddered through me. My heart broke once again. I was a Jew, but my life was not complete. The towering wall of beaten, scarred stone rose before my eyes. I was filled with a sense of timelessness. I looked out upon the swaying, sorrowing people — now my people — praying at the Wall.

I stood at the world's holiest site, remnant of the glorious Temple that once graced the earth. I stood there as part of G-d's inner circle. At the same time, I was acutely aware of our painful exile. The desolation of the surrounding hills; the swarms of Muslims who walked about so haughtily. The pain and suffering of so many; the ill, downtrodden, and brokenhearted Jews throughout the centuries who begged and pleaded for redemption — all reminded me that we must yearn for more. I had arrived at my destiny, I felt more whole than ever before, and yet I knew that something was still missing.

I had been praying all my life, turning my heart to the Creator of the heavens and stars and begging Him to help me on my life's journey. I promised to serve Him, but didn't know how. Empty and alone, I was ignorant of the truth, clawing at the earth as I slowly, laboriously climbed the rugged terrain of the expedition that had been my life.

I hadn't been able to understand what G-d had done with all

my prayers, why it seemed that He had led me away from Him to the backwoods culture of the country folk where I lived in abject poverty, struggling to educate my children to become leaders and men of G-d. Where had He filed my prayers away?

Yet under the blackest blanket that seemed to cover my life, no one knew that I still nurtured the tiniest wisp of a flame, of hope in G-d. Then He brought us to Atlanta, where my children took their own path to Judaism. I was left out in the dark, pleading to gain admittance through the hallowed doors of Judaism, until that momentous day six months before, when finally I stepped through the portal of my destiny.

Now my soul raced to find my place among all the women who seemed to roil with prayer and connection to Hashem. I restrained myself and walked toward the plaza, filled with an intense thanksgiving that I was at last able to connect with my G-d amid a crowd of other yearning souls.

The
Judean Hills

Jerusalem, hills surround her

And so our wandering family finally joined the Jewish People
and are finding serenity, challenges, growth, and triumph —
among the mountains of Jerusalem!

CHAPTER 16

"Arise and Depart"

I belonged in Israel. The two weeks I spent in Jerusalem convinced me that my boys had been right. I had fallen in love with the land. This was where I wanted to raise my children, where my grandchildren would be born.

While still in Israel, I spoke to Rabbi Daniel Belsky about making *aliyah*, and he sent me to the office of AACI, the Association of Americans and Canadians in Israel. The staff suggested that I visit an absorption center, which I did immediately. While there I met a woman I knew. She told me that her children were very unhappy at the absorption center. I wanted our family's *aliyah* to be a good experience for our children, so I nixed that idea. I also spoke to another woman Rabbi Belsky suggested I see. We shared a cup of tea; she was extremely upbeat and positive. I enjoyed my visit with her. On my way out, she warmly promised, "Come to Israel. You're going to make the best friends you ever had here."

After a very fulfilling two weeks, in which I had been wined and dined while I soaked up loads of encouragement and quality time with my sons, my trip drew to a close. I was able to leave in peace, hoping that I would soon return with the rest of my family.

I said goodbye to my boys and set out for the airport. Until that point, my stay in Israel had gone smoothly, remarkably free of the tests and struggles that had so characterized my life. However, after a lengthy delay at the gate, our pilot came out to tell us that he had to cancel our flight due to dangerous flying conditions.

Was I ever surprised by the hue and cry of my fellow travel companions! Some passengers began to argue with the pilot and insist that he fly anyway. We were told that we would be given vouchers for a free meal at the airport restaurant before being put up overnight at a nearby hotel. It had been many hours since my last meal, and I was ravenous. I didn't have much information about the state of *kashrus* in Israel, but I figured that surely a Jewish airport in a Jewish country would have kosher food.

I noticed some religious-looking people on line in front of the restaurant's take-out counter, so I got on line too. As I waited, I debated with myself, wondering whether or not my sons would eat at this restaurant. This was back in the days before cell phones were commonplace. I had no way of contacting them to receive a definitive answer, no money on me, and nothing else to eat. My thoughts kept going back and forth. I was hungry; it sure looked kosher; after all, this is Israel — and yet in the back of my mind I knew that my sons probably wouldn't eat here.

When my turn came, I ordered a mouth-watering serving of lasagna and asked the man behind the counter to heat it up for me. Out of the corner of my eye I noticed a family of Yerushalmi Jews walk right by us, completely ignoring the line in front of the restaurant. I watched how they sat down in a quiet corner and began to eat their own food. A moment later, I caught sight of an obviously religious woman and asked her if the restaurant was kosher. Her answer was a resounding no. I canceled my order and walked away. With my empty stomach rumbling in protest, I proudly withstood my test and made my way to my hotel room, where I fell asleep, still hungry.

The next day, I boarded a flight back to Baltimore. I was happy to see that my children had been well cared for in my absence. The Rings had gone so far as to hold a mock wedding so that my children wouldn't feel bad about missing our family's first *simchah*.

When I consulted Rabbi Porter about the possibility of moving my family to Israel, I was pleasantly surprised to find him so encouraging. I had expected him to veto the idea, but he had met my boys earlier that year when he had visited Israel, and he had been very impressed by them. He felt that it would be beneficial for me personally to move to Israel, and would do my family a world of good to finally be reunited. Estie was only in the seventh grade, and so, as long as we moved that summer, he told me that it would still be possible to move her to a new country. Waiting a year would mean that Estie would be high-school age, and this would be too difficult for her.

Rabbi Porter also coached me in the correct attitude toward Israeli culture. He told me about the dynamics of a group of neighbors in a building in Yerushalayim. The drains on a number of the building's porches emptied directly onto the property of a neighbor below. The downstairs neighbor would wash her patio, only to have the dirty water from the porches upstairs spill down and mess up all her hard work. The drains problem was a big sore point with this new American family. Dissension prevailed. And then one of the neighbors suddenly passed away, leaving behind a widow and many orphans. The American family saw how residents of this building took it upon themselves to collect enough money to allow the widow to care for all her children comfortably for many years.

In telling me this incident, Rabbi Porter wanted me to realize that I could either be put off by the strong personalities of my future neighbors, or instead focus on the flip side: the intense love and concern that they displayed toward one another in times of challenge.

At our last meeting, Rabbi Porter picked up a Shabbos *siddur* and began to read from the *Kabbalas Shabbos* prayer: "Arise and depart from amid the upheaval; too long you have dwelled in the valley of weeping, He will shower compassion upon you."[1]

When I broached the subject of *aliyah* with my children, they were thrilled. I also realized that there wasn't much of a future for me in Baltimore. Even with my grueling work schedule, which for the last half of the year had included three jobs, I was unable to fully pay my children's tuition. The time had come for us to move on.

My older sons were on the lookout for an apartment for us, and although I originally had my heart set on living in Yerushalayim, when we were offered a brand-new apartment in an outlying community for the same rent I had been paying in Baltimore, I decided to go ahead with it. The apartment I rented was part of a brand-new neighborhood consisting of about 1,000 housing units. Although the street I would be living on was already inhabited, much of the neighborhood infrastructure was not yet in place. Before the move, I had so much on my mind, between work and single parenting, that I didn't consider this fact or how it would affect me personally. I just didn't have the head for dealing with all the myriad details that our impending move necessitated.

I began the *aliyah* process in Baltimore and was put in contact with a few other families who were also moving that summer. My new acquaintances were quite caught up with analyzing the feasibility of bringing a lift and researching which appliances they were best off bringing with them, how they would support themselves, and where they would live. All of this was just too much for me. With the exception of a few pieces of furniture that a friend offered to ship for me, I decided to leave most of my possessions behind.

During this time, my cousin came by to pick up my car and drive it over to the home of his brother, my brother-in-law, who was buying it from me. Before he left with the car, he was going to drop the things I was shipping to Israel off at the home of the family

---

1. Translation from ArtScroll *Linear Siddur.*

sending the lift. When he saw how little I was sending, he asked, "Where do you think you're going — to the Promised Land?" In all honesty I'd have to say that yes, I was headed to the Promised Land!

Other than my child support, I was moving across the world with very little in the way of financial resources. I had no savings, no job, not even a degree or marketable skills to speak of. I didn't know the language, and had no family to help me out. I was thrilled that my sons were learning full-time in yeshivah, and I knew that they weren't going to be able to help me financially. Yet I was not afraid. I trusted that G-d would help me. My maternal grandparents had moved to Israel as gentiles in the '50s, remaining Christians but taking on several Jewish practices over time, including the Jewish holidays. If they had managed to stick it out during the difficult period immediately following the establishment of the State, I would surely be able to make it as a Jew in the Land of the Jews!

We were allowed to bring a large number of boxes with us on the plane, so I gave each child three boxes to fill with whatever items they would like to transport. I packed my pots, pans, and dishes, as well as most of my books and personal papers.

My friends in Baltimore threw a goodbye party for me and gave me a beautiful send-off. I had been in Baltimore for just one year, and yet I had made many wonderful friends. Practically everyone I knew showed up at the party and shared heartwarming memories.

One woman whom I barely knew told everyone how I had once helped her out during carpool. I had learned the hard way that I couldn't count on others to maintain my car. Once I had the gas-station attendant add oil to my motor. Shortly after, the engine started to smoke. I investigated, only to find out that the attendant had added too much oil. Realizing that I had to keep my vehicle in good shape, I had no choice but to learn the ins and outs of basic car maintenance.

The muffler on my old car gave me a lot of trouble, so I kept a bunch of wire hangers in my trunk in case of an emergency. One morning as I was driving carpool, I noticed a station wagon in front of me whose muffler dragged so low that it sparked as the car went over bumps in the road. A second look showed me that the car was loaded with kids and was being driven by a *frum* woman. I followed her as she pulled over, and I got out of my car to offer my assistance. I pulled some hangers out of my trunk, crawled under her car, and proceeded to wire up her muffler. After years of being on the receiving end of people's help, I was thrilled to help another Jew in distress! The woman called me that night to tell me that her husband was impressed with my handiwork; he said that it was the best job anyone had ever done on their muffler.

I had made some great friends in Baltimore. There was something about the simple and nonmaterialistic lifestyle of Baltimore's *frum* community that made many of the women I came into contact with so down to earth and easy to relate to. Baltimore's *frum* community is located in the city itself, rather than in an upscale suburban area, and I believe this lends a certain unpretentiousness to the lives of its community members. And yet these same unspoiled women showered me with love and generosity. At my goodbye party I was presented with everything I needed to set a beautiful Shabbos table: a lovely tablecloth, an elegant set of dishes and silverware, and a magnificent wine decanter. I was deeply touched. The thoughtful gifts left me looking forward to the wonderful *Shabbosos* and *Yamim Tovim* I hoped to spend together with all my children in *Eretz Yisrael*.

Just days before we left the United States, I received an exciting phone call from Jerusalem. My second son Nosson was seeing a girl seriously and it looked like they were going to get engaged! She was from Baltimore, and her parents wanted to meet me. The three of us met in a restaurant and we spoke about our children. I found it unbelievable to make the acquaintance of these intelligent and highly educated professionals who were about to become Nosson's in-laws.

In almost any new venture a person begins there will be those who challenge this leap of *emunah*. I was now flying halfway around the world with little income and few possessions, and there were those who questioned my sanity. On a whim, one night before I left I purchased a small decorative cactus and left it on the windowsill of the preschool I had worked for, with this note:

> *Cactus*
> *If, from above,*
> *these homely prickly things*
> *are given enough moisture in the desert*
> *to endure —*
> *how much, much more*
> *will Hashem allow*
> *the Jew upon His land*
> *to blossom?*

Aliyah entailed a slew of procedures and paperwork (this was in the days before Nefesh B'Nefesh streamlined the process!), but the benefits of making *aliyah* made all the hassle worthwhile. As a family of *olim*, we were entitled to free airline tickets, extra baggage, transportation from the airport to our destination, rent subsidy, free medical care, a child-allowance stipend from *Bituach Leumi*, and other benefits.

My children eagerly anticipated their first airplane trip. Everything about the bustling airport — from the check-in counter and security to watching the planes take off outside the departure gate — was new and exciting. It was hard for me to imagine that the same children who had once run about barefoot in the mountains were about to become world travelers. I recalled my little ones' excitement at their first encounter with a shower when we moved to Atlanta, and I laughed. It was amazing to think about how much broader their world had become since those days.

During the flight, my kids had a lot of fun trying out all the functions of their airplane seats. They kept themselves busy, reading goodbye letters from all their friends and methodically working through wads of chewing gum. I slept for the first time in days. Left to their own devices, they managed quite well, other than a little incident in which the contents of a packet of salad dressing ended up dripping down the blouse of the well-dressed woman sleeping next to one of my little girls.

We disembarked in Israel's Ben-Gurion Airport and were met by a representative of the immigration office holding up a little sign with our family's name on it. We followed our escort to the airport's branch of the Ministry of Interior, where my exhausted children were treated to refreshments as our paperwork was processed.

When asked for my name, I made sure to give the clerk my Hebrew name. From that point on, I was legally known as Tzirel Rus Massey. I was presented with my *teudat oleh* and welcomed as an official Israeli citizen. I was surprised by the speed of the naturalization process. I was moved to know that, just like any other Jew, we were awarded Israeli citizenship under Israel's Law of Return.

Ever since my sons had rented an apartment for us, I had been telling everyone that I was moving to Rechov Zevel. When the officer from the Ministry of Interior was processing my immigration papers, he asked me for my street address, and was a bit taken aback by my cursory answer, "Rechov Zevel 9." He looked me straight in the eye and said, "*Geveret, zevel* is garbage. Would you like to try again? You're moving to Rechov Zhvill."

We proceeded on to the baggage-claim area and loaded up a staggering amount of carts with our boxes, which we then struggled to maneuver through Customs into the arrivals hall beyond. Excited shouts and high-pitched squeals filled the air as my older sons ran to greet us after years of separation; my youngest girls were excitedly scooped up into the arms of their adoring big brothers. I watched them, my eyes misting over.

After we finally regained our composure, my boys confidently navigated our luggage carts through the exit and out into the balmy night air of Tel Aviv. We loaded up the two waiting *sheiruts* with our many boxes and set out on the long drive to our new home.

As we neared our destination, our *sheirut* began to ascend the winding mountain roads of the Judean Hills. Finally we approached the military checkpoint and were waved through by soldiers in flak vests holding rifles. We traveled on until the guard at the city gates allowed us passage through the barbed-wire fence surrounding the settlement. In the inky blackness, I wondered what had possessed me, a single mother with young children, to move out to this new community in the West Bank. *Maybe I should have checked this out a little better,* I thought as we drove through the gate and on into deserted streets below.

The next morning, I awoke to the warming rays of Israeli sunshine streaming through the bedroom window. I washed, dressed, and looked around my new apartment. Bathed in the brilliance of the morning sunlight, the world looked very different. I went from room to room, taking stock of all the furnishings, and my heart expanded with gratitude.

Hearing of our move, Rabbi Pavlov of She'arim had kept his eyes open for good-quality used furniture. Whenever he found something he felt we could use, he picked it up and transported it to our empty apartment. There were enough beds in our three bedrooms for our entire family, a cozy couch in the living room, and a fully functional kitchen. There was even a washing machine all ready and waiting for me on the little laundry porch off our bathroom. All this was due to the hard work and generosity of Rabbi Pavlov and my sons.

It seemed that my new life in Israel was to be a far cry from the deprivation I had experienced during my years in the Appalachian Mountains. That first day we were all very excited to finally be together as Jews in our brand-new apartment in *Eretz Yisrael.*

I soon made the acquaintance of some of my neighbors and was impressed by how warm and inviting they were. I hit it off particularly well with Michal Appelbaum, a friendly woman from Atlanta whose daughters were about the same age as my own. In time, our girls became very close. I just loved watching how they all

Watching the sun set off the porch of our apartment

played house together. Their play was nothing like what I remembered from my own childhood back in California. Our little ones covered their hair like little Jewish mommies, pulled out tablecloths and candlesticks, and pretended to make Shabbos.

The beginnings were tough. I had heard about a beautiful park at the entrance of our town and determined to treat my kids to an outing. I hadn't reckoned on how delicate my girls had become after four years of city living. I also didn't realize something that every Israeli takes for granted: the park is not the place to be during the early afternoon hours, when the Mediterranean sun shines in all its intensity. As there was not yet a good public transportation system in place, we hiked half an hour in the blazing summer sun to get there. The outing was a failure; my daughters were totally miserable.

The mounds of boxes strewn throughout my apartment began to get to me, demanding that I sort through them and unpack.

Other than a few kitchen cabinets, there were absolutely no shelves, hooks, or closets in my brand-new apartment. By the third day, my adrenaline had evaporated and I was feeling completely overwhelmed. I crawled into bed and stayed there for a day or two until I slowly pulled myself back together.

We spent our first Shabbos in Yerushalayim, in the home of Rabbi Daniel and Shoshana Belsky in Mattersdorf. During that Shabbos, Rabbi Belsky said, "May Hashem bless you that the great feelings of inspiration you feel now upon moving to *Eretz Yisrael* stay with you always." I answered with a heartfelt "Amen."

I was determined to make the next Shabbos at home. I was excited to put the beautiful gifts I had received from my friends in Baltimore to good use. First, though, everything had to be *toiveled.* The *mikveh* was located all the way up the hill; there were no buses and we were not yet serviced by a taxi company. Every day, my sons hauled one or two boxes of dishes and silverware up the hill, until all was done.

On Thursday I made a huge batch of *challah* dough. I eagerly anticipated the delicious fragrance of baking bread that would soon fill my home, but when I slid the trays into the oven I had pre-heated, I realized that my oven was broken!

Not one to give up easily, I grabbed tray after tray of braided loaves, knocked on my neighbors' doors, and, aided in my Hebrew by a little neighbor girl, introduced myself. "Hi, I am Tzirel Rus and I've just moved here from Baltimore. My oven is broken and I was wondering if you would be willing to bake these for me?"

My new community was wonderfully supportive. Every Friday a young man stopped by with an envelope of money that he had collected for our family. I would then quickly run over to the store and buy whatever I needed for Shabbos. Often, my account at the grocery store mysteriously contained more money than I had remembered depositing.

On Friday afternoons, Shaul, Eliyahu, and Yishai would come home from yeshivah and round up the family to help them quickly wash the floors and get the house in shape for Shabbos. Then they'd all go outdoors and play Freeze Tag or Capture the Flag before Shabbos. After all we had been through, I loved seeing my kids playing and having a good time together.

How I loved our beautiful *Shabbos seudos*. I was very proud of my large close-knit family seated around my table and very happy to be able to help others as well. My sons would often bring home bachurim from Ohr Somayach, and since I never quite knew how many to expect I made sure to put up a big pot of *cholent*. As my sons' voices blended with those of their friends, my home was filled with the sweet sound of *Shabbos zemiros*. Even Binyamin's pet parrots would chirp along, enhancing the beautiful symphony of Shabbos.

Our neighborhood was relatively young, and most of the families around us were just beginning to build their lives. We were

Our first *Erev Shabbos* in our new home in *Eretz Yisrael*.
The beautiful table settings were a goodbye gift from my friends in Baltimore.
Two of my sons are in the background.

one of the few families that boasted teenage children, and so our neighbors also enjoyed the melodious sound of *zemiros* that welled up from our apartment and spilled out through the building.

The best part of living in Israel was knowing that I was finally able to mother all my children again. My fifth son, Yishai, left my home in Atlanta at the tender age of 14 to join his brothers in Israel. He had been pretty homesick and never tired of thanking me for relocating so that we could all be together again. His gratitude for the most basic things — from providing him with a home to washing his clothes — told me how sorely I had been missed.

For the most part I saw adjusting to life in Israel as one big adventure. The fact that I had moved around a lot throughout my adult life probably made me more flexible and open to change. Still, this was the first time I had actually moved out of the United States, and I had to learn to manage in a different country with a foreign language. But I have always welcomed challenges and I saw managing in a Hebrew-speaking country as a particularly worthwhile challenge. My friends advised me to converse with the locals in English, since a good many Israelis do know basic English. In the event that the person I was speaking to couldn't manage in English, I would resort to pantomime. Somehow or other we usually managed to communicate.

Since I have a hard time reading Hebrew, when shopping I generally rely on the pictures on an item's packaging. For the most part this system worked; there were, however, one or two glitches. I still remember my daughter's cries as she ladled hot *cholent* into bowls. I had bought what I thought was a cheap cut of meat. "Ew, gizzards! Mother put gizzards in the *cholent!*" emanated from the kitchen. No one was willing to eat gizzard *cholent*, and so I ended up throwing it all out.

It seemed to me that the greengrocer yelled at me every time I went in, especially when I tried to pay him a little something on my account. As he yelled at me in Hebrew, I adamantly stood my ground in English. "This is all I can pay you now, but I will pay you off eventually," I would say over and over. I finally decided, *That's it, as soon as I get this balance paid off I'm not shopping at this store anymore.*

One day, as his son sat at the cash register, he seemed quite adamant in explaining something to me as I tried to pay him. Finally, after he made a few calls, the mystery was solved. The "yelling proprietor" had been trying to tell me that I didn't owe him any money, and I was just adding cash to my account! Yet all in all I didn't let my poor command of Hebrew inhibit me from acclimating to life in Israel.

There are just so many things I love about living here. After being lonely for much of my life, I particularly enjoy the experience of living in an apartment building and having wonderful neighbors close by. I remember being asked to accept delivery for my neighbor's meat order when she was out. In all the years I had lived in America, nothing like that had ever happened to me! I love living in such a trusting society that merchants think nothing of leaving housewares and clothing on display outside their stores.

And the children! I remember once, with my red-plaid shopping cart piled high, I passed through a group of about 15 young boys just coming out of *cheder*. Suddenly my bag of green apples toppled over and scattered in umpteen directions.

I steeled myself to be embarrassed by uproarious laughter, to see apples slipped into boys' pockets and look-at-the clumsy-old-lady sneers, followed by a few swift kicks to send the rolling apples even faster down the hill . . . all normal "boy behavior" in the world that I'd inhabited for so many years. Instead, as if with one mind and heart, this group of young boys rushed to intercept each apple and return it, with shy smiles and laughter, to my basket!

How wonderful to be part of such a holy nation!

CHAPTER 17

Finding the Joy

The new school year was fast approaching. My children needed schools, and this became the focus of my attention. The *Litvish* community of our small town was still in its infancy and there weren't all that many options to choose from. There was only one choice for both Estie and Binyamin, but a new Bais Yaakov had opened up that was just perfect for my younger girls.

When the first day of school rolled around, I had to figure out who to accompany to school first. As a single mother, I was outnumbered five to one. There was no way I could be in all three schools at once. I realized that the three youngest girls had each other and that Estie was outgoing enough to manage on her own, and so I set off with Binyamin on that exciting morning. Together, we walked over to the *cheder* where he was to attend the sixth grade. After seeing to it that he was settled in the right classroom, I walked down to the cottages where my daughters' new school conducted classes.

To my surprise I found that in my absence both Shira and Leora had taken the initiative of skipping themselves a grade so that they would be in the same class as their friends, the Appelbaum girls. I felt that it would have been wise to keep them back a year to give them more time to catch up on their Hebrew, but the principal decided not to disturb the status quo. Instead, she adopted a watch-and-wait strategy. No one ever had the heart to put them back, so they remained in their chosen grades.

I was delighted when Shira and Leora acclimated well. Estie, however, had a very hard time in her new school. There was a huge culture gap between her and her Israeli classmates. A few weeks into the year, we switched her to the Bais Yaakov of Telshe Stone, with its larger body of English-speaking girls.

Although it took some trial and error until Estie finally found herself in a school that suited her, her warm and outgoing personality helped her forge a number of local friendships.

Shortly after moving to Israel, I began attending Rabbi Avraham Stern's weekly Shabbos *shiur*, through which I met and began a friendship with Shoshana Bracha Berger, an intelligent *"frum-from-birth"* fellow American. Shoshana Bracha was something of

My little Bais Yaakov girls in a candy store in Geulah

a mentor to many of the younger women and recent returnees to Judaism who sought her advice and guidance. I developed a practice of walking Shoshana Bracha home from the *shiur* every Shabbos, even when it was out of the way. I had a lot to discuss with her, as there was still so much I was trying to learn and understand.

Interestingly, Estie became best friends with Chaya Berger, Shoshana Bracha's daughter. The Bergers had also recently emigrated from America, giving Chaya and Estie a lot of common ground. I was happy to see my daughter building a strong relationship with the daughter of my own friend, and I was grateful that she was spending so much time in such a lovely *Torahdik* home.

Though the girls did not attend the same school, since the Bergers' children were enrolled in *chassidishe* schools, Chaya and Estie still spent their afternoons in each other's company. They even went together to help straighten up the apartment of Chaya's ailing uncle, who was divorced.

It wasn't easy for Estie to adjust to Israeli culture, but thankfully we had the support of a prominent family in Yerushalayim, with whom my sons were close. As principal of a seminary for English-speaking girls, the mother offered to help Estie acclimate to life in Israel.

While my children were adjusting to their new schools and our new environment, I enrolled in a government-run *ulpan* in Har Nof. Each day, I traveled an hour and a half until I alighted at the very last stop in Har Nof, feeling rather queasy after the long ride on curvy mountain roads. I wish I could say that going to *ulpan* was worth the hassle. Despite the effort I invested in learning Hebrew, I was unable to follow the lessons. By the time my 18-year-old teacher declared that I was too old to learn a new language, I had already given up.

In retrospect, I regret having spent my first year in Israel attending *ulpan*. It proved to be a huge waste of time and energy. By the end of each day, I was worn out and unavailable for my children. I wish that I had been more fully present in their lives while they were adjusting to a new language and culture.

In our neighborhood, there were few American boys around the ages of my youngest sons. Fortunately, after having been separated for so long, Yishai and Binyamin were very happy to finally be together. They spent their evenings thoroughly enjoying each other's company.

In spite of all the trouble we had adjusting, I was thrilled to live in Israel. I couldn't understand how people could complain about the government offices and how long it took to process paperwork or get a phone line. As a veteran of the United States welfare programs, I was actually very impressed with how efficiently things were run in Israel. I had been used to navigating an extremely long and frustrating paper trail back in the United States every time I needed to verify my name and address for one of the government benefit programs. Just transferring my Medicaid coverage from Georgia to Maryland took five months! But here in Israel they trusted me; I no longer needed to produce endless lists of references in order to prove who I was and where I lived. It was an incredible feeling to be living among Jews in a Jewish country, where people actually trusted one another!

When I walked the streets of my growing community, I felt a deep appreciation for each and every brick and tile used in its construction. I would marvel at how much the Jewish people had gone through during the bitter years of exile, how much blood had been spilled, how many tears had been cried until we had reached this point in time. I just couldn't understand how people didn't appreciate the tremendous blessing we have received, to have been born into a time period that is relatively peaceful when compared to the generations that preceded ours. Not only have we been spared the agony of the Holocaust and the horror of pogroms, but on top of all the goodness that Hashem has bestowed upon us, He even granted us the special privilege of living in *Eretz Yisrael*, the land our ancestors yearned to see for thousands of years! How dare we complain! So we have to wait on line and learn to manage without our favorite American brands, but so what; we are alive, safe, healthy, and living in the Holy Land!

Despite my failures in *ulpan*, I reveled in my new lifestyle. No longer did I have to wake up in the morning to milk a cow, stoke a fire, draw water, bake bread, or help my kids plant and harvest acres of farmland. All I needed to do was walk down the street to the grocery store and load up my cart with luscious Israeli produce!

I wasn't frightened by the rawness of my developing community, since hand in hand with the inconveniences that the town's pioneers had to endure there was also a deep sense of camaraderie and even excitement as we joined together to develop that which we found missing. After living so long in social isolation, I had my independent streak. Since I had no one to follow, I had been forced to look within and draw from my own wellspring of faith and fortitude to find my own way. When women complained to me about the lack of organized social events and *shiurim* and the like, I told them, "Here we have to roll up our sleeves and go to work. After all, this is a young community and we have to build it up!"

An excerpt from a letter I wrote to my friends back in Baltimore during this time succinctly sums up my feelings:

"...It was so much harder back in Georgia to climb even the smallest hill while I was surrounded by gentiles and only had a tenuous thread of connection to my Creator. Now, as I reside among the people who know Hashem so intimately, I feel that I, too, have been given the ability to access Him more directly than ever before. I sense a greater strength to my prayers, and feel that they ascend directly to the Master of the Universe.

"I feel that all of my life's experiences have been to bring me to this moment. Hashem had always put me in situations where I had no one to follow, compelling me to blaze my own path. Here in this growing town, I feel a sense of destiny. With G-d's help I will get to pioneer and blaze new trails, only this time I am building on holy soil amid a holy nation. This time everything will be forever."

Sometime during my first year, a young mother on my block asked me to open my home for a parenting class she was organizing. I was a bit uncomfortable with the suggestion. After all, who was I, a relative newcomer to Judaism, to host a group of Jewish-from-birth women? But Miriam insisted that my home would be perfect, and so I agreed.

Unfortunately that particular parenting class was never really much of a success, and after some time it dwindled down to just our speaker, Miriam, and me. Often, I couldn't even be there since the class would coincide with the morning that I was supposed to be at the unemployment office in Jerusalem. Even so, hosting that class was a real eye-opener for me. I had been in awe of the *frum* community and felt that I didn't have much to offer. This experience gave me the confidence to make my own contribution.

I felt it vitally important that our community have *shiurim* for women, as I looked to the future especially for my daughters and daughters-in-law. Not long thereafter I made the acquaintance of Devorah Fastag, a highly intelligent and learned woman, who readily agreed to give a series of lectures in my home. This weekly *shiur* was a huge success, and it moved to the home of my friend Hemla Levitt, where it continued regularly for many years. Devorah also introduced me to several concepts that I really admired, such as *hisbodedus* — solitary meditation — and rising at midnight to mourn the destruction of the Temple.

Hemla and I had a lot in common; both of us hailed from California and were very grateful to have exchanged that culture for the beauty of our Torah community. As two of the oldest women on our block, we enjoyed getting out for an evening stroll together every now and again. While we sat outside one night schmoozing, we heard a car slowly make its way up the street, a Hebrew message blaring from the loudspeaker. Obviously a funeral, we surmised, and we continued our conversation in subdued tones. We stopped a passerby and asked who had died, hoping the tragedy wouldn't hit close to home. The passerby swallowed a smile and explained that no one had died; the announcement was simply informing the public about a sale on diapers!

The months passed, and I gradually became acclimated to life in Israel. There were still, though, some hiccups along the way. One of the most memorable was the incident with the Arab taxi driver.

My *tzedakah* boxes had become filled to the top with coins. I contacted the respective charities and asked what they wanted me to do with the money. They told me to count it out, send in a check for that sum, and keep the small change.

In anticipation of my next trip to Yerushalayim, I sat down and organized my coins. I filled a number of sandwich bags with 200 10-*agurot* coins, knotted them up, and piled them into my purse.

I got off my bus and flagged a cab to Mattersdorf. I didn't realize it at the time, but my driver was an Arab. When we pulled up in front of my destination I handed the driver the 20 NIS fare in the form of a heavy bag of *agurot*. I prepared to be on my way. The driver screamed at me, and I feared that he was after my blood. I sprang out of the car and ran up a nearby hill. The driver followed, hot on my heels. I managed to outrun him and I ducked into a garage where a group of mechanics was working on cars. With all those *Sabras* around, I felt I was safe. I stood in the middle of them as the mechanics and the driver yelled back and forth for a while.

Finally, one guy who knew some English filled me in on what was going on. It turned out the driver wanted to know if I had any larger money on me. He demanded to see the contents of my purse. Hesitantly, I complied. I unzipped the purse hanging from my shoulder. Four more bags of coins fell to the floor with a crash. The mechanics burst out laughing. That was the last time I ever attempted to pay for anything with a bag of coins!

Holiday preparations made a particular impact on me. What a contrast this was to my outsider status as a little girl. Since my parents didn't celebrate pagan holidays, as a little girl in public school I felt different and excluded. When I close my eyes I can easily conjure up the image of my 6-year-old self back in Garden Grove, California. I stand off to the side, dressed in school clothes, silently watching my classmates. I hold the smooth, cool pole in the schoolyard. I walk around and around in an endless circle, trying to distract myself from feeling alone and awkward as I watch the other children in costume marching merrily in the Halloween parade.

Up until now, that was the story of my life. Somehow I was always different from those around me. Our Sabbath observance had kept me from performing in the school orchestra, displaying my goats at the annual goat show, and participating in the Orange County Fair. Somehow it seemed that everything exciting always took place on Saturday or was somehow tied up with a pagan holiday. One way or another, I was always left out.

In Israel, one of the sensations I savored was living in sync with those around me. I particularly recall my first *Motza'ei Yom Kippur.* That very evening, the entire neighborhood got to work constructing their *succos.* This was to be the first time the Yom Tov of Succos would be celebrated in my brand-new neighborhood, and so we were all in the same boat. The streets echoed with the sounds of *succos* under construction. The late-night quiet was banished by the screeching vibration of drills biting through concrete and stone. Yet, as the neighborhood prepared as one for the upcoming holiday, no one seemed to mind the noise.

The preholiday preparations don't come close to the joy felt during the holidays themselves. Imagine stepping outside and seeing entire apartment buildings sporting *succos* on every porch, while lively music spills into the streets from the many *Simchas Beis Hasho'eivah* celebrations taking place around the city. Can you picture the beauty of gazing out into the cold, dark winter streets and seeing the flickering lights of Chanukah *menorahs* brightening up the windows of every home? And when the festivities of Purim spill over into the streets as countless costumed children rush to and fro delivering *mishloach manos* and groups of *bachurim* sporting monogrammed jackets dance and sing their way through the streets, my heart sings along with my beloved people as we engage in the special *mitzvos* of the day.

I remember telling my friend Shoshana Bracha of my plans to spend my first Israeli Simchas Torah together with my sons in Ohr Somayach. Shoshana Bracha and her husband are Boyaner *chassidim*, and she encouraged me to take advantage of my time in Yerushalayim to stop in at Boyan as well. I had so much *nachas* watching my sons enthusiastically taking part in our celebration of the gift of Torah learning. I saw them from above, linked hand in hand with the pulsating crowd below as they circled the *bimah* again and again in a never-ending dance of pure joy. They were at one with the yeshivah, intertwined in ecstatic celebration of the eternity of Torah learning and the newfound connection to the everlasting word of G-d of many of the yeshivah's students.

Once the *hakafos* had died down at Ohr Somayach, I set off on a 20-minute hike through Geulah to the Boyaner *beis midrash*. My first exposure to the rich *Chassidus* of Boyan on that memorable Simchas Torah was incredibly uplifting. I saw the Rebbe of Boyan dance the same sacred dance that had been passed down through the Ruzhiner dynasty from his ancestors before him. I absorbed the infectious joy of thousands of *chassidim* joined in celebration. I had never encountered such an emphasis on joy; there is something so uniquely Jewish about the attribute of *simchah* that I finally was able to tap into as part of the Jewish nation. I find it very interesting that throughout the years of my relentless search for the truth I had read countless books on all the world's religions, including Judaism, yet somehow I had never come across the concept of *Chassidus*, a movement that I now found myself drawn toward with a force that surprised me by its strength.

Though every *Yom Tov* brings its own thrill, nothing quite compares to the pulsating joy during the celebration for a new Torah scroll at a *hachnasas Sefer Torah*. Each time I stumble upon one of these most beautiful events, my heart catches in my throat. How I love to watch the young boys holding their flaming torches aloft as they lead the procession. Then comes the decorated van, fully outfitted with colorful flashing lights and loudspeakers spreading joyful tunes though the streets. I chuckle delightedly at the many pajama-clad children visible from the balconies of their homes above.

The tempo builds and my excitement mounts. Finally, I spot

Our first and only bar mitzvah, when my son Binyamin accepted upon himself the yoke of Torah and *mitzvos*. Rabbi Daniel Belsky is seated at his left.

the *chuppah*. The velvet canopy is danced down the streets, supported by exuberant men dancing on air, giving honor to the brand-new Torah Scroll cradled lovingly in the arms of the rabbi dancing beneath. I don't attempt to stop the tears filling my eyes and trickling down my cheeks as I wordlessly thank G-d for bringing me close and giving me a share in the everlasting union that exists between Hashem, the Jewish people, and the holy Torah.

If not for the tenacious hold that the G-d-fearing People of Israel maintained over the Torah — through gas and fire and endless wandering — there would have been no Tree of Life for me to grasp. For that alone I will always be grateful to the Jewish nation, for preserving their magnificent heritage under the most trying conditions so that I, too, am privileged to taste of her beauty.

During these years, for the first time I began to reflect back on my life with a fresh understanding. Before, I never could figure it out. Back in the States I had known people who for years worked from nine to five every day, went home, and changed into their slippers at exactly 5:55, sitting down in their easy chair to watch the news. Once a year they took a vacation to Las Vegas, blew all their savings, and came back home to their routine. Every day my life was full of disruptions, sabotaged goals and dreams, tests that called for unending patience, prayers not being answered — and, all the while, me wondering, *Why am I having such a crazy life?*

After I became Jewish, the answers were becoming much clearer. All along it had been Hashem masterminding my life to bring me to the Jewish people. The tools and the people He brought into my life were exactly what I needed to make this voyage.

CHAPTER 18

A Blessing Fulfilled

Rabbi Nachman Bulman, *zt"l*, had blessed my sons that our family would go from *simchah* to *simchah*. Beginning with Dovid's engagement, this blessing was fulfilled many times over. Five days after we moved to Israel, Nosson announced his engagement to a friend of Dovid's wife.

At first I was wary of my role as mother-in-law. I had come across so much negativity on the topic over the years. I didn't want to scare off my new daughters-in-law, and so I resolved to give them plenty of space. Over time, I realized that I spoke with everyone else significantly more than I talked with my sons' wives. Perhaps I was holding back a little too much. Eventually, I loosened up and began to develop a more natural relationship with them.

My beloved family was greatly enriched by the presence and personalities of my wonderful daughters-in-law, and I looked forward to our family being extended further. Fortunately, I didn't have long to wait. My house was in a state of chaos and I was up to my elbows in Pesach preparations during our first year in Israel when Shoshana Belsky, daughter of Rabbi Bulman and sister of Toby Katz, called to suggest a *shidduch* for my third son, Shaul.

Although I already had two married sons, I was still pretty new to the whole *shidduch* concept. I didn't trust myself to get very involved. The rabbis at Ohr Somayach had guided my two older sons through the process of *shidduchim*, and I was happy to leave this suggestion in their hands as well.

I discreetly called Shaul outside, where we were able to speak privately about Rebbetzin Belsky's suggestion. We had heard a lot of nice things about this English-speaking girl who had grown up in Yerushalayim, and so we decided to go ahead with it. The couple met a few times over the Pesach break, and then Shaul brought the young lady to meet Rabbi Bulman. Rabbi Bulman spoke with them for a little while and then asked if they were ready to make a *l'chaim*. I was floored when Shaul called to tell me he was engaged. Once I got to know his wife, I was able to see that she was indeed perfect for him!

Baruch Hashem, the *simchos* just kept coming. During the following Succos, a contingent of rabbis from Ohr Somayach came to our little town to take part in the *bris* of one of my grandsons. After the *bris*, the rabbis set off together down the street to meet the bride of my fourth son, Eliyahu. We were definitely going from one joyous occasion to the next.

On top of all that, we were also blessed to have G-d provide for all of our financial needs. I had a large family to feed. Shabbos after Shabbos I hosted my married kids, as well as many students from Ohr Somayach. Then there were the holidays, with all of the expenses they entail. Somehow, we always had what we needed. There were, of course, many times when I had absolutely no idea where I would get the money to pay a bill, but inevitably everything fell into place.

Thus passed three happy years full of blessing and growth in Torah. My finances, though, were getting more difficult, until one day I could no longer pay the rent. I fell three months behind, and that knowledge cast a pall on my daily activities. I felt terrible that I owed so much money. I consulted with Rabbi Stern, who calmly told me not to worry. He reassured me that it would all work out in the end.

I believe Rabbi Stern asked Yisrael Eisenstark, *z"l*, and his good friend Yishai Elfenbein, *yblc"t*, to help me find affordable housing. I was eligible for housing from the Ministry of Absorption, but they didn't have any housing projects for immigrants in any of the *chareidi* neighborhoods. At the time, the Ministry of Housing was actually constructing a housing development in our town, designated for families who qualified through the Social Services department. We hoped that I would be granted one of the new apartments. Moving my file from the absorption ministry to the housing ministry was a bureaucratic challenge that I would never have been able to navigate without the help of Rabbis Eisenstark and Elfenbein.

How many times had I walked into a government office only to find that there were 200 people on line ahead of me? How often had I tried to make myself understood using a combination of English and sign language? Yet with these two leading the way, I felt like I was in the cradle of G-d's care. Somehow, they knew how to navigate the confounding labyrinth of lines and waiting rooms, effortlessly gaining us entry to any official we needed to visit. With his characteristic charm and passion, Rabbi Eisenstark would manage to get all my documents signed and stamped, while Rabbi Elfenbein's imposing figure cast a spell of its own.

Finally, unbelievably, the apartment was mine. Before moving day, these two men looked over my furniture and appliances to determine what was in good condition and what needed to be replaced. It was decided that I would get a new desk, refrigerator, and couch. This was the first time in all my life that I actually got to choose my own furniture! They treated me like one of their own family and made sure that all of my needs were met, even going so far as to have a patio put in for me.

It's difficult to describe the intense feelings of joy and gratitude that accompanied me as I crossed the threshold of my new apartment. After having spent my entire adult life making do with very

My oldest grandson, learning to become a *"gemarakup"* during a visit in our new apartment

little in the way of materialism, here I was, almost 50 years old, and Hashem was finally giving me a home of my very own! Not only was it mine, but it was a sturdy structure built of stone upon the holy soil of *Eretz Yisrael*, and outfitted with new furniture and appliances! What more could I possibly need?

My neighbors were primarily Hebrew-speaking Sefardim, and I got on well with them. I greatly admired the lovely Yemenite upstairs who, together with two other women, completed *Sefer Tehillim* daily for a friend in crisis. Thank G-d, her friend eventually experienced an unbelievable turn of events that set her life back on track.

I had a particularly interesting experience during the time I spent in that apartment. I don't remember the specific details of how and why one of my Hebrew-speaking neighbors got upset with me, but I do remember that as a result of our little spat, I began to keep my distance. Although hurt by her anger, I was also upset at the thought of maintaining a cold war with one of my neighbors. In the face of our language barrier, I felt helpless. I felt uncomfortable asking a third party to get involved. I was stuck.

One day while I was busy baking *challah*, another neighbor knocked on my door and demanded to know what I was cooking. When I told her I was making *challah*, she declared that I had to give her a loaf! "Why?" I asked, taken aback. She told me that a pregnant woman in the building was so taken by the aroma of my baking loaves that she needed to sample a piece. The Talmud mentions that if a pregnant woman smells and then craves a food, she should be given that food to eat, lest the unborn child suffer any danger. I had never heard of such a thing, but I happily handed over a fragrant loaf of fresh-baked *challah* for the anonymous pregnant woman in my building.

A few days later, I was outside schmoozing with the woman who had requisitioned one of my *challah* loaves when she pointed to the woman I'd had trouble with, mentioning that she was the mystery recipient of my fresh-baked *challah*. The expectant mother smiled at me through her window and waved in gratitude. I was astounded by the wondrous ways of G-d, Who saw how badly I wanted to patch up my relationship with my neighbor and arranged for it to happen!

I would have been happy to live in my little apartment for the rest of my life, yet Hashem had other plans for me.

My daughter Estie had become very close with a girl called Rochel Berger, the daughter of Reb Avrum Berger and the first cousin of Estie's good friend Chaya. Estie and Rochel had learned together in Europe, and now they were both back in Israel.

One day I was walking along the streets of my new neighborhood, a few hundred yards behind Estie and Rochel. I was impressed by how well the two of them got along, when suddenly I was struck by a powerful thought. I remembered hearing that the Berger family had once considered me as a potential *shidduch* for Reb Avrum, Shoshana Bracha's divorced brother-in-law — and Rochel's father.

Avrum spent his mornings learning in his older brother's *kollel* and was the father of seven children. Although I understood that Reb Avrum suffered from a health condition, I was deeply moved that the Berger family thought me worthy of joining their respected family. At that time, nothing had come of the suggested *shidduch*, yet as I observed the warmth and friendship that had sprouted between our daughters, I began to think of Reb Avrum Berger once again. A voice deep inside whispered of the possibility of our building a home together.

During the seven years since my divorce, I had not given much thought to the idea of remarriage. If G-d wanted me to marry, I figured He would help me out. Way back in Atlanta, before my divorce, I was compelled by the state of Georgia to attend a workshop on marriage. A psychologist had addressed the crowd and shared his own personal experiences. He told us that he got remarried immediately after his divorce without taking the time necessary to heal. Not surprisingly, his second marriage also ended in divorce. He left us with a strong warning not to remarry without first exploring the reasons behind the failure of our first marriage.

I thought some about what to look for in a husband the second time around. I was adamant that I would only consider a man who was both a father and a Torah scholar. I considered it the highest privilege imaginable to build a home with a man who spent his days engrossed in Torah learning. It was also vitally important to me that I find an experienced father for my children. From what I had heard about Reb Avrum, he was a friendly and upbeat person who spent his days learning Torah. He even had the added advantage of living nearby and being the brother-in-law of my dear friend Shoshana Bracha. To top it all off, he was a Boyaner *chassid*.

For some time I had felt drawn to *Chassidus*. Boyan in particular made a favorable impression on me. I was deeply inspired each time I attended a *tisch* or holiday celebration and saw hundreds of men come together in song and dance to celebrate their relationship with the Master of the Universe. I loved the atmosphere of a *beis midrash* charged with the passion of men who know beyond a shadow of a doubt that theirs is a religion of truth.

All things considered, I realized that I was quite interested in meeting with Reb Avrum Berger. I asked my friend Faigel to suggest the *shidduch*. I was thrilled when she called and told me that she'd managed to set up a meeting.

The evening I met the man who would become my second husband wasn't particularly memorable. There was no interesting symbolism, no hints of an other-worldly experience. I did not experience a blinding flash of recognition telling me that he was "the one." Neither of us were youngsters, taking our first halting steps into the world of adulthood; rather, we were two mature individuals, graduates of the school of hard knocks.

I sat across the table from Avrum, and we spoke of our dreams and aspirations, of our values and goals, and of course about the possibility of blending our precious families. Avrum was short and obviously frail, but a wide smile lit up his face and his blue eyes shone with happiness and a loving acceptance of the bitter trials he had endured. I was impressed by his warmth and gentleness of spirit. He shared with me his deep love of prayer.

During the course of our meeting, it became obvious to me that his illness greatly limited him. I mentally took a step back and asked myself if this was something I could get over. I took stock of the abilities that had been building up for decades within me, born of my lifelong struggle for truth and refined in the furnace of suffering. Looking within the deepest recesses of my soul, I felt that I would be able to look past the outer shell that clothed the soul of the special man sitting across from me. I felt that I could build a deep relationship with the wonderful person I sensed he was.

I so much wanted to marry a man who spent his days immersed in Torah learning that those closest to me didn't have the heart to tell me that my aspirations were rather unrealistic. After all, how many single fathers in my age bracket still spent their days in the study hall? And yet, perhaps because I wanted it so badly, Hashem fulfilled my dreams anyway.

At that point it wasn't clear to me how functional Reb Avrum actually was, but I was prepared to marry him, care for him, and build a home together with him, as long as he was learning Torah. I knew it would be a special privilege to share my life with a man who constantly forced himself to rise beyond the constraints of his ailing body to study the holy words of our Torah.

The opportunity for me to marry into such a wonderful family was nothing less than a dream come true. I greatly loved and admired the Jewish people and was honored to join their ranks, but on some level I still felt like a stranger. I perceived myself as belonging to the outer circle of this holy nation, and I longed to make it to the hallowed inside ranks. I wanted a deeper, more intimate connection with the Jewish nation. Marrying Reb Avrum Berger would finally make that dream a reality.

I could hardly believe that someone like him would be interested in someone like me. Interestingly, Avrum felt the same way. Long ago he had heard that my family had moved to town, as it seems we generated quite a bit of conversation. He also used to read the advertisements I placed about the speakers I brought in and some of the programs I designed to inspire the English-speaking women of my community. When the match was first suggested, he assumed that I would never agree to even meet him! And yet Hashem had obviously been pulling the strings for a number of years so that one day we would become husband and wife.

Once we decided to marry, we were advised to spend time building a solid relationship before the wedding took place. That way, we would have a stable foundation in place to support the formidable task of blending a family of 17 children. Even before we were officially engaged, we went for premarital counseling. We spent a good deal of time together, sharing our past experiences and developing a system for building a joint future. We decided that it would be best to be proactive, and instead of falling into the pattern of being caught by surprise by each other's plans and family issues, once we were married we would meet weekly to discuss things in advance. We set aside *Motza'ei Shabbos* as our own special time together.

After our marriage, we would eat our *Melaveh Malkah* meal in Reb Avrum's office, making it clear that we were not to be disturbed. We would use our weekly date to discuss our impressions of the previous Shabbos and plan out the events of the upcoming week. From the way each child was adjusting to our marriage to the particular needs and issues of our growing kids as they came up, all was discussed during that special time. In retrospect, I think this was one of the keys to the success of our marriage.

Not long before I made the acquaintance of my second husband, my ex-husband converted to Judaism and moved to the neighborhood. Having him nearby was really quite helpful. My two youngest sons sorely missed their father, and they were thrilled to finally have him back in their lives. An unofficial joint-custody arrangement was put into effect for the boys. At the time of my remarriage, Yishai and Binyamin were living up the hill with their father, and most of Avrum's children were either away at yeshivah or likewise living with relatives. Out of 17 of our children, only six actually lived with us: my four daughters and two of his daughters. My apartment was too small to accommodate our expanded family, and so we rented a larger place.

On my wedding day, my dear friend Elana came by to style my *sheitel* and transform me into a blissful bride. I wore a lovely cream-colored suit. Our wedding was a small yet joyous affair held in the Boyan *beis midrash*. The Boyaner Rebbe attended our wedding, and I was led to the *chuppah* by Avrum's mother and my dear friend Shoshana Bracha.

Although our children did not attend the *chuppah*, they came later for the reception and dancing. I was surrounded by my nearest and dearest and enveloped in the love and joy of all those who cared for me. The *beis midrash* resounded with enthusiastic dancing, and

The Boyaner Rebbe *shlita*
at my *chuppah*

At my *chasunah*. My son Shaul is shaking hands with the Boyaner Rebbe.
To his right is Rabbi Samet.

248 • THE MOUNTAIN FAMILY

our guests' passionate *berachos* accompanied Avrum and me as we set out to build the miraculous promise of our new life.

The plan was that Avrum and I would spend the first month of marriage alone together. My daughters were supposed to stay with their father, while Avrum's daughter was hosted by Shoshana Bracha. After two weeks, my girls began to slowly trickle back into our home. Not long after, Avrum's daughter Rochel packed her bags and joined us as well, soon to be followed by her younger sister, Shulamis, from America. Blending had officially begun.

Although Avrum was a warm person and not at all overbearing, blending our families did not come easily. When raising my daughters, I had found it nearly impossible to be both mother and father. Sheer necessity forced me to surrender the maternal role somewhat in favor of a more paternal role. Understandably, this created a degree of distance and resentment in our relationship. Upon our marriage, I was eager to relinquish the official role of father and bestow it on Avrum, thus freeing me up to be more feminine and empathetic. Casting Avrum in the role of disciplinarian proved to be a bad move. I knew my kids more intimately than Avrum ever could, and where I would have let many of their antics pass without comment, treating them as a passing phase, he tended to take them more seriously.

We were already going for counseling, and we brought up the strained stepparenting dynamic. Our counselor told us that we had to give up the idea of becoming either father or mother to our stepkids. Instead, our aim was to take on the role of aunt and uncle toward our spouse's children. Like an aunt or uncle, we stopped disciplining and making decisions regarding each other's children. It took some adjustment, but the results were certainly worth the effort.

Reb Avrum and I worked together to adopt a fairly tolerant approach to raising our six daughters. Over time, I had learned that it wasn't worthwhile to meet my kids head-on while they were going through one of their stages. They had been through a lot and had been forced to make many adjustments in life. Which other girls their ages had moved from the country to the city, lost a baby sibling, coped during my depression and subsequent divorce, converted, moved from Atlanta to Baltimore and from there to Israel? I was careful not to push them too hard. I had seen that immigrant children often don't adjust well to their new culture, and so I decided to cut my kids some slack so that they wouldn't buckle under the pressure of all the changes they needed to undergo.

Our backgrounds couldn't have been more different. Avrum had grown up in Crown Heights, and had gone to *cheder* with the Boyaner Rebbe. And me? Southern California and the Appalachian Mountains are a long way from Crown Heights.

With all that, Avrum and I found much in common. There is something about painful life experiences — no matter what their source — that draws together fellow survivors. Our past histories, in which we had both engaged in backbreaking labor, removing metaphorical stones and battling the parched and hardened earth, had resulted in dark, loamy soil from which our shared future would sprout. The vagaries of our lives forced both of us to rise above our physical limitations and develop a more spiritual perspective on life. This strength became the cornerstone of our relationship, the basis for the deep understanding that developed between us. We became true partners in every way. More, we were each other's biggest fans.

Besides our goals of building a home of Torah for ourselves and our children, we both passionately loved *Klal Yisrael*. We couldn't stand to hear anyone speak badly of a fellow Jew. We scorned division and strife and yearned for the unification of our nation, the return of our people to both Torah and the Land of Israel, and the coming of *Mashiach*.

Although Avrum and I were obviously very well suited, it took some time until our children were able to accept our new family. A well-meaning *rav* had said that it was inevitable that there would be significant problems in blending our families. My daughters were adolescents at the time and naturally highly sensitive about the way they and their families appeared to others. Not only were my daughters forced time and again to swallow their discomfort about our unusual family background, but now I also expected them to redefine our family image altogether. In the eyes of a teenager just about the only thing worse than a new stepfather was a handicapped stepfather. It was quite an adjustment for my girls, yet the grace and courage my husband showed in winning my daughters' acceptance went a long way in smoothing things over.

With the passing of time, the same girls who struggled to accept my new husband in our home spoke with awe about the love and understanding that Reb Avrum had shown them during those hard years of adjustment. Day after day he greeted them with the warmest of smiles, completely disregarding the cool and disinterested responses he received in return. Although Avrum was limited by his significant health issues, he tried to give to the family in whatever way possible. Since he got up early every morning, he offered his services as the household alarm clock. He knocked on the door of anyone who wanted to be woken up early. If any of my daughters showed the slightest sign of illness, he offered to schedule a doctor's appointment for them, something I was unable to do since I couldn't speak Hebrew. He was genuinely concerned for their well-being, frequently asking how they were feeling and whether or not they had slept well.

As teens, my girls didn't appreciate his concern about their sleep and health, something that they took for granted. Avrum's physical suffering was lost on them, but as they began to taste a little bit more of life's challenges, they received new insight into Avrum's everyday heroism.

Before my remarriage, our family had identified as *Litvish*, or Jews of Lithuanian extraction, although I personally had a strong interest in *Chassidus*. Sensing that my daughters might consider my bringing a *chassidish* stepfather into their home as another potential source of friction, Avrum reverently hung up pictures of Lithuanian

Torah giants. He often recounted the teachings of both *chassidishe* Rebbes and *Litvishe gedolim*, saying, "*Eilu v'eilu divrei Elokim chaim!* These and these are both words of the living G-d!" By showing sincere respect for the rabbis who had guided our family before our marriage, Avrum taught even my youngest children an invaluable lesson in respecting differing pathways to Hashem.

The way in which Avrum conducted our Shabbos *seudos* underlined his great sensitivity to my feelings. He knew that I didn't understand Hebrew, and he was concerned that I felt left out as he chanted *Eishes Chayil*. To show how much he appreciated my efforts in running our home, Avrum read through the entire "Woman of Valor" a second time during the meal — this time in English. It is due to Avrum's dedication that I finally learned how to *bentch* in Hebrew. Week after week, he'd patiently sing a few lines of the *bentching* with me after the meal, each time adding a phrase. Eventually, I mastered the entire *bentching*. Understandably, my daughters found our joint *bentching* sessions quite uncomfortable.

Me bentching in my son's succah

None of their friends' mothers sang the *bentching* along with their husbands! Then again, none of their friends' mothers became Jewish in midlife.

Beginning married life with a houseful of teenage girls painted those years with splashes of bold color. Yet Avrum and I stayed focused on our goals, continued to develop our own relationship, and made sure never to discuss any differences of opinion in front of the children.

Early in our marriage I saw that Avrum had great difficulty walking. His balance was off, and his gait clumsy. At home he'd walk with one arm against the wall, but it was obvious to me that to safely navigate outside the house, he needed a walker. I knew my daughters would be mortified, and I was concerned that calling any more attention to Avrum's differences would only alienate them further. Still, my husband needed a walker and I was determined to do something about it.

We found a sturdy walker with a large pouch for carrying belongings. I decided to get everyone used to this new piece of equipment. Wanting my family to have positive associations with Avrum's walker, I placed my little grandchildren in the pouch and wheeled them around. I also pretended that our new walker was really the perfect shopping cart for carrying my groceries home from the store. My teenage daughters had a fit when they saw me pushing a walker laden with bags of groceries through the streets. They were only too happy when I decided to relinquish my cart so that Avrum could use it to get around.

The walker greatly enhanced Avrum's independence. It granted him greater mobility, as well as new opportunities to give to others. He decided that it would be his job to carry my heavy ArtScroll *Chumash* and *siddur* home from *shul* each Shabbos, slipping them carefully into the pouch of his walker. (Of course, our community has a *mehadrin eiruv*.) Whenever I decided to spare him the trouble and carry them home myself, he was very disappointed.

For all the benefit he received from the walker, it did call greater public attention to Avrum's disability. When someone mentioned that he found it depressing to see Avrum dependent on a walker, Avrum dubbed it his "*simchah*-mobile." Perhaps this was also why he began his practice of jumping. Not one to allow his disabilities to slow him down, Avrum realized that he could get people to laugh with one of his spontaneous jumping sessions. He'd grip the walker for support and startle his companion by jumping up and down in earnest, something no one would expect of a man who walked with so much difficulty. Jumping became a hallmark habit that Avrum used to express his joy or to bring a smile to the face of a friend.

Avrum's daughter Rochel told me how her father used to sit on the floor and play with them when they were little. Chess and checkers were regulars, yet Avrum's all-time favorite was the Israeli game of *chamesh avanim,* or "Five Stones." A game very similar to its American counterpart, jacks, Five Stones demands dexterity and coordination. This should have been completely beyond the limits of Avrum, who suffered terribly from tremors, yet it was a game that he enjoyed and even excelled at.

Avrum and I encountered significant challenges in melding our families together. Still, with conviction and perseverance we forged ahead and built our own relationship. Our happiness spilled over, filling the walls of our home. When maturity and perspective dawned, our children appreciated the atmosphere of joyous dignity that Avrum and I had nurtured since the day we stood under the *chuppah.*

CHAPTER 19

Small Man, Big Heart

My husband's lifelong battle for health shaped his unique personality. Not only was his childhood marked by physical suffering, but his unusually small stature and inability to run and play also made him a target of other children's harassment.

Instead of feeling bullied, though, as a child Avrum felt secure in the knowledge of his parents' devotion and protection. His loving family tried their best to shield him from harm, yet they also did their utmost to give him as normal a childhood as possible. Since he was bright, they encouraged him to do well in school, and they even sent him to camp with other boys his age. One year he boarded the bus to camp with an oxygen tank in tow, another humbling experience in the life of a very unassuming personality.

The relationship that Avrum had with his older brother was unique. When Avrum moved to *Eretz Yisrael*, where his brother had made his home, they decided to meet to learn each day. From this beginning eventually came an English-speaking *kollel*. Later each was to claim the other started it. Every morning they ate breakfast together at Avrum's house. Thus began the years of *davening*, learning, and being there for each other on a daily basis, each calling the other brother his biggest rebbi.

Every afternoon and evening his older brother's family pitched in to help him with laundry and meals. Special jokes and laughter were shared to help ease the burden of constant daily pain that the younger brother, Avrum, carried so gracefully. Throughout their lives they enjoyed this rare brotherly camaraderie: truly soul mates.

Instead of making him bitter, Avrum's suffering made him particularly sensitive to others' pain. His loving heart intuitively homed in on others in distress, impelling him to find a way to lift their flagging spirits. He would slowly walk the streets of our neighborhood, pushing his walker ahead of him, all the while scanning the sidewalk for someone in need of a kind word or a heartfelt blessing. People often stopped him in *shul*, in the street, or at the doctor's office in order to unburden themselves of their troubles or ask for advice. He was particularly sought after by those who were trying to build successful second marriages. He often advised these husbands to take their wives on vacation.

I once asked him why he made such an effort to greet everyone with a smile. I was astounded by his answer. Avrum explained that although he was a *baal yissurim,* he nevertheless managed to keep a smile on his face. However, he noticed that many of the people he encountered truly did not look happy. He reasoned that if he was capable of being happy despite his great physical suffering, then all of these unhappy people must be suffering even more than he, and therefore he must cheer them up!

Although his illness certainly impacted his everyday life, Avrum was a lot more functional than many healthy people. He was very disciplined and had learned how to strike a balance between attending to his bodily needs and the needs of his soul. His state of health was quite precarious and minor alterations in either the time or quantity of the food he ate were liable to land him in the hospital. Over time we realized that even joyous stressors such as family *simchos* and *Yamim Tovim* would throw his sensitive body out of whack, necessitating yet another hospitalization. Avrum took his doctors' recommendations very seriously and religiously followed their medical advice, even though it was at times inconvenient or uncomfortable to do so. Yet he rarely complained and didn't allow his condition to get in the way of his making the most of life. As his son was to say later, "My father was a man broken on the inside and broken on the outside, but he wasn't a broken man."

When we were engaged, I would often hear him washing the dishes during our phone conversations. After we married, I relieved him of all such mundane tasks, preferring instead that he spend his time learning Torah. And learn he did, for the better part of each day. He got up bright and early at 5 a.m., after having gone to sleep the night before at 11:30. Although he took a brief afternoon nap, he certainly didn't spend much time in bed, considering his state of ill health. If he was sick, he went to the hospital; if he wasn't in the hospital, he was up and about, making the most of every minute.

Even during his frequent hospitalizations, Avrum managed to accomplish wonderful things. As my son Dovid said, "Reb Avrum never complained about anything. And I mean never. Even when he was seriously ill and on his way to the hospital, he'd say, 'Hashem's sending me off to draw His distant children nearer to Him!'"

In the hospital, he kept up with his learning, and on the occasion that he fell behind he would catch up when he returned home. Unlike most people visiting the emergency room, who are intent on getting the care they need, Avrum focused on the needs of the medical staff. He knew they were likely overworked and underappreciated, and more likely to receive complaints than thanks. He decided to be the one to compliment them.

Arriving in the emergency room, the first thing he'd do was ask the doctors if they had eaten breakfast. Usually, they would mention having had a cup of coffee. "That's not enough," Avrum would insist. Sometimes he asked the medical professional if he'd been on vacation recently. If the answer was no, Avrum would encourage him to indulge in some much-needed downtime. He warmly thanked the doctors and nurses who cared for him, even when they struggled to draw his blood and had to prick him numerous times. Not surprisingly, the emergency room staff would fight for the privilege of attending him, and the two internal medicine wards vied for the right to have him admitted to their ward!

Avrum knew that people usually complained about hospital food. Yet he recognized how hard the cook worked to cater to the varying diets of the entire hospital. He wanted the cook to know that he appreciated his efforts, and so he often sent him regards. On one occasion, Avrum asked that the cook come meet him so that he could personally thank him for all his hard work.

Everyone who met Avrum during his hospital stays came to love the short and friendly man who had a smile and a kind word for all. He often spoke to our children about the importance of greeting people with a smile. "With one smile, you can make someone's day," he said. His roommates always became his close friends, and he even made a point of chatting with people in the elevators. It was amazing to see the transformation that took place among the other occupants of the elevator. By the time we had exited at our floor, everyone was smiling and happy. Once, as we were being discharged, I heard an old, gravelly voice calling from behind the curtain. "Avrum! Avrum!" I hesitantly pulled back the curtain. Lying in his hospital bed was an elderly Arab. He didn't want to miss out on saying goodbye to Avrum!

One of Avrum's hospital friends was a Holocaust survivor. The man bitterly declared that he was an atheist. Avrum had just been reading about the Klausenberger Rebbe, *zt"l*, who had lost his entire family in the war. Inspired by what he had read, Avrum felt that he had something to share with his suffering roommate. He spoke of the Klausenberger Rebbe, who had once been asked by a fellow survivor, "Why did they take the best and leave the rest?" The Klausenberger sat and wept with him.

This story seemed to touch Avrum's roommate deeply, rewarding Avrum with yet another new friend. The two men kept in touch even after leaving the hospital. In fact, Avrum called the man every *Erev Shabbos*. At one point, this former atheist called to let us know that he was on the road to recovery and that he had been thanking people for praying for him. He even came to visit us and was shocked to find that religious Jews actually lived in such a beautiful and well-run city. As the Boyaner Rebbe once told Avrum, it seemed that his mission in life was to draw estranged Jews closer to Hashem. Indeed, Avrum made a *Kiddush Hashem* wherever he went.

Aside from his many hospitalizations, Avrum also put in a regular appearance at the local health clinic. It was difficult not to notice him. As he ambled down the halls pushing his walker, all the health care personnel, including nurses, doctors, and pharmacists, made a point of greeting him. The doctors' eyes would light up as Avrum affectionately shook their hands and wished them well.

Avrum needed to have his blood drawn weekly, and when he would approach the lab and ask if anyone was available, the nurses and lab technicians would even argue over the privilege! He used to divide his veins among the staff members: He would say, "This is Michoel's vein, this is Miriam's, and this is Nurit's..." Michoel, an immigrant from the former U.S.S.R., often won the rights to draw Avrum's blood, since as the only male working in the lab he was the only one who could actually give Avrum a hug, which he didn't hesitate to do. It was Michoel who said of him, "He was a small man with a big heart."

The laboratory staff explained that it was difficult to work on Avrum. On occasion it took as many as 12 punctures to get a good vein, while a second nurse held down his trembling arm. The nursing staff felt terrible about causing Avrum so much pain. Avrum reassured them: "Don't worry, don't worry, it's not your fault, it's my veins. Each puncture was preordained in Heaven." Not only would he gratefully thank them for their effort on his behalf, he never even let on that he was in pain.

Speaking about Avrum, Nurit, one of the lab technicians who also happened to be his former neighbor, described him as "one of the most special people" she knew. He was well loved by all the children of their building and made a habit of rewarding her daughters with a piece of chocolate whenever they brought home a good grade. She doesn't recall ever having heard him utter a negative word, and he never complained, although he certainly had what to complain about.

She described how friendly he was and how he would greet every doctor with his characteristic warmth. He didn't reserve his affection for his own physicians but would greet them all. He'd stop a strange doctor hurrying by and exuberantly call out, "Hi! How are you doing?" Perplexed, the doctor would turn to him and ask, "Do I know you?" To which Avrum would always reply, "Sure, we met at Har Sinai!"[1] After having his blood drawn, he would thank the nurses and wish them that they merit to meet soon in Yerushalayim. It was clear to all that he awaited the redemption with every fiber of his being.

When Avrum saw a soldier he would go up to him, grab his hand, and gush, "Thank you so much for all you do for us, for risking your life to protect us!" Sometimes the soldier would shrug it off and say, "No, you are protecting us with your *davening* and your learning!" They would argue back and forth for a bit, and Avrum would give the soldier a blessing: "Hashem should watch over you and protect you…"

Avrum was always happy and upbeat, except for those times when he came across flyers from *tzedakah* organizations collecting money for orphans and families in distress. At those times he would visibly sadden, and with a heartfelt sigh say, "Oh no, not another one; how can we stand it." He ached when he heard about the suffering of other Jews.

Torah learning was Avrum's refuge. When challenges arose that threatened to drag down his spirits, he would be heard saying, "I

---

1. The Torah was given to the Jewish nation on Mount Sinai. Our Sages teach that the souls of all Jews, including future converts, were also present at the giving of the Torah.

can't think about it, I'm just going to throw myself into my learning." He never went to sleep at night without first taking stock of all that happened that day and evaluating whether or not he had reacted appropriately or if he needed to improve in any particular area. He was someone who constantly worked on himself to become the best husband, father, and Jew possible.

As devoted as Avrum was to the service of G-d and his fellow man, he made sure never to forget about me. Although our marriage was complicated by the needs of all our children, their spouses, and our grandchildren, Avrum always made sure that I knew how important I was to him. He was available for me whenever I needed his wise advice or emotional support, giving me his full attention and really hearing me out. We had both been through a great deal, and had learned how to hold back from saying anything that would spark an argument. I tried to keep in mind that the more I built up my husband, the greater the husband, father, and Torah scholar he would become. Against the backdrop of all the pain we had endured, the beauty of our marriage shone bright.

Not only did Avrum care about me, but he genuinely cared for all of my children and their spouses as well. He found creative ways to keep all 17 of our children in mind when he prayed. On Shabbos, during the recitation of the Priestly Blessing of the *Shacharis* prayer[2] he kept his children in mind, and he thought of mine during *Birkas Kohanim* of *Mussaf*. It took a great deal of concentration to focus on the needs of all our children and their spouses, but since they meant so much to him he made sure to figure out a system that worked.

In the glow of the 20 Shabbos candles I kindled — besides two for Shabbos, there was one for each of our 17 children, and one for my beloved Leah Rose — we spent many beautiful Shabbos meals together. Avrum and I sat at opposite ends of our long table, and

---

2 In *Eretz Yisrael Birkas Kohanim*, the Priestly Blessing, is recited daily.

my sons and sons-in-law pressed close to Avrum as he kept them spellbound with his endless stories.

One of Avrum's favorite stories was about the Rebbe Reb Elimelech of Lizhensk and his brother, Reb Zishe of Anapoli. During the brothers' voluntary "exile," they were once thrown into prison. Conditions in the crowded cell were primitive, and a chamber pot stood in the center of the cell. At first the brothers were saddened that they would be prohibited from learning Torah and praying. When they thought further, they realized that their incarceration in the dank and offensive conditions was all part of G-d's will. As such, it was not an impediment to happiness. The two rabbis began to rejoice and dance around the pot. Soon, their fellow cellmates joined in the dancing, and the lively ruckus drew the attention of the prison guards. When they learned that the chamber pot was the reason for the commotion, they immediately removed it from the cell. Once again, the two spiritual giants were able to learn and pray.

For Avrum, this story symbolized his life's work. He worked hard to see all that life brought him — whether pleasant or painful — as Hashem's will, and thus a reason for rejoicing.

He was extremely sensitive to the needs of my children, giving special attention to those who he felt needed an extra dose of fatherly love. He made sure to compliment the children, "Mother and I are so proud of you for such and such…" Wanting to include everyone in the family *seudah*, Avrum would ask the children to suggest *zemiros* for the family to sing. He loved it when the boys would repeat Torah thoughts at the table, yet he never asked them to speak since he himself didn't like being put on the spot. He loved to tell jokes and had an excellent sense of humor.

The love and warmth that Avrum lavished upon my children was absorbed by them and reflected back upon us. They deeply respected my husband, and stood up for him when he entered the room. The children took his health problems in stride. When he was hospitalized, they pitched in with shopping and cooking for

Shabbos so that I was free to spend my time at Avrum's bedside.

We spent the first two years of our marriage in a rental apartment. A year or so into our marriage Avrum and I heard about a new building project going up near the Boyan *shul* at the top of our town. Since it was really difficult for Avrum to get around, I was quite excited about the idea of moving closer to the *shul*. We spoke to the real-estate agent and chose a nice five-room apartment with a quaint little garden in the building right next door to the *shul*.

It took the better part of a year for the financial details to be worked out and make use of our *aliyah* rights. Finally, we were ready to make a down payment. Amazingly, the apartment we had chosen a year earlier was still available! It just goes to show that when something's meant to be, it will all work out. We have merited to fill our new apartment with many happy memories of large family *Shabbosos* and *Yamim Tovim* over the years.

Avrum was called upon to help maintain quiet in *shul*. Anyone caught talking would be handed one of these little cards — with a candy attached to sweeten the message.

I did my best to enroll the children in schools that suited their personal temperaments, but when that didn't work out with some

"It's forbidden to talk during the prayer service"

of my teens I was flexible enough to think out of the box. Two of my daughters were actually homeschooled here in Israel during high school. Thanks to the efforts of a number of talented teachers living in the community, Leora and for a time Shira were provided with an excellent Jewish education tailored to their interests and strengths. We also put a lot of thought into setting Leora up in an appropriate apprenticeship. We wanted her to learn a trade from a woman who would also be a role model. Thus Leora became Morah Simi's assistant preschool teacher, and after her marriage she opened her own private preschool.

I was careful to honestly consider the needs of my children, choosing to ignore the dire warnings of those who insisted that taking my girls out of "the system" would be a death sentence to their already "compromised" *shidduch* prospects. I knew that G-d is the Ultimate Matchmaker, and that He would be there for us as He always had been. In retrospect it is clear to me that He led each of my daughters upon her own path.

When the time came, *baruch Hashem*, we had no shortage of marriage prospects for my girls. Estie married a *chassid* from New York at the age of 19. Shira attended high school in Jerusalem and then became a wig stylist. She later married an English-speaking young man from Southern Israel, and they belong to the *Litvish* community. Leora also identifies as *Litvish*, and Devora's husband is *chassidish*.

Hashem looked after my sons as well, sending them wonderful women of valor as wives. Our 10th wedding, that of my son Binyamin, was particularly memorable. I took special pride in preparing decorated brooms for each grandchild old enough to dance. Under twinkling chandeliers, I led my grandchildren in symbolically sweeping Binyamin, last of our children to marry, out the house. Joy welled up inside me at the sight of Binyamin's radiant bride, standing before us. I danced with winged feet, and my heart soared. I was the matriarch of a large family. I had grandchildren. And I was a Jew.

CHAPTER 20

Circles of Love

The years moved on by, molding and shaping Avrum and me and our children into a large blended family. Happy memories, holidays shared, and milestones celebrated created a new entity composed of very disparate parts. How I remember that first time Avrum's boys and my own single sons joined us for Pesach. Our teenage sons took upon themselves the task of Pesach cleaning and arranging the fish tank. It was obvious how much fun they were having together, so I didn't mind the hours upon hours spent on that single task. I was thrilled to see how much they enjoyed each other's company; so what if they spent the better part of the night engrossed in a game of chess? As long as they were developing a relationship, I wasn't complaining!

Avrum and I watched our children come to understand each other, even becoming a source of support for each other. The attention my mother-in-law lavished upon my daughters also went a long way in creating a cohesive family unit. She went out of her way to buy my daughters all sorts of beautiful things, from linen sets to Shabbos clothing. Each gift let my daughters know that they were cared for and considered part of the family.

One day in the early years of my marriage I met a young friend who commented on how happy I looked. Her own mother had remarried, and she had noticed that her mother became much stronger after remarrying. Her words made me realize even more how much I appreciated having someone to talk to and make decisions with. Additionally, as a newcomer to Judaism, I was particularly happy to finally have one definitive approach to *halachah*. Up until this point I had relied on my sons to guide me, since they were by far more knowledgeable than me. The problem was that often each of my sons followed different halachic opinions, and I would be left confused. Marrying Avrum gave me strength and stability in many different areas of my life!

Avrum urged me to continue developing my strengths and helped me to compensate for my weaknesses. From organizing speakers to getting involved in antimissionary work, he encouraged and supported me all the way. At one point I was contacted by a woman whose nephew had become involved with a missionary on his college campus. A young woman had approached him, befriending him and offering a host of well-used lines to steer him away from Judaism. Unfortunately, he didn't have a strong enough background to provide any rebuttal, but I was only too happy to help out. His aunt would email me his questions, and I would send back the answers. It was the least I could do for my people.

Years earlier, I had joined a writing group run by Faigel Safran. It was Faigel who subsequently recommended that I move on to Sarah Shapiro's writing group in Yerushalayim. Without Avrum's encouragement, I never would have gone. I gained a great deal from the experience. I always loved writing, but throughout high school the papers I proudly turned in were returned to me with a bunch of red marks. My teachers didn't seem to care as much about the content of my work; they were after perfect spelling and grammar. Sarah saw the beauty in each of us and what we had to share, irrespective of commas and quotation marks.

Avrum also encouraged me to attend Rebbetzin Heller's weekly

Torah class in the Old City. Every week women originating from all corners of the world walk over the ancient stones of the Jewish Quarter to Sara Yoheved Rigler's home and soar intellectually, emotionally, and spiritually with the Rebbetzin. In addition to her profound wisdom, I was enriched by her example of a highly spiritual and yet balanced *eishes chayil*.

Over the years, our children married and began families of their own. Still, our own home remained a magnet, and Shabbos and *Yom Tov* saw married children and grandchildren crowded around our table. I loved the way Avrum interacted with my sons and daughters-in-law. He made everyone who entered our home feel comfortable and valued, and he developed a special relationship with each one. People were so important to him that he always remembered previous conversations he'd had with them, often referring to them. He took a sincere interest in each family member and the projects he was involved in. He delighted in their successes, was pained by their troubles, and always tried to strengthen their marriages by praising the good qualities of each spouse in front of the other.

As a boy, my youngest son-in-law, Devora's husband, had attended Camp Ohr Shraga, a camp Avrum had also attended, albeit 30 years earlier. The warm and welcoming atmosphere of Camp Ohr Shraga had been the highlight of Avrum's childhood. On the *Shabbosos* that my son-in-law was present, Avrum would sing the *niggunim* that were sung in camp, all the while recalling those wonderful summers.

This newest son-in-law knew Avrum's rebbi from his Yeshivah Torah Vodaas days nearly 40 years ago. After my daughter's engagement, Avrum asked the *chassan* to buy him a set of tapes of Torah classes from his former rebbi, and when he received them he listened to them faithfully each day. Every time he saw my son-in-law, he made sure to thank him for changing his life!

A few weeks before our 10th anniversary, my daughter Shira and her husband came up from the southern town of Ofakim to spend Shabbos with us and her sisters. Unfortunately, Avrum took ill that Shabbos and had to be hospitalized. With Shira's sincere encouragement, her husband offered to accompany Avrum to the hospital.

Watching Avrum wrapped in blankets and gently lifted into the ambulance, Shira was struck for the first time by the full extent of his suffering. When Avrum noticed her hovering presence, he called out, "I'm sorry for taking your husband away from you. Have a good Shabbos and enjoy your sisters." Deeply touched by Avrum's concern in the midst of his own suffering, Shira ran back into the house, where she broke down in tears. "Hashem, how can one person suffer so much!" she cried. "Please bring an end to his suffering …."

Shira couldn't have known it then, but the full measure of Avrum's allotted suffering had almost been filled. Just six weeks later, Avrum was taken from us.

In December of 2011, Avrum and I celebrated our 10th wedding anniversary. Both of us independently called my mother-in-law and told her that these had been the best 10 years of our lives.

A few weeks later, my dear friend Lisa Elon came to Israel from Atlanta to visit. Our mutual friend Jackie had since moved to Jerusalem and the two of them made plans to come and see me on Wednesday morning. I was on a local bus when they called to tell me that they had arrived. Avrum was out at *kollel* and the front door was unlocked, so I told them to go on in and wait a few minutes until I got back.

Just as my bus pulled up in front of my building, Avrum's doctor in Hadassah Mount Scopus Medical Center called to let me know that my husband was in an ambulance on his way in.

Although I had accompanied Avrum to the hospital numerous times, I was completely shaken up by the doctor's call. A half-perceptible whisper told me that this time was going to be different. With a heavy heart, I entered my building. Then I remembered Lisa and Jackie waiting for me inside. What was I to do? How could

I go ahead and schmooze with my friends while my husband's life was in danger? But then again, I hadn't seen Lisa in years. How could I just ignore her?

I took a few moments to collect myself and put a smile on my face. I greeted Lisa and Jackie warmly. Only after acknowledging my visitors did I tell them that Avrum was on his way to the hospital. Shortly thereafter I received word that he was being transferred to Hadassah Ein Kerem. When we heard that the transfer was underway, the three of us jumped into a cab and sped off to the hospital.

We sat outside the Emergency Room watching all the comings and goings, entirely focused on not missing my husband's arrival. Finally, a group of paramedics ran past us with Avrum's stretcher. They brought him to a little cubicle, where a neurologist examined him. Avrum was conscious and obviously in terrible pain, which he did his best to mask. When the doctor asked him if he could smile, he answered, "For you, of course!" As usual Avrum used his charming sense of humor to keep our spirits up.

Suddenly, a neurological team entered, raised the sides of the bed, and took off down the hall with Avrum. My brother-in-law and I raced behind, trying to keep up. We reached the operating rooms. A surgeon came out to talk to us, explaining that a ruptured aneurysm had caused massive bleeding in Avrum's brain, necessitating emergency surgery. The surgery itself was relatively safe, but the blood that had already accumulated in his brain was threatening his life. The critical point would come in three days' time when we'd see how Avrum's body handled the clotted blood pressing on his brain. Before he headed back into the surgical suite, the doctor turned to us, "If you have any words to say, now is the time to say them."

In a state of shock, I looked over at Avrum. I longed for a few moments of privacy, yet the hum of activity around us made that impossible. Something inside told me that I must say goodbye — yet how could I say goodbye to my life's partner? I looked into

Avrum's pain-filled eyes and asked for forgiveness. Tears blurred my vision as Avrum asked for mine in return. And then he was gone, swallowed up by the cold steel walls of the operating room and a team of surgeons fighting for his life.

I sat down to pray, grateful that Lisa and Jackie were by my side. Two dear and comforting faces from the past now gave me strength, just as they had 20 years earlier at the bedside of Leah Rose.

After a number of hours, we received word that the surgery had been a success. Avrum was taken to the ICU for recovery, and Jackie took me to her home in Jerusalem to spend the night.

Early Thursday morning I was back at the hospital. Avrum was in a drug-induced coma, and we were only allowed in his room for short periods at a time. We called in his children from overseas. On Friday morning, Avrum's vital signs grew weak. The family gathered around his bedside. Heartbroken, we watched as his weak and battered body slowly loosened its hold on Avrum's lofty soul.

Jackie is a seasoned hospice volunteer, and she drew on her extensive experience to help me prepare myself. She also reached out to Avrum's children, helping them to see and understand the process taking place before them. She coached them to grab hold of the opportunity to express their final words of love and appreciation to their dying father, so that they would have some closure upon his passing.

Clear Divine Providence brought my son Yishai in from America just before Avrum's aneurysm. I found it such a comfort to have him at my side during this time. I spent Shabbos at the hospital together with my son, brother-in-law, and Avrum's sons. The end was drawing near, and we were no longer limited to short bursts of time at Avrum's bedside. To buoy our spirits, Avrum's oldest brother began to sing *zemiros* and our sons joined in. Avrum seemed to stabilize for a while, although his vital signs remained low.

That Shabbos, our songs formed a circle of love around the bed of my dying husband. As Jews have always done, we transcended our immediate pain, focusing instead on the special place in time and space where day-to-day life is suspended and the peace of Shabbos reigns. We thus gave tribute to Avrum, a man whose life personified the soul's ability to rise beyond the limits of a broken body and spread light in the darkness. That Shabbos we serenaded Avrum, escorting his soul on its journey to a place that is all and always Shabbos.

Shabbos came to an end. Avrum was still with us. There was no way to know how much longer it would be, and so I accepted my brother-in-law's offer of a ride back home. As I walked through the door, my daughters pounced on me, anxious for news of their beloved stepfather. Five minutes later, the phone rang. We were called back to the hospital. A neighbor took me and my daughters and their husbands back to Hadassah Medical Center.

On the way, my cell phone rang, and a nurse asked to speak with me. I refused to take the call. I was escorted to the hospital by my children's smothered whispers of *"Baruch Dayan HaEmes."*

Back in Avrum's room, we asked for his forgiveness. Each child took some private time to spill out some thoughts and spend a little more time with him.

Eventually we left, going to the home of Avrum's youngest brother in Yerushalayim. In keeping with the Yerushalmi custom, Avrum was laid to rest that very night, while the sanctity of Shabbos still hung in the air.

Numb with grief, overtaken by a deep chill that spread through my limbs, I huddled together with all our daughters on the women's side of the funeral home, listening to the eulogies. I noticed nothing of my surroundings, other than the eloquent words of my devoted brother-in-law and the sobbing of Avrum's daughters, which blended with the cries of my own girls. It struck me then that no outsider would be able to differentiate between Avrum's children and my own. In that moment of searing loss, I finally knew that we had indeed become a family.

All of Avrum's family piled into our home for the week of *shi-*

vah. His father, brothers, and sons sat in the living room, and his mother, daughters, and I sat in a bedroom. In finding Avrum, I had found peace after many trials and tribulations. Now I was a widow, but I was not alone. I thanked Hashem many times over for bringing me into such a wonderful family. Even as we mourned together, they enveloped me in a warm blanket of love and acceptance.

When my baby died I didn't sit *shivah*, but I cried for years. In Avrum's passing, I was granted the gift of *shivah*. It is an incredibly powerful experience. I felt cared for and comforted by the Jewish people, and I marveled at how the deep wisdom of the Torah's laws were so in sync with my emotions.

One afternoon I got up from a nap feeling the renewed pain of my open wound, with absolutely no desire to talk to anybody. I sat down on my low chair and looked at the two women who had come to comfort me. I said nothing. According to Torah law, one is only allowed to speak to a mourner after the mourner has acknowledged him. For many long minutes, the three of us sat in silence. Although no words passed between us, my grief was mirrored in their faces. The Torah laws provided the perfect guide at a time when even words failed.

In the days following *shivah* I asked all those I met, "Do you have any idea what it's like to have almost every one of your friends, relatives, and acquaintances come visit you in the span of just one week?" From Jerusalem, Bnei Brak, Tzefas, and Zichron Yaakov visitors came to comfort us and soothe the bitterness of our loss. There were the listeners, the weepers, the askers of questions, the storytellers who shared their experiences with Avrum, the intellectuals who spoke of *gilgulim* and preordained times, and the spiritual ones who brought us words of inspiration and comfort. My in-laws, neighbors, *shul* friends, doctors, and nurses: each visitor brought along a tiny part of Avrum, the part he or she had known and loved. And as I became acquainted with each color that sparkled from the prism that was Avrum's personality, I cried all over again.

Each story was a gift. I heard about Avrum's last day in *kollel*. How he collapsed, how CPR was performed, and an ambulance was summoned. As Hatzalah wheeled him out of the room, Avrum looked up at these men he had spent hundreds of hours through- out the years studying with and called out, "I love you all!" Those were the last words he spoke in his beloved study hall.

The varied personalities of my visitors brought me comfort on a number of different levels. Each one's offerings appealed to a different aspect of my own character, a satisfying experience for us multifaceted creatures. My phone was not working well during the week of *shivah*, and afterward we found over 100 messages on my voice mail, testimony to the many people who reached out to us even though they were unable to come. It was like one great big bear hug from *Klal Yisrael*.

My children's tributes were particularly meaningful. As Shira said, "He never, ever criticized us." And in the words of Dovid, "Reb Avrum had so much warmth, respect, and intelligence. He knew when to leave things alone and when to speak up. Everyone loved him, the Arabs he encountered and all the bus drivers in the city. Perceptive as well as tremendously empathetic, he had a unique gift of knowing what to say to each person. Reb Avrum had a deeply held *ahavas habriyos*, love for G-d's creations. He didn't love just Jews, but every human being he encountered."

The week of *shivah* was a time of mixed emotions. I was both devastated by my loss and happy to be together with Avrum's chil- dren, and my children, who were mostly in the kitchen, helping out behind the scenes. I was honored to have my home filled with many Torah scholars and respected personages, yet it was heart- wrenching to lose Avrum and bid farewell to the happiest years of my life. Still, I was relieved that he was no longer suffering. So often I'd heard him say, "I just want to be well!" Now he was no longer in pain; his soul had at last moved beyond the constraints of his disabled body.

Having traveled a long, dark journey with Leah Rose's passing, I had been forced to strengthen my belief and trust in G-d. The coping skills I had developed over the years helped me handle Avrum's death without getting lost in the grief.

During the *shivah*, one of my callers told me that as the soul of the deceased first begins its ascent on high, the family below experiences much blessing. Indeed, in the year of Avrum's passing we merited many happy tidings. We have seen the birth of many babies in the family, as well as the marriage of Avrum's youngest daughter.

Yet for all the *simchos*, there have also been times of loneliness and challenge. Even as the family gathers around on *Shabbosos* and holidays, Avrum's seat remains empty. And still there have been moments when the pain of his loss lessens somewhat, times when I open my heart to feel Hashem's deep love.

One of those times was this past Chanukah. It was *Motza'ei Shabbos*, the 25th of Kislev 5773, and I was on my way back home from a Shabbos spent with my children. The bus swayed from side to side as we traveled through the dark night, twisting and turning out of the picturesque northern village, where my children live, back down to Yerushalayim. I glanced over at my three grandchildren returning with me and saw them nodding off into the peaceful world of slumber. I set aside the nagging thoughts of the logistics involved in transferring my sleeping crew and all of our belongings onto the connecting bus, and relaxed into the upholstered seat.

I watched the peaceful nighttime countryside and let my mind wander back over the events of Shabbos, the past week, and the recent months. It had been a hard year, full of ups and downs, progress and setbacks, and through it all *nachas* amid the pain. Hashem had really challenged us this year, pushing a number of my married children to new heights of *emunah* and *bitachon* as they struggled through their own custom-designed trials. And yet my children have rallied, supporting each other with so much love and caring.

That Shabbos we had welcomed the newest little Massey into the covenant of Avraham Avinu, a precious new life full of untapped potential, a pure sweet gift from Hashem. In the afternoon I returned to my son's home to grab a few minutes of much-needed rest. As I slept, my granddaughters gathered in the dining room for their weekly *Tehillim* group. The youthful trill of their voices chanting the timeless words of King David filled my children's small home with a melodious harmony so perfectly holy and pure.

The beautiful voices penetrated my room, transporting me gently from the world of my dreams briefly back to the present before returning me to the days of my youth and the vision of my own mother reciting her beloved Psalms. Mother clutched her book of Psalms in times of stress and challenge. It was those Psalms that helped her through the dark months of her grief after my father passed on, leaving her bereft and rudderless. And now, in my own vulnerable state of widowhood I remembered the strength she drew from those Psalms, and felt my bruised heart relax into the soothing caress of the ancient words borne aloft by my granddaughters.

My thoughts returned to the present and the long bus ride stretching before me. That night was the first night of Chanukah, and the anniversary of the first Jewish holiday we celebrated as a family. In the darkness of Lookout Mountain, on a hastily constructed *menorah*, we had kindled lights of warmth and hope. Just a year later, on the very first night of Chanukah, Leah Rose slipped away from us.

I remembered my first Chanukah as Mrs. Berger, celebrated with such joy by just Avrum and me a few short weeks after our wedding. I eagerly soaked up every cherished moment we spent together that evening, our first holiday as a couple. That night, Avrum introduced me to his family's beautiful *minhagim*. I watched as he placed a little table opposite our door and lovingly set up his *menorah*. As Avrum kindled the first light, I felt the prickle of tears in my eyes. He began to sing his haunting version of *Maoz Tzur*, and the tears spilled over and coursed down my cheeks. For the first time I was a Jewish wife standing faithfully, lovingly at my husband's side.

As the years progressed, Avrum was no longer able to set up the little table on his own. Eventually, he wasn't even able to prepare his *menorah* by himself. His arms trembled and flailed, making it all but impossible for him to fill the little glass cups of oil. Watching him struggle to kindle those lights was a lesson in perseverance. It took many long minutes until finally he was able to hold his candle over the wick long enough for it to burst into flame. Last year, the tremors had gotten so bad that I had held each little glass cup so that Avrum wouldn't knock them over as he lit the *menorah*.

Yet how I missed those times! Even though it hurt to see Avrum struggle so, at least he was still with us. I sat on the bus, envisioning my homecoming that evening. The apartment would be dark. Worse, it would be empty of the joy and love that Avrum radiated. I hadn't had time to set up the table and *menorah* before my trip. I couldn't even remember if I was supposed to light from right to left or from left to right. My children had all flown my nest to build homes of their own. This would be my first Chanukah on my own, all alone.

By the time I had delivered my grandchildren to their parents, it was late. I was devastated at the thought of entering my empty apartment to kindle the Chanukah lights alone. As my key turned in the lock, I was greeted by a wonderful surprise: my youngest daughter, her husband, and children had lit up my lonely home.

On the very first Chanukah night since the passing of my dear husband, it was my newest *chassidish* son-in-law, who had shared such a beautiful relationship with Avrum, who helped me set up my *licht*. We filled the small cups of Avrum's silver *menorah* with the purest of olive oils, produced by my children up north. My son-in-law coached me through the lighting. Together we kindled a flame that dispelled the heavy darkness of night. Warm memories of my dear husband filled my home and heart with happiness, reminding me that a Jew is never truly alone.

The months passed by, bringing more holidays and more *simchos*, each one beautiful and yet bittersweet. Each milestone takes me by the hand and teaches me that life continues on.

This past Lag BaOmer, my sister-in-law and I decided to join the thousands traveling to Meron to mark the *yahrzeit* of the great Talmudic sage, Rabbi Shimon bar Yochai. We journeyed through the night, and at 5 a.m., with just a few kilometers to go, we decided to circumvent the crawling traffic and make our way to the tomb by foot.

Squeezing ourselves between the buses clogging both lanes, Shoshana Bracha and I linked arms with her sister, sisters-in-law, and nieces to form a chain of women making our way up the mountain in the freshness of dawn.

A handwritten list detailing the names of my children, Avrum's children, and our grandchildren was firmly tucked in between my *siddur* and my *Sefer Tehillim*. Finally we reached the entrance to the tomb. The first sounds of the sunrise *minyan* could be heard from over the *mechitzah*, mingling with the happy strains of song from the band outside. The music enveloped me, reverberating off the ancient stone walls, wrapping me in chords of yearning, opening up my heart before my Maker until I was nothing more than prayer itself. The outer mask I wear to shield others from the raw ache of my loneliness fell away, completely exposing my vulnerability. I lost myself in prayer, beseeching G-d to help me, our children, and our children's children serve Him in happiness and good health. I sat on the stone steps, weeping. I was surrounded by thousands of people, and yet I was alone with my Creator.

When I felt ready, I left the tomb with Shoshana Bracha at my side and caught a fresh egg sandwich from the overflowing boxes above thrown down to the women by the volunteers. I was touched once again by the thoughtful kindness of my special people. So much work and love went into welcoming the hundreds of thousands of people who converge on Meron each year.

Shoshana Bracha and I decided to head over to the large tent erected especially for those who have come to celebrate their son's first haircut. My niece and her family were among those celebrating, and so we decided to wait for them in the tent.

I entered the tent and was immediately mesmerized. Hundreds of dancing men whirled about in the center of the tent, their wives looking on from the bleachers above. At the very center were dozens of little boys — yesterday's babies — bobbing up and down on their father's shoulders. Grandfathers, uncles, and brothers formed circles inside circles of exuberant participants in a human chain of love and joy that seemed to stretch back through the generations and forward into the future.

I have heard music before, but the hymns sung in my youth couldn't touch the authenticity and vibrancy of those songs. I have seen crowds of spectators gather to watch impressive feats of sportsmanship, but the vitality of yesterday's athletes falls short of the burning enthusiasm I absorbed on that day. Professional athletes train for years and push themselves hard, yet even they will age out of the game. Yet love of G-d is never outgrown, and those *zeidies* were dancing and sweating right alongside their sons and grandsons. The rings and rings of circles celebrating the launching of those boys onto their own cycle of service reassured me of the continuity of our people. Even after my dear husband had passed on to the World of Truth, I paused to think of a grandson who carries his name and who would soon claim his own place in this cycle of life.

The day faded into evening. Shoshana Bracha and I headed out, down the hill to the buses and the drive home. I sat beside my sister-in-law, feeling so full that I had no need to talk.

The words of a woman I had encountered in my youth rang true for me on that day as I journeyed back to my own home in *Eretz Yisrael*: "Honey, there's a hole inside each of us that only G-d Himself can fill."

Epilogue

W hen I last visited the home of my youngest sister, Lesa, I was fascinated by her antique candlesticks, enthralled by their possible significance. They had been passed down in my family, from mother to daughter for generations. What I couldn't understand was why I never knew about them.

Lesa believes that although our family was affiliated with Christianity for centuries we are, in fact, descendants of Jews. She feels that Mother suppressed her Jewish heritage during Daddy's lifetime. When I spoke with Lesa about her theory, a conversation I'd once had with my mother's sister, Aunt Mary, came to mind: "You know, Mother and Daddy always said we were Jews from Spain."

As I contemplated my Aunt Mary's words, scattered impressions and snippets of long-forgotten conversations, which I had long ago written off as strange, reawakened within me. There was the time when I was just a little girl and I overheard someone mention that Grandpa Dugger had said that we were Jews. In my mind's eye I can still see how Daddy dismissed the idea with a disbelieving grunt and a wave of his hand. If Daddy felt so strongly about our supposed Jewishness, I was convinced that he must have been right.

I also understood that Mother didn't believe that we were Jewish. It wasn't quite what she said that led me to that conclusion, it was more how she referred to Jews. I remember her telling me about Israel's astounding capture of Adolf Eichmann from under the noses of the Argentinean government. I heard both the amazement as well as the distance in her voice each time she said, "Those Jews are so smart!"

Although my memories of my parents would lead me to believe that there is no substance to our supposed Jewish roots, I do in fact have a number of memories that point to a possible Jewish connection. Like the summers I spent with Aunt Naomi and Uncle Gordon up at the ranch in Washington. Each night, my uncle prayed for the peace of Jerusalem, a prayer the likes of which I have never heard any self-respecting Christian say. Some of their fellow congregants in their place of worship were also pretty strange. Each Sabbath I had been struck by the sight of a group of elderly bearded men sitting together on old benches at the front of the room. It wasn't just their long beards that caught my attention. Their entire manner was unusual, and the way they sang seemed to me entirely bizarre. Till this day I can still hear their gruff voices bellowing out the words to some Germanic song that sounded something like, *"G-tt es der libi…"*

They say that Uncle Gordon himself hailed from a family of German-speaking Sabbath-keepers in North Dakota, yet when he went to Israel to help Grandpa Dugger with the magazine he was publishing, he learned that the German he spoke was in fact Yiddish. Today I wonder if perhaps those old men I saw singing in "German" all those years ago weren't Christian after all.

Growing up, I didn't see much of Granma and Grandpa Dugger, since they passionately loved the Land of Israel and decided to settle there. In time it seems that they began to identify with her Jewish inhabitants. As a child, I resented the fact that my beloved grandparents had chosen to live among Jews.

Granma Dugger wrote a magazine column entitled "Life in Israel." Spanning 30 years, this became something of a journal of her personal experiences. As I read through her writings, I was astounded by the many positive things she had written about the Jews:

"The smallest child of the Orthodox Jews will not so much as pick a flower on the Sabbath."

"All tourists…marvel how the people of Israel have caused this land to blossom and bring forth fruit."

"It is the custom in the synagogues to pray for rain at the end of the Succot period. The answer came promptly this year. Within two days there was a lovely warm and soaking rain from Metulla to Eilat."

"I was sorry that my husband printed an old picture of us. We do not look much like that picture now, being about 15 years older. Besides, now I always wear a covering on my head…"

Her entry marked May 1959 read, "I always wondered why Rachel was not buried in the family burial place at Hebron eighteen miles farther south." I find it ironic that she struggled with this question, whose answer would one day be well known by her many Israeli great-great-grandchildren while still in preschool!

(Catherine) Great-great-great Grandma Grimm

Grandma Grimm was born March 25, 1828, was married at 15, and had 238 descendants at her death at the age of 92. She would faithfully light her candles on Friday night.

It is clear to me that along with following some Jewish practices, my ancestors felt a deep connection to the Jewish people. Lesa and her family lived in Israel for a while, and about a decade after Daddy's death Mother lived with Lesa in Israel for a year. It was in Israel that Lesa confronted Mother with the possibility of her having Jewish roots, citing her long-held family practices of soaking and salting meat as well as circumcising their 8-day-old sons. At first Mother denied that possibility, but over time she began to open up just a little bit.

Once, as Mother watched Lesa form invisible circles in the air before covering her face and making the blessing over her Sabbath candles, she called out, "That's just the way Granma Carpenter did it!"

She then recalled how as a young girl she had watched Granma Carpenter lighting candles in her back room just before sundown. She was mesmerized by the sight of her Granma covering her eyes with her aged and wrinkled hands as she prayed for her children after candle lighting.

My Great-great-great-grandmother, Granma Catherine Bowers Grimm, and her children, including my Great-great-grandmother Arminda Mira Carpenter..

All of this has sparked my interest in researching my lineage and looking for a definite Jewish ancestor. I have traced my matriarchal line back through the years, from Oregon to Nebraska and Missouri, then back to Indiana and Ohio, until I encountered my earliest documented ancestor in America: Susanna Leslie (Walther), who married in Lancaster, Pennsylvania, in 1749 and bore 11 children.

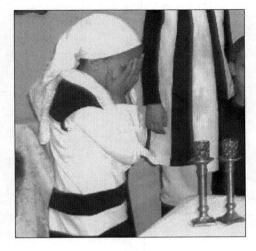

Seven generations after Granma Grimm, my oldest daughter's oldest daughter awaits the day when she too will light the Shabbos candles, as a Jew from birth.

With Susanna, my research dead-ends. There is no documentation of her country of origin or of the names and burial places of her parents. Was this a deliberate attempt on her part to hide her past? Or were these records lost through some other means? I have no concrete proof, yet as my study of genealogy continues more and more pieces of the puzzle come together. I am confident that one day the complete picture will come to light.

And as for me and my "mountain family"? We pray that we merit continued tranquility and growth in *Eretz Yisrael*, basking in the light of Hashem's Torah and His people.

The Next Generation

Estie's Story

Estie was my sixth child, and yet she holds the distinction of being my first daughter. The austere conditions in which I managed my home on the mountain slowly drained me of my femininity. I was too busy with survival to begin to think about my clothing, appearance, or beautifying my home. I was much more concerned with keeping my house warm, my husband and five sons fed, and educating my children. Yet as my little girl grew, I found my own innate femininity begin to thaw in the sunshine of her girlish delight in flowers and pretty dresses. I still marvel at the princess our family managed to produce in the raw backwoods culture of Appalachia.

Here is a brief glimpse of Estie's life, through her own mind's eye.

Even when I was little I knew that I didn't want to be like the people on the mountain. We were raised with a strong inner pride, and I always felt a cut above the simple country folk. In retrospect, I find it interesting that despite being raised in poverty I never felt poor. I have no recollection of deprivation, and I do not remember ever going hungry or even feeling cold. It seems to me that I was so filled up with love that I never noticed what I lacked. We were considered poor even by hillbilly standards, but I was never jealous of the other children on the mountain. It was clear to me that we were somehow different and special.

My earliest memories of the time we spent living on the mountain are mostly positive. Although I do remember being terrified of snakes, I also have many pleasant memories of my early childhood. Nestled in the warmth of my loving family, I grew up secure in the knowledge that I could count on my parents and my older brothers to keep me safe.

I fondly recall my mother's lessons. These went well beyond the classic textbook curriculum. My mother made a point of teaching us concepts such as caring for others, anger management, self-control, and taking responsibility for one's actions. When I was about 4 years old, my mother's sister Anita got engaged, and she chose me to be a flower girl at her wedding. I was very excited, and the best part of it all were the gowns my aunt commissioned for all of her flower girls and bridesmaids. I was given two beautiful dresses, one yellow and one purple. I was even able to take one of my dresses back home with me.

There was a family on the mountain that lived in a trailer and had a pool in their backyard. When we returned from Aunt Anita's wedding, Mother explained that this family was quite poor and didn't have enough clothing for their children. Since they had a plastic swimming pool, I had assumed that they were rich, but I trusted Mother; if she said they were poor, then poor they must be. One morning, Mother and I put the dress in a bag and left it on the doorstep of the trailer for the little girls in the family. The happiness I experienced from that act of giving has stayed with me all these years.

To teach us to be sensitive to others — including people who were mentally deficient and thus generally shunned by the mountain folk — Mother would occasionally take us to visit a woman she greatly admired. Mrs. Shipman was a very special woman who devotedly cared for her three retarded sons. These boys — actually fully grown men — received excellent care and were always well dressed; their clothes were neat and clean and freshly ironed. Their mother hand-washed all their diapers and saw to her sons' many needs while maintaining a happy and upbeat attitude. Mother taught us to think about what sort of gift the "boys" would most enjoy. We brought a candy bar for one, a toy car for another, and a book for the third. I still remember the look on Lester's face as he rocked back and forth in his chair, happily flipping through the pages of his new book. This was another of Mother's great lessons, designed to teach us the joy of giving and to delight in the happiness of others. Her lesson was a success.

Mother felt strongly about developing our characters, and in addition to the "field trips" that taught us to become givers, she had two other powerful tools: sharing stories of other people's lives so that we would learn from their mistakes, and the use of carefully considered punishments when necessary. When I was 5, I once tore off all the buttons of one of my shirts. I wondered how Mother would respond. Mother never trained us to say "I'm sorry." She wasn't interested in us mumbling a string of meaningless words. She wanted a change in behavior. Until this day I am impressed by how she responded to my loss of control. I was calmly yet firmly informed that it would be my responsibility to mend my blouse by sewing all the buttons back on. I was only 5 years old and did not know how to sew. Mother sat with me and patiently taught me how to sew buttons so that I would be able to take responsibility for my actions and fix that which I had damaged.

Mother would tell us a powerful story to impress upon us the great danger of unbridled anger. She told us about a happy couple who got into an argument. In a moment of anger, the husband threw a pair of scissors at his wife, tearing open her face from the nose all the way down her cheek. The large, ugly scar left was a constant painful reminder of her husband's lack of control, and she ran off to New York, the city they had always dreamed of living in, and spent the rest of her life living in seclusion. Although the forlorn husband crossed the Atlantic in search of his wife, the couple was never reunited. The story imprinted upon us the lesson of how one moment of anger can ruin an entire life.

As the oldest Massey daughter, I certainly held a place of distinction in my family. While I was given special attention, I also had to carve out a niche for myself. Figuring out just who I was and what was expected of me was an ongoing process. I remember watching Elijah and Jesse climbing a huge tree near our home. It was obvious how much they loved climbing, savoring the thrill of the challenge as well as the satisfaction of reaching a perch high into the sky. I was inspired to follow their lead. The only problem was that I didn't particularly enjoy climbing trees. Not one to give up easily, I worked hard to develop a liking for my brothers' exciting sport. Try as I might, though, I never did learn to enjoy tree climbing. I just couldn't stand the resulting scrapes and scratches that

My sisters and me

my brothers so easily took in stride. Finally, reluctantly, I decided that tree climbing just wasn't for me.

One year, my older brothers bought two little dogs as birthday presents for me and my younger brother, Benton. They were adorable little beagles which we named Tramp and Trotter. We didn't give them much attention. We rarely took them out for a walk or to play, and due to their small size we had to keep them tied up close to home to prevent them from becoming tasty meals for wild animals. I had no idea that our pets were that vulnerable, and I felt that bad that they spent their days tied up. The day came when I could no longer endure seeing my pet suffering the injustice of living under such confining conditions. In a selfless act of mercy, I decided to let my dog go free. When no one was looking, I untied my furry little pet and happily watched him scamper off into the freedom of the beautiful world beyond our yard. He never returned.

Later that night I overheard my brothers discuss the mysterious disappearance of my dog. My little act of heroism lost its luster when I heard them say, "He's probably been eaten by the coyotes by now." To this day I feel a bit silly admitting that it was I who let him go.

However, I found other opportunities to save helpless little creatures. My father would often bring home honey from one of the many beehives we kept on Husky Farm. I was excited by the sweet and sticky mess that inevitably formed in our backyard when transferring the honey, but I just couldn't stand the sight of the poor bees that got trapped. Once again, I stepped into the role of heroine, and at the tender age of 6 I officially opened a bee hospital. I would wash down the struggling little fellows, carefully gauging the amount of water I used: too much and they would drown, too little and they remained prisoner. I was ecstatic every time one of my patients actually got free! One morning I ran outside barefoot to check on my bees and stepped on one of my patients, who had no mercy for his would-be savior and viciously stung me. My entire leg swelled up, and I was unable to walk for an entire week. I relinquished my dream of rescuing creatures in distress.

I remember going with my grandfather to draw water from the well. I must have been about 3 years old when I noticed that Grand-dad collected water in buckets that he had gotten from a nearby baking company. I was delighted to discover that one of the lids still had traces of dried-up cake frosting, and quickly snuck a lick. Granddad saw what I had done and carefully admonished me not to sample the frosting for fear that it might contain traces of lard. As soon as he turned his back, I went for another lick and was caught in the act. This time Granddad was rather stern with me, and managed to impress upon me that eating a possibly forbidden food was not something that I wanted to do.

As I grew, my parents' religious beliefs became more and more a part of my own life. It was clear to us that there was a Creator, and yet I was also aware that my parents were still searching for the true religion. I, too, was caught up in the quest, and anxiously awaited the time when we would find our path. I remember attending a *bris* one Friday night at the Conservative synagogue in Chattanooga, Tennessee. It was a classy, black-tie affair, with waiters dressed in tuxedos circulating through the crowd with trays of hors d'oeuvres. I was very curious to see what sort of goodies sat atop that big tray, yet when the waiter asked me if I wanted anything I was too shy to say yes. I was surprised to see that the baby's mother was dressed in a very undignified manner. I knew that my parents would be upset with that, and I was not at all surprised that that turned out to be our last Shabbos at the Conservative synagogue in Chattanooga.

As far as I remember, the next stop along our family's quest in search of G-d's people was an Orthodox *shul*, also in Chattanooga, Tennessee. Eight of us kids packed like sardines into our small Pinto. When we arrived, a number of congregants ran over to watch two adults and eight children spilling out of a tiny car. In contrast to our brief exposure to Conservative Judaism, our relationship with Rabbi and Rebbetzin Katz developed into a friendship that endures more than 20 years later.

In fact, it was at the Katz home that I had my first taste of Manischewitz wine, which has remained my favorite. The *challah* was great, but I was scared off by the gefilte fish, which I thought was soggy bread with a fishy taste. I was thrilled with my purple velvet dress with the white lace collar that I got to wear to *shul*.

On our first visit to the Katzes' house, Rebbetzin Toby Katz told me that she was going to teach me how to pray. "The first thing you need to do," she said, "is take the gum out of your mouth." With that introduction, she managed to impress her 7-year-old pupil with the seriousness of prayer.

Even though the congregation in Chattanooga was primarily composed of senior citizens, I loved going to *shul*. One Shabbos I was surprised to find a little girl my age in *shul*. I was very excited by the opportunity to finally have a Jewish friend. Tightly grasping the hand of my 3-year-old sister Suzy, I lost no time in getting to know the first Jewish girl my age I had ever met. Was I ever shocked when I heard her call her own little sister a brat! I protectively clutched Suzy to shelter her from the harsh words this little girl had spoken. I stalked off, determined not to keep company with the likes of such a girl!

The five youngest Massey children: Jenny, Benton and Suzy, Debra and Lyn

It wasn't until we moved to Atlanta that I finally made friends with Jewish girls. The drive out to Atlanta was even longer than the trip to Chattanooga, but it was certainly worth it! We had many wonderful experiences during the three years that we lived in Atlanta. The community was very warm and accepting, and I loved our neighbors, the Elons. Their daughter Mimi became my first Jewish friend. I remember our first Shabbos in Atlanta, and how I excitedly got dressed in my Shabbos clothes. I thought I looked great in my colorful plaid skirt and coordinating yellow T-shirt, emblazoned with a picture of a wolf under a beautiful sunset. *Baruch Hashem*, my fashion sense has developed quite a bit since then!

The Elons hosted us that first Shabbos in Atlanta, and Mimi and I began a serious *chavrusa* in *alef-beis*. I was an eager pupil and she was a very devoted teacher. Although I much preferred playing at my friends' houses, they seemed to flock to ours. My active brothers had a host of creative games that they had come up with over the years, and just watching them immersed in play kept my friends transfixed for hours!

My younger sisters and I were thrilled with the modern conveniences of life in the big city. We still chuckle over Suzy's excitement upon discovering that our new home had a little room that sprayed water from the ceiling and made prickles on your back! I loved the hustle and bustle of city life, and my naturally extroverted nature blossomed in the faster-paced culture that thrived around us. The only thing I really had difficulty adjusting to was wearing shoes. I missed the feel of the soft and forgiving earth under my bare feet. I went through my fair share of skinned knees until experience finally taught me that which my early childhood environment hadn't: when living in the city, you had to walk the walk and talk the talk to keep out of trouble. I had left the flexibility of country life behind, and now I had to learn to conform to society.

At some point during our first few months in Atlanta, I became aware that my mother was suffering from some sort of pregnancy complication. The stability of my loving family that had nurtured me from when I was an infant began to crumble. I remember the community pulling together to support us during that very difficult time when Leah Rose hovered between life and death. People sent in meals, and teenage girls came over to help care for my younger siblings. For all the support the community offered us, nothing could compensate for the gaping void that appeared in my sheltered life with the breakdown of our family unit. In my mind's eye, the wonder of joining the *frum* community in Atlanta was seriously marred by the death of my baby sister, Mother's pain and suffering, and my parents' subsequent divorce.

There was, however, a magnificent silver lining to the dark cloud of my family's bitter experiences: the magical experience of learning in Atlanta's Jewish day school. The best years of my Jewish school experience were spent in the cheery classrooms of grades four through six in Atlanta. Many of my classmates' parents had come to Atlanta in order to teach Torah to nonaffiliated Jews, and their accepting attitude rubbed off on their daughters. Everyone in the class wanted to sit next to me, and I was unanimously accepted as one of their own even though I hadn't yet converted. When one of our teachers called on me to read from the *Chumash*, I got overwhelmed and burst into tears. There was an uproar in the classroom as 10 9-year-old girls began shouting, "But she doesn't know Hebrew!" Some of the more empathetic girls even came over to comfort me.

Although only my older brothers actually converted while we were living in Atlanta, we all knew how to fit in. The food and snacks we brought to school were purchased in Kroger's, Atlanta's kosher grocery, and since we had lived a very sheltered life back on the mountain we hadn't been exposed to inappropriate concepts or coarse language. Unfortunately, some of the new friends we encountered hadn't been protected as well!

During my second year in the day school, Rabbi Rosenbaum, our principal, introduced a school motto: "I am a worthwhile person because I am a *tzelem Elokim*, and everything I say and do must show that I am a *tzelem Elokim.*" This sentence was displayed on the walls of the school, and every student recited it daily before class began. Those words had a profound effect on me, and during my first years in Israel they were a balm to my spirit as I struggled to find my place in an entirely new culture. The knowledge that I am a worthwhile person and that I have been given the mission of representing Hashem in this world is something that I carry with me always, and no one can ever take it away from me. Today, this is the message that I seek to instill in the minds of my own precious children.

Ever since my parents came to the conclusion that Orthodox Judaism was G-d's true religion, I was able to completely accept their judgment and didn't doubt that they were correct. I took to Judaism as a fish to water, and was anxiously awaiting the day we would finally convert. If we had to move to Baltimore in order to finally become Jews, I wasn't going to stand in the way of progress.

Baltimore was a whole new experience. I was very excited to begin living as a full-fledged member of the Jewish people. I had no doubt that this was the true religion; it felt so real to me and not foreign at all. I didn't have the slightest sense that I was giving up anything or sacrificing in any way by becoming a Jew.

In Baltimore, my mother finally managed to extricate herself from the fog that had clouded her sunny personality since Leah Rose's passing. We became very close with our new neighbors, the Rings, and their support and warmth went a long way in easing the fear and discomfort we children experienced from living in a new neighborhood. Although we only lived in Baltimore for one year, I made a number of good friends, and kept in touch with my old friends in Atlanta as well. In fact, my old friends missed me so much that my class decided to chip in and buy me a plane ticket back to Atlanta so that they could see me.

We were very excited when Dovid became a *chasan,* and the Rings saw to it that we had a lovely time with them during Mother's trip to Israel. They even held a mock wedding for us so that we wouldn't feel left out.

Mother came home from Israel very inspired and immediately began to arrange our family's relocation to Israel. Unfortunately, I did not share her enthusiasm; in fact, I was quite nervous about making *aliyah*. I was still recovering from our difficult years in Atlanta and was finally beginning to adjust to our new life in Baltimore. The news that we would now be moving to Israel hit me like a ton of bricks. Ever since I had my first taste of Bamba, I knew that our brothers in the Holy Land represented an entirely new culture; I mean, who would think to combine *peanut butter* with cheese curls?

I had a hard enough time learning the ropes at my new school in Baltimore; I was scared to start all over again in yet another school, in a new country, in a different language. Perhaps it was the reassuring words my principal in Baltimore scrawled on the bottom of my report card that gave me the courage to begin again. In addition to the grades that summed up my first year in a large, mainstream Bais Yaakov, she penned, "Keep trying and you will reach the stars."

We arrived in Israel in the middle of the summer, and although I was happy to finally be reunited with all my brothers, especially Yishai, who had been my companion back home, I was anxious about getting into a new school. I was only 13, and wanted nothing more than to find a school that would accept me into their eighth grade.

I finally did get accepted into the Bais Yaakov of our neighborhood, but the culture gap between me and my Sefardi classmates was just too big for us to bridge. I soon transferred to a Bais Yaakov in another town that boasted a larger American student body. The girls were nice, but due to the spotty transportation, I had to board with a local family. There was one aspect of that experience that I really enjoyed, and that was learning *halachah*. Since I had had to learn any relevant *halachos* in order to convert, I was well versed in *halachah*, and I was surprised to find that my knowledge surpassed that of my Israeli counterparts! In recognition of my achievements, my principal presented me with a set of *halachah sefarim*.

Unfortunately my success was short-lived, since I wasn't accepted to a high school that suited me. A well-known rebbetzin who had a close relationship with my family allowed me to sit in on the classes in her seminary and join them for trips as well. The girls were very friendly and went out of their way to make me feel included, yet once again I found myself adjusting to an entirely new mentality. Though I was excited to once again be in the company of fellow Americans, my new friends were primarily from New York, and their big-city mentality was nothing like the unassuming companionship I had experienced back in Atlanta. It took me time to realize that by asking me questions, my new friends were trying to involve me in conversation, and not simply prying.

Meanwhile I had become friends with Chaya Berger, whose family had moved to Israel from the Midwest. Chaya attended a Yiddish-speaking school, so we never did end up going to school together. Interestingly, our mothers also were very close friends. I was quite frustrated at this point since I realized that my place wasn't really in a seminary with girls who were four years older than me. Chaya realized that something had to be done, so she took action. She took it upon herself to teach me a rudimentary Yiddish. After extensive practice I was finally able to say, *"Ich vill lernen in Biyan*—I would like to learn in Boyan."

As soon as I had mastered the complexities of my first Yiddish sentence, Chaya called up the principal of her school to try to get me accepted. The principal told me she had a better idea; she would help get me into a school with girls my own age. Recognizing that I would do best in an English-speaking environment, she pulled some strings and got me accepted to a seminary in Europe.

Before I was accepted, I was warned about the dress code and told that I would need to wear beige stockings. After all I had been through wearing beige stockings was nothing, but in this country

I was once again on unfamiliar turf and had to find my way in a community that was different from anything I had yet experienced. Not only was this the first time that I learned with *chassidish* girls, but they were European to boot! I started to wonder if something was wrong with me; for so long I had been trying to find my place in society, and yet I still felt terribly lost. In retrospect, I now understand that my feelings didn't come from an innate confusion but were the result of constantly transferring from community to community. I was 15, and yet this was the seventh major adjustment I had made — beginning with Appalachia.

The seminary did have the advantage of being an international school, so I wasn't the only foreigner. I became good friends with the other American girls, and I also spent some time with the Israelis. I had a distinct advantage over the Israelis in that I was completely fluent in English. I still chuckle at the memory of an outing I took with my fellow Israelis shortly after arriving in Europe. I remember how we ran to catch our bus, and even pushed our way on as the locals looked on incredulously. After we were already seated, we observed with mounting surprise how the proper European travelers waited patiently in their queue for their turn to board the bus. We were absolutely shocked to see that the bus driver actually waited for everyone to be seated before he pulled out of the bus stop! At that point we all realized how out of place our own behavior had been when contrasted with proper European etiquette.

No one in sem had any inkling that I was a *giyores*, and my colorful background remained a secret during my sojourn abroad. For the most part I did my best to blend in; I made some good friends and spent a lot of time visiting the local nursing home. I had always enjoyed the company of senior citizens, so I decided to take the two-year course offered by the seminary in caring for the elderly. Even though I didn't quite find myself that first year, I told everyone back home that I loved school, and so the Bergers decided that it would be a good experience for Chaya's cousin

Rochel. That's how I found myself in seminary the following year with my future stepsister.

Rochel was in the grade beneath me, but since she was the cousin of my friend Chaya I made sure to develop a relationship with her, and we actually became quite friendly. By my second year I began to understand a bit more about *Chassidus* as well as the surrounding culture, and I felt more comfortable. I realized that at the core of *Chassidus* was the all-important relationship with one's Rebbe, and over time I also came to appreciate the more feminine approach to education that prevailed in sem. The focus in my sem was to prepare the students to become excellent homemakers rather than career women, and as such practical *halachah* and *hashkafah* were emphasized more than academics. We had sewing classes and were taught how to *kasher* chickens and liver, as well as given an excellent grasp of *halachah*.

It was during my second year in the sem that my mother got engaged to Rochel's father.

I spent my first year back in Israel as a preschool assistant in the morning and attending Pninim Seminary in Yerushalayim in the afternoons. It was good to be back with my family, yet I now had to deal with another major adjustment, my mother's remarriage. I had heard many disturbing stories about stepparents, so I was wary about my mother remarrying.

After we returned to Israel, Rochel would come over to our house to visit, and my sister and I would sometimes go visit at her house. It wasn't long before I realized that my future stepfather was a really warm and friendly person, and yet it wasn't until after their wedding that I was finally able to accept him.

We spent the first couple of weeks after my mother's wedding living with my father, and when we came back home I was immediately struck by how happy my mother looked. I was 17 years old, and for the first time since my baby sister had died I finally felt that I was able to stop worrying about my mother. I sensed that she was well cared for, and for the first time in many years I felt free to be a kid. Until I let go of the burden, I hadn't even realized how responsible I felt for my mother.

My mother and stepfather created a warm and cozy atmosphere in our new home. A real blending took place and all of us children felt welcome, although for some of my siblings the adjustment was more difficult and took more time than it did for me. My stepfather conducted beautiful Shabbos *seudos* and would go through the entire family and bless each of us with success in whatever it was we were working on at the time. I was very impressed with how organized my stepfather was and how closely he adhered to his self-imposed schedule, despite his health issues. Of all the many adjustments I had had to make during my childhood, becoming accustomed to a stepfather and stepsiblings was by far the easiest.

Becoming a Jew wasn't difficult for me, but finding my own place within contemporary Jewish society was a process. As a young teen I *davened* fervently and asked Hashem to please help me get accepted to a good school, and yet I had much difficulty in this area. In retrospect it is obvious to me that none of my prayers were wasted. Today, *baruch Hashem*, my children all learn in the best schools, and one of my daughters is in the same school as the daughter of my friend Chaya! My children have wonderful friends, and they feel very at ease in our community. It's incredible to think that they were given by right of birth a sense of belonging that has taken me years to cultivate.

Project Galilee[1]

S habbos morning. I stride through the quiet village streets, past a lone plow and an old tractor, the proud symbols of man's mastery over the earth. My sights are set on a loftier destination: the magnificent *shul* built by Baroness Rothschild.

As I walk, I marvel at the quaint beauty of the village's homes. In the gardens, flashes of yellow and orange peek through the verdant green leaves of fruit trees. Goats and sheep run about in the backyards and occasionally I catch sight of a horse. I continue up the brick path that leads to the *shul*, the symbol of Torah in this quiet northern town. I enter at the side and climb the stairs to the women's section.

The plush elegance of the upholstered seats catches me off guard. Such luxury seems somehow out of place in this rural village. I choose a seat right up front, so that I can peer down through the wrought-iron *mechitzah*.

I take in the sight of the *rav*, a Vizhnitzer *chassid* dressed in his Shabbos finery, his princely *shtreimel* crowning his head. Another magnificent *shtreimel* is seen down below, worn by the *chazzan*, the *rav's* son. A couple of Chabad *chassidim* join the mix, swaying in their frock coats, *gartels* swinging at their sides. The local farmers lend their stoic presence to this congregation. Dressed in button-down shirts pulled tight over muscular frames and tucked

---

1. All translations and quoted explanations in this chapter have been taken from ArtScroll's *Chumash, Stone Edition*

neatly into blue jeans, they seem to blend right in, in spite of the shiny white *kippot* perched upon their heads. The *gabbaim* are both veterans of the IDF, who, once secular, have found their way back to Hashem and His Torah. The *Litvishe* element is comprised of a distinguished South African *rav*, a family of new *olim*, and my children. Here is a microcosm of the Jewish people, and I thrill at the sight.

I open my *siddur* and join the *davening*, proud to be part of this wondrous picture. Soon the *chazzan*'s baritone can be heard chanting *Mussaf*, his powerful voice accompanying our words of prayer. And then, finally, the climax of the morning: a dozen young boys scurry around borrowing *talleisim* from the congregants and then assemble in a semicircle facing the *aron*. The *chazzan* arranges them in height order, their symmetry lending another layer to the lofty atmosphere. He begins and then all at once their high-pitched voices burst into song, as they and the *chazzan* alternately sing the beautiful lines of *Anim Zemiros*.

Their sweet voices wash over me, penetrating my heart. I am lifted upon wings of song to a different dimension, above time and space. The years begin to fall away. Ten, 20, and then 30 years fall away until I am again Sheryl, a young and idealistic Christian mother, struggling to raise my large family in the wilderness. Isolated and alone, I rise above the penury of my primitive surroundings, borne aloft by the vision of the goals I have formed for my children. I beseech G-d to make my dream for them a reality, and inspire my precious offspring to become beacons of truth that will spread G-d's holy light in the far-off corners of the world.

Sheryl of my past and Tzirel Rus of my present merge as I open my eyes and look down upon the *cheder yingelach* below. Ten eager faces search my own, waiting for their *Bubby's* approval. I give a little wave and smile down on my grandsons. My own song of praise silently soars up to the heavens, for Hashem has certainly answered my prayers. My dream has materialized far beyond the scope of anything I could have imagined when I was raising my children in the wilds of the Appalachian Mountains.

Feeling more at home in a rural setting, five of my six sons have chosen to live in the verdant hills of the Galilee. Located just ten minutes from the Kinneret, dotted with a number of naturally occurring springs and crisscrossed with hiking trails and vacation cabins, their village draws thousands of vacationers each year. Its fertile grounds are rich in vegetation, producing tomatoes, herbs, onions, garlic, cucumbers, cabbage, and lettuce, as well as significant amounts of wheat, oats, and hay. Groves of beautiful fruit trees bursting with almonds, dates, pomegranates, citrus fruits, and olives give the town the feel of paradise.

The history of this agricultural town is almost as varied and colorful as the many different crops it produces. It was established in the year 1901 on lands bought by Baron Rothschild. Though a good part of today's residents are secular, the village's first *cheder* was established generations ago by the grandparents of Israeli MK Rabbi Meir Porush. Long before it became common, the farmers were known for their *shemittah* observance, thanks to the influence of one of the village's mayors, a man named Amos, considered to be one of Israel's first *baalei teshuvah*.

The rav of the town's main *shul*, a Vizhnitzer *chassid* by the name of Rabbi Sinai Meyer Frankel, has been behind much of the religious development of the town today, having facilitated the establishment of both the local Chabad and Breslov communities, as well as building up his own *shul*. He was the youngest rabbi ever to be ordained by the Rabbanut, and he first came up north at 19, before he was married.

After beginning their married lives in either Yerushalayim or its surrounding towns, my sons felt a yearning to return to a rural setting, where they would come into closer contact with nature and Hashem's creations. Dovid is passionate about living in the lap of nature. There, he comes into daily contact with G-d's handiwork. He is fond of quoting the Gemara (*Yevamos* 63a): "A person who doesn't have land of his own is not considered a complete person."[1] The Gemara continues and quotes the verse "G-d gave the earth to the children of man."[2] It explains that a person should grow his own produce instead of purchasing it from others even though the cost may be the same, since the produce a person has sown himself brings more blessing.

Dovid also enjoys quoting Rabbi Samson Raphael Hirsch, who wrote: "Unless we are very much mistaken… Jews will ultimately return to agriculture, their ancestral pursuit, which they loved and which was intimately linked with their original destiny as a nation."[3]

Dovid is concerned about today's youth, who grow up in cities of concrete and spend many hours plugged into electronic devices. He feels so strongly about it that he has taken the initiative of bringing his brothers up to the small, idyllic farming village where their children can grow up surrounded by nature, under the watchful eyes of their devoted parents. Originally my grandsons learned in the cities nearby, but after a number of years the logistics became impossible to maintain and, together with a few other local families, my sons established their own school. Not only do my grandsons learn the standard *cheder* curriculum, but the Gemara comes alive as they learn the Torah laws necessary for the proper handling of livestock and the observance of the special *mitzvos* that apply in the Land of Israel. Dovid is a man of vision, and he is just beginning to reap the fruits of his labor as he observes his sons and

---

1. According to one interpretation, this literally refers to land for planting.

2. *Tehillim* 115:16.

3. *Talmudic Judaism in Society,* p. 223. The entire quote is: "Unless we are very much mistaken, there is no question but that given freedom, equal rights, and the time needed to become adept at this particular occupation, which really requires training and habituation from early youth, Jews will ultimately return to agriculture, their ancestral pursuit, which they loved and which was intimately linked with their original destiny as a nation."

Three of my grandsons

nephews living a life that combines love of Torah and its laws with the agricultural experiences of his own youth.

Dovid reflects on his work: "I spent most of my childhood in the mountains. Those magical days spent in the forest cultivated a strong connection to G-d and His creations deep within me. When you plant something, you take little seeds and put them in the ground, but you don't know if it's going to grow or not. You've got to leave that to G-d. The process gives you the feeling of partnering with Hashem.

"Growing vegetables has got to be a much better pastime for children than playing video games! Not only does working the land connect you with the Creator, but I have personally grown in Torah since I moved to this farming community. People have no idea how many Torah laws you need to know just to plant a vegetable garden in Israel! Aside from the laws of *kilayim*, the forbidden planting of mixed seed[4] (also prohibited outside of the Land of Israel), there are many commandments that are specific to agriculture in *Eretz*

---

4. *Leviticus* 19:19: "You shall not plant your field with mixed seed."

Yisrael. For example; there are laws pertaining to harvesting such as *pe'ah*,[1] as well as the obligation to separate the *terumos*[2] and *maaseros*,[3] tithes from produce, wine, and olive oil, and the once-in-seven-year practice of *shemittah*![4]

"Raising animals involves many complex laws with *bechoros*,[5] firstborn males. For example, is one permitted to purchase a male sheep from a non-observant Jew who is not familiar with these complex laws? The owner of a large herd will definitely have a number of firstborn males but may be unsure which ones are first-born. Therefore we generally consider all male sheep as being of questionable status. It is not permitted to derive benefit from an animal of questionable status.

"A lot of interesting questions have come up over the years, which have necessitated rabbinical guidance. For example, due to a misunderstanding, my son once bought two male lambs of questionable status. I wasn't even sure if it was permissible to sell them back to the farmer from whom he had purchased them. After much back-and-forth discussion among the local rabbis as well as

---

1. *Leviticus* 19:9: "When you reap the harvest of your land, you shall not complete your reaping to the corner of your field."

2. *Numbers* 18:8–20: "Hashem spoke to Aharon: And I — behold! I have given you…. And this shall be yours … all the best of your oil and the best of your wine and grain … the first fruits of everything that is in their land …" This refers to special gifts that the Torah obligates us to give to *Kohanim*.

3. *Numbers* 18:21: "To the sons of Levi, behold! I have given every tithe in Israel as a heritage in exchange for the service that they perform…" There are other tithes, however, that do not go to the Levi, such as the "second tithe," which is taken after the Levite tithe and is eaten in Jerusalem (*Deuteronomy* 14:22–27), and the tithe for the poor (ibid. 26:12).

4 *Leviticus* 25:1–7: "When you come into the land that I shall give you, the land shall observe a Sabbath rest for Hashem. For six years you may sow your field and for six years you may prune your vineyard, and you may gather in its crop. But the seventh year shall be a complete rest for the land…"

5 *Numbers* 18:15–17: "But the firstborn of sheep or the firstborn of a goat you shall not redeem; they are holy …." The firstborn males of kosher animals — cows, sheep, and goats — are sacred from birth and are given to the *Kohanim* to be brought as offerings.

halachic authorities in Yerushalayim, we were told that it was permitted to annul the sale and exchange the male lambs for females.

"On another occasion, some of our chickens were clawed by a mongoose. A kosher animal that has been mortally wounded is no longer considered kosher.[6] Since anything that issues from a nonkosher animal is also nonkosher, we also had a problem with our eggs. We brought our dilemma to the attention of a halachic authority and were told to wait and see if the chickens recovered within 21 days, at which point the eggs would be considered kosher retroactively.

"Then there was the time I was walking to *shul* on Shabbos and noticed three horses trotting down the main road on their way out of the village. Now that was an interesting question in returning lost objects![7] Was there a permitted way to catch the horses and bring them back, since it is not permitted to trap animals on Shabbos?"

My sons and a number of other families make up the basis of Rabbi Frankel's community. Most of the other families and farmers in their neighborhood are secular. My children have become something of an example for the local farmers, who now approach them with their halachic questions. One man wanted to know if perhaps my son could find a leniency to permit him to cut down a fruit tree that his boss asked him to remove. When told to remain firm and not destroy the tree, the man stuck to his principles.

My grandsons have made an impact that is all their own on the spiritual climate of the village. Over the years they have enjoyed a warm and respectful relationship with a local farmer called Itzik. Dressed in blue jeans, with sun-bronzed skin and muscular arms,

---

6 *Leviticus* 14:24: "An animal that had been torn to death." The Talmud expounds: "The animal did not die of its wounds...rather the animal had been mortally wounded ... or the animal had a disease or wound in a vital organ that would cause its death within twelve months" (*Chullin* 42a). In both cases, the meat may not be eaten even if the slaughter performed was a valid *shechitah*.

7 *Deuteronomy* 22:1: "You shall not see the ox of your brother or his sheep or goat cast off, and hide yourself from them; you shall surely return them to your brother."

Itzik looks like a typical *Sabra* farmer. He owns many acres of farm-land and livestock, and a few of my grandsons have helped care for his sheep.

Once, while tending the sheep, my young grandsons asked Itzik the time, explaining that they needed to break for the afternoon prayers before completing their chores. It was an emotional Itzik who later related the episode to my son. The discipline and self-control that such young boys were able to display brought tears to the eyes of big, burly Itzik.

People often wonder if my sons are concerned about their children absorbing negative influences from their secular neighbors. Yet I truly think that my grandchildren are growing up firm in their fear of G-d and *mitzvah* observance. Torah comes alive for them in their day-to-day experiences. They are not religious just because everyone expects them to follow *halachah*. My children spend time with their boys, discussing their interactions with the locals and providing them with answers to any questions that come up. A Torah-observant child cannot just go with the flow in their farming community; he has to stand up for the right thing and at times defend religious practices to their secular neighbors. If anything, this has made my grandchildren stronger and more committed than many young men their age living in more established communities.

The village *cheder* is reminiscent of the small *chadarim* in the *shtetls* of old. There are two separate groups, one for the older boys and one for the younger. The oldest group of 12- to 14-year-olds is composed primarily of my grandchildren, since most of my sons' families started off with boys before the daughters were born.

In this rural environment the boys have the opportunity to take an interest in farming and agriculture. Not only do they work for the local farmers, but they also have animals of their own, including donkeys, horses, sheep, goats, chickens, geese, and ducks. Two of my sons are accomplished *sofrim*, scribes, and one supervises the *kashrus* in some of the factories in the Galilee under the auspices of the Eidah HaChareidis.[1] One of my sons as well as a number of my grandsons have recently begun to train as *shochtim* in nearby Teveriah. I am very thankful to the One Above for my sons and their many accomplishments, seeing an echo of the educational methods I used decades ago in our home school being put to practice in their *cheder* today.

My sons have recently begun to produce their own olive oil. Last year they bought the olives from two of Itzik's olive groves. Each grove was approximately ten dunams, or five acres, in total. The groves boasted two types of olives, manzanilla and Syrian, and some olives were as large as plums. After seeing such large olives we can really understand where the Talmudic measurement of a *kezayis*[2] comes from!

After the first rains of the season they got to work. First they surveyed the olive trees, looking for any that were still off-limits due to the prohibition of *orlah*, using the fruit of a tree within three years of its planting.[3] Only one such tree was found, which they marked. After determining that the two groves were close enough together that you could see one from the other, my sons were told that they only had to leave *pe'ah*, a corner of the field for the poor, from one grove. Many people do not leave *pe'ah* these days, since it is not practical for the poor to come and harvest fields, and not taking *pe'ah* does not affect the *kashrus* of the produce. Yet since my sons have a deep reverence for the special *mitzvos* pertaining to agriculture in Eretz Yisrael, they set aside 1/60 of the olives on the trees, which later were picked and distributed to the poor.

For the picking, the boys were divided into teams, with several children for each tree. They made use of a number of different olive-picking methods, depending on the height of the limbs and

---

1. The name of a widely accepted Kosher-certification organization.

2. A halachic measure that literally means "the size of an olive."

3. *Leviticus* 19:23: "When you shall come to the land and you shall plant any food tree, you shall treat its fruit as forbidden; for three years they shall be forbidden to you, they shall not be eaten."

whether or not the olives were clinging to the branches. First they beat the limbs of the trees, which sent the loosest olives raining down onto the tarps spread below. Next they cut down the very tall limbs that stuck up out of reach, and then used either a hand rake or a battery-operated olive picker to clean the branches of the remaining olives. Some boys collected the fallen olives and dumped them into crates, and others pulled out the leaves from between the olives. Harvesting olives is very enjoyable and therapeutic work that even attracted guest pickers from out of town.

Soon their crates were full with 300 to 400 kilos of olives. Each crate could produce about 60 liters of oil. The boys were careful not to let the olives sit too long between picking and pressing so that the oil would not become acidic. Every two to three days they headed off to the press with anywhere from three to six tons of olives. Finding an appropriate olive press took some arranging. They needed a press with a *kashrus* supervisor to ensure that only non-*orlah* olives had been processed there. Many of the larger olive presses had a minimum of 50 tons of olives, which disqualified their private operation.

The whole project took about a month from start to finish and produced about 3,000 liters of top-quality olive oil. The boys separated *terumah* and distributed it to *Kohanim* well versed in the laws. Since everyone today is considered to be ritually impure,[1] even *Kohanim* who are sure of their lineage may not eat *terumah*, but they may derive benefit from it. In this case the *Kohanim* were able to use the boys' homemade olive oil for burning. Then the boys separated the other tithes, and distributed the *maaser ani* to the poor. The rest of the oil was either divided up among the families who were involved in the project, given away, or marketed in Yerushalayim as olive

---

1. Anyone who has either come into contact with a dead body or has been in the same building as a dead body is ritually impure. One who has come into contact with a dead body can transfer his state of impurity to others with whom he comes into contact. The only way to purify oneself would be via the sprinkling of the ashes of the Red Heifer, which has not been possible since the destruction of the Holy Temple, roughly 2,000 years ago.

oil meeting the strictest halachic standards and sold in bulk before Chanukah of the following year. My grandsons' olive oil was a great success and sold out very quickly, rated by some as the purest olive oil available in all of Israel.

Olive oil is well known since Biblical times for its special propensity to encourage excellence in Torah learning by increasing intelligence.[2] The boys involved seemed to gain a lot from the olive harvest. Dovid is not surprised; he has consulted with many *rabbanim* over the years, and has gotten a lot of support for his educational approach. As one rabbi told him: "The most important value you could possibly give your sons is a love of learning and Judaism, even at the cost of knowing less Gemara." *Baruch Hashem*, we have thus merited to raise children who are enthusiastic about their Torah learning and their *mitzvah* observance.

I personally have found much meaning in my sons' project. The fact that they sold their olive oil before Chanukah touches a chord deep within me. I feel a special connection to Chanukah, the first Jewish holiday our family ever celebrated. The Bible had been part of my life ever since I was a little girl, but much of it was locked away and undecipherable to me until I became a Jew and was able to tap into the Oral Torah. Chanukah is the holiday of the Oral Torah, which is the key to true understanding of the Written Torah, and it is through the light of the *menorah* that the Oral Torah shines forth into the homes and hearts of the Jewish people.[3]

Back in Baltimore I was moved to tears at the sight of the preschool's *Kohen Gadol* project. I felt very left out and cut off back then, since even young Jewish children knew more than I. But Aharon the High Priest also became disheartened when his tribe made no contribution to the inauguration of the Tabernacle. Hashem comforted him, giving him the privilege of lighting the *Menorah*

---

2. *Samuel II* 14:2: "And Yoav sent to Tekoa, and he took from there a wise woman..." *Rashi* explains, "Since olive oil is found there, therefore intelligence is found there."

3. See *Ohr Gedalyahu* on Chanukah.

We have merited to see the fulfillment of the blessing in *Psalms* 128:3:
"Your children shall be like olive shoots surrounding your table."

in the Tabernacle, which the commentaries say hints at the future holiday of Chanukah and the subsequent *mitzvah* of kindling the *menorah* throughout the generations.

Like Aharon, I also felt the pain of lost opportunity: I had missed out on so much Jewish education during the first four decades of my life. And just as he was rewarded by the "kindling of lights" throughout the generations to come for his yearning, so I also feel Hashem took note of our deepest desires and has comforted us with the Chanukah gifts of oil and lights. Throughout the lengthy darkness of our past on those mountains a tiny light flickered, but now a flame of eternity burns brightly, as our progeny delight and delve into Torah and *mitzvos*!

Glossary

agurot — Israeli coins of the smallest denomination, equivalent to one-tenth of a shekel.

aliyah — lit., "going up"; here, immigration to Israel.

Anim Zemiros — a song of honor chanted after the Sabbath morning service.

Avraham (Avinu) — Abraham (our forefather).

Avraham HaIvri — lit., "Abraham the Hebrew" or "Abraham on the other side"; the Biblical figure Abraham, the appellation alluding to the idea that he left paganism behind and believed in only one G-d, in contrast to the rest of the world.

baal chesed (pl. *baalei chesed*) — one who performs acts of kindness.

baal teshuvah (pl. *baalei teshuvah*) — one who repents; those who return to Torah-true Judaism.

baal yissurim — one who bears the burden of suffering.

bachur (pl. *bachurim*) — young man; an unmarried young man, used to denote a student in a yeshivah.

Bais Yaakov — the *Chareidi* schools for girls, originally established in Poland in 1917.

Baruch Dayan HaEmes — lit., "Blessed is the True Judge," the blessing recited when one hears of a death.

Baruch Hashem — lit., "Blessed is Hashem"; "thank Hashem"; an expression of appreciation of Hashem's goodness.

bechor (pl. *bechoros*)— firstborn male.

beis midrash — a study hall where Torah is learned, often used as a synagogue as well.

ben Noach (pl. *b'nei Noach*) — lit., "a son of Noah"; those who observe the seven commandments given to Noah and his descendants after the Flood.

bikur cholim — lit., "visiting the sick," referring to the Torah commandment to care for the ill. Many Jewish communities have a *bikur cholim* organization that provides services for those in need.

bimah — table or platform in the synagogue from which the Torah Scroll is read.

Birchos HaShachar — blessings recited during the morning prayer service.

Birkas Kohanim — blessings recited by the *Kohanim* during a prayer service, recited daily in Israel and on holidays in communities outside Israel.

bitachon — lit., "trust"; trust in Hashem.

Bituach Leumi — National Insurance in Israel.

Boyan — a Chassidic dynasty named after the town of Boiany in Ukraine.

bris (bris milah) — circumcision of male infants, generally performed on the eighth day after birth.

Bubby — (Yiddish) Grandma or Grand-mother.

Chabad shaliach — An emissary of Chabad Lubavitch sent to do out-reach among nonreligious Jews.

challah — loaves of soft wheat-bread traditionally eaten during Sabbath and holiday meals.

Chanukah — Hanukah.

Chassid (hassid) (pl. *chassidim; hassidim*) — 1. pious man. 2. the follower of a Rebbe.

chassidish — hassidic.

Chassidus — The study of Hassidic thought.

chavrusa — study partner or partner-ship.

chazzan — cantor; one who leads the prayer service in the synagogue.

cheder (pl. *chadarim*) — school, usu. an elementary school (spec. for Jewish studies).

chesed — kindness; lovingkindness; acts of beneficence; charitable giving.

chillul Hashem — desecration of G-d's Name.

cholent — (Yiddish) a stew prepared before Shabbos, simmered over-night, and traditionally eaten at the Shabbos-day meal, often consist-ing of meat, potatoes, beans, and barley.

chuppah — a wedding canopy beneath which the wedding ceremony takes place.

daven — (Yiddish) to pray.

davening — (Yiddish) praying; prayers.

Derech Hashem — a book of Jewish thought written by Rabbi Moshe Chaim Luzzatto in the 17th century.

Eishes Chayil — *Proverbs* Chapter 31, verses 10-31, traditionally recited before the Friday-night Shabbos meal, depicting a woman of valor.

emunah — faith; belief in G-d.

Eretz Yisrael — the Land of Israel.

Erev Shabbos — the day before the Sabbath, an often busy time dur-ing which families complete their preparations in honor of the com-ing day of rest.

frum — (Yiddish) religious; Torah observant.

gabbai (pl. *gabbaim*) — (Yiddish) syna-gogue sexton; person responsible for the proper functioning of a syn-agogue or other communal body.

gartel — (Yiddish) belt worn to distin-guish between the upper and lower parts of the body, worn by some men during religious observances.

Gemara — the Talmud.

ger (pl. *geirim*) — a convert.

geirus — conversion (to Judaism).

geveret — Ma'am or Mrs.

gilgul (gilgulim) — reincarnation of the soul into another living being to atone for past sins.

giyores — female convert.

hachnasas Sefer Torah — the joyous cer-emony in which a new Torah Scroll is first brought to a synagogue.

hakafos — the encircling of the *bimah* seven times on the holiday of Sim-chas Torah, while dancing with the Torah Scrolls.

halachah (pl. *halachos*)— Torah law.

halachah shiur — a class on Torah law.

Har Sinai — Mount Sinai, the mountain upon which the Torah was given to the Jewish people. The souls of all future members of the Jewish people, including the converts who would convert throughout the generations, were also present at that time.

Hashem — literally, "the Name," a respectful way to refer to G-d.

Hashgachah — Divine Providence.

Kabbalas Shabbos — literally, "welcoming the Shabbos"; part of the Friday-night prayer service.

kallah — Bride.

kasher — The process by which appliances and utensils that were not fit for usage according to Torah law are rendered fit for use.

kashrus, kashruth — Jewish dietary laws.

kedushah — Holiness, sanctity.

Kiddush — a. mandatory blessing over wine expressing the sanctity of Shabbos or Festivals. 2. A reception after Shabbos morning prayers at which Kiddush is recited and refreshments are served.

Kiddush Hashem — sanctification of G-d's Name.

kippah (pl. *kippot*) — skullcap worn by religious Jewish males; *yarmulke*.

Klal Yisrael — Jewish people in general; the community of Israel; the Jewish nation.

Kohen (pl. *Kohanim*) — a member of the priestly family descended in the male line from Aaron; *Kohanim* performed a number of services in the Temple. Although there is no Temple today, there are still a number of laws pertaining specifically to *Kohanim*.

Kohen Gadol (pl. *Kohanim Gedolim*)— the high priest who served both in the Tabernacle and later in the Temple. The first high priest was Aaron, the brother of Moses.

Kol Nidrei — opening prayer recited at the onset of Yom Kippur.

Kollel — learning program on a postgraduate level, usually providing stipends for its full-time participants; yeshivah whose students are mostly men who are married.

Kosel — the Western Wall.

Lag BaOmer — the 33rd day of the *Omer* (the period between Passover and Shavuos). It is also the anniversary of the death of Rabbi Shimon bar Yochai, a day that is often marked by bonfires in Israel and, in Hassidic circles, by the first haircut of 3-year-old boys.

licht — (Yiddish) lit., "lights"; candles.

Litvish — lit., "Lithuanian"; adjective describing non-chassidic Jews of Eastern European extraction.

machateineste — one's child's mother-in-law.

machzor — holiday prayer book.

makolet — small grocery store.

Maoz Tzur — song traditionally sung after lighting the *menorah* on Hanukah.

Maseches Shabbos — a tractate of the Talmud dealing primarily with the laws of the Sabbath.

mashgiach — 1. spiritual guide in a yeshivah; dean of students. 2. *kashrus* supervisor.

Mashiach — the Messiah.

masmid (pl. *masmidim*) — an exceptionally dedicated Torah scholar who spends much time immersed in Torah study.

Meah Shearim — one of the first Jerusalem neighborhoods built outside the Old City walls.

mechitzah — a partition separating men and women during prayer.

Megillah — literally, "scroll"; also refers to the Scroll of *Esther* read on Purim.

Melaveh Malkah—meal eaten on Saturday night in honor of the departure of the Sabbath Queen.

menorah — candelabrum used to hold the Chanukah lights.

Meron — site of the burial place of Rabbi Shimon Bar Yochai, a Torah Sage who died on Lag BaOmer almost two millennia ago.

meshulach (pl. *meshulachim*) — an itinerant fund-raiser; charity collector.

mezuzah (pl. *mezuzos*) — small parchment scroll in a casing, affixed to a doorpost and containing the first two paragraphs of the *Shema* prayer.

mikveh — ritual pool made under specific halachic specifications used for both purification and conversion.

minhag (pl. *minhagim*) — a custom.

mishloach manos — gifts of food sent to friends on Purim.

Mishnah — teachings of the Tannaim that form the basis of the Talmud, the Oral Torah.

mitzvah (pl. *mitzvos, mitzvot*) —a good deed; one of the 613 commandments; a Biblical or Rabbinic commandment.

morah (pl. *morahs*) — woman teacher.

Moshe Rabbeinu — Moses, Our Teacher.

Motza'ei Shabbos — Saturday night; the time of the departure of the Sabbath.

Motza'ei Yom Kippur — nightfall following Yom Kippur.

Mussaf — lit., "additional"; supplementary prayer service added to the morning services on festivals.

nachas — satisfaction; pleasure, usually from one's children; spiritual or emotional pleasure.

Ner Yisrael — a prominent yeshivah in Baltimore founded in 1933 by Rabbi Yaakov Yitzchak Ruderman.

netz minyan — a quorum for prayer at the earliest time permitted to recite the morning prayer.

niggun (pl. *niggunim*) — Jewish tunes or melodies, often sung during special occasions.

Noahide movement — the group of gentiles that seek to learn and observe the seven commandments that the Bible demands of the sons of Noah.

Ohr Somayach — a yeshivah in Jerusalem for returnees to Judaism.

olah chadashah — a recent (female) immigrant to Israel.

olim — immigrants to Israel.

Parah Adumah — the Red Heifer.

parnassah — livelihood.

perek — chapter.

peyos — sideburns or sidecurls, worn by Orthodox Jewish males.

pesukim — verses.

Purim — holiday established by Queen Esther, commemorating the Jewish survival after a decree that they would be annihilated in Persia in fifth-century BCE (see *Esther* 9:31-32).

rabbanim — Rabbis.

Rabbi Shimon bar Yochai — a Sage who lived during the Roman occupation of Israel; he is mentioned many times in the Talmud and is believed to have written the *Zohar*, the first book of Kabbalah.

Rebbe — Hassidic Grand Rabbi.

Rebbetzin — *rebbetzin* (Yid.) — rabbi's wife; also used to refer to a respected Jewish woman.

rechov — street.

Rosh Hashanah — the Jewish New Year.

schach — the roof of the *succah*, generally made from leaves, branches, or bamboo.

Sefer Tehillim — The Book of *Psalms*.

Sefer Yeshayahu — The Book of *Isaiah*.

seudah (pl. *seudos*)— a festive meal eaten on the Shabbos or holidays; a meal, esp. a meal served on Shabbos or *Yom Tov*. Traditionally there is a festive meal eaten on Friday night after services, as well as at noon or late morning on Saturday. A smaller third meal — *shalosh seudos* — is eaten late on the Shabbos afternoon shortly before sunset.

Shabbos (pl. *Shabbosos*) — Saturday or the Sabbath; the Jewish day of rest.

Shabbosdik — appropriate for the Sabbath.

Shacharis — the morning prayer service.

shadchan (pl. *shadchanim*) —matchmaker.

sheirut (pl. *sheiruts*)— semipublic taxi service in Israel.

sheitel — (Yiddish) wig. Orthodox women cover their hair after marrying, often with a wig.

shemiras halashon — guarding oneself against improper speech, such as gossip, slander, and other forms of forbidden speech.

shemittah — the Sabbatical year, occurring every seventh year, during which the land is not worked. This law only pertains to the Land of Israel.

Shemoneh Esrei (lit., "18") — the prayer, originally 18 blessings but now 19, that forms the central core of each weekday prayer service.

sheva berachos — 1. the seven blessings recited under the *chuppah*. 2. festive meals, celebrated during the week after a wedding, at which the seven blessings are recited.

shidduch (pl. *shidduchim*) — 1. match, esp. a marriage match. 2. proposed marriage match.

shiur (pl. *shiurim*) — Torah lecture.

shivah — the weeklong period of mourning observed after the passing of a close family member.

shtreimel — a fur hat commonly worn by Hassidic males on the Sabbath and holidays.

shul (Yid.) — synagogue.

siddur (pl. *siddurim*) — a prayer book.

Sifrei Torah — Torah Scrolls.

simchah (pl. *simchos*) — 1. joy; happiness. 2. a celebration, esp. a celebration of a family milestone such as a wedding, bar mitzvah, or a birth.

Simchas Beis HaSho'eivah — gathering held on the intermediary days of the Succos holiday, which includes music, dance, and refreshments, commemorating the Water Libation Ceremony performed in the Holy Temple in Jerusalem.

Simchas Torah — the festival immediately following Succos honoring the cycle of the Torah.

sofer (pl. *sofrim*) — scribe who writes religious materials such as a Torah Scroll, a *mezuzah*, *tefillin*, etc.

succah (pl. *succos*)— booth in which Jews are commanded to dwell during Succos.

Succos — Tabernacles; the festival during which one dwells in a *succah* and takes the Four Species.

Taanis Esther — the Fast of Esther, the day before Purim, when Jews fast in remembrance of Queen Esther's fast before risking her life to visit King Achashveirosh without an invitation.

tallis (pl. *talleisim*) — prayer shawl; four-cornered prayer shawl with *tzitzis*, worn during morning prayers.

Talmud — the body of Oral Torah.

Tanach — acronym for *Torah, Ne-veim, Kesuvim.*; the written Torah, including the Five Books of Moses, the eight books of Prophets, and eleven books of Writings.

tefillah (pl. *tefillos*) — prayer.

tefillin — phylacteries, small black leather boxes containing parchment scrolls inscribed with Biblical passages, bound to the arm and forehead of adult Jewish males during the weekday morning prayer service.

teudat oleh — a legal document attesting to one's status as a new Israeli immigrant.

tisch — (Yiddish) lit., "table"; a chassidic gathering around a Hassidic Rebbe.

Tishrei — the first month of the Jewish year which contains the holidays of Rosh Hashanah, Yom Kippur, Succos, and Simchas Torah.

toivel — to ritually purify via immersion in a *mikveh*.

Torah — the Bible or Old Testament; can refer collectively to both the Oral and Written Torahs given to Moses on Mount Sinai.

tzedakah — charity.

tzaddik — a righteous man.

tzadekes — a righteous woman.

tzelem Elokim — lit., "image of G-d." Man was formed in the image of G-d and therefore each human being is deserving of respect.

tzitzis — four-cornered fringed garment worn by Jewish men and boys; fringes at the corners of a *tallis*.

ulpan — a school teaching Hebrew to new immigrants.

Yaakov — our forefather Jacob.

Yerushalayim — Jerusalem.

Yerushalmi (pl. Yerushalmim) — Jerusalemite.

yeshivah — a school of Jewish studies; a Torah academy.

Yesimcha Elokim k'Efraim u'ch'Menasheh — literally, "May G-d make you like Efraim and Menashe." This is the traditional blessing that Jewish parents bestow on their sons on Friday night and before Yom Kippur.

Yiddishe — (Yiddish) Jewish.

Yiddishkeit — (Yiddish) — Judaism; the Jewish way of life..

yingelach — (Yiddish) little boys.

Yitzchak — our forefather Isaac.

Yom Kippur — the Day of Atonement.

Yom Tov (pl. *Yamim Tovim*) — a Jewish holiday.

zechus — merit; privilege.

zeidy (pl. *zeidies*) — (Yiddish) Grandpa or grandfather.

zemiros — songs sung at Shabbos and festive meals.

zt"l — an acronym for *zecher tzaddik l'vrachah*, meaning "may the memory of this righteous man be for a blessing."